To Renata,

In great appreciation for your continuing support.

With best wishes,

ONE-ARMED
ECONOMIST

ONE-ARMED ECONOMIST

ON THE INTERSECTION OF BUSINESS AND GOVERNMENT

MURRAY WEIDENBAUM

Transaction Publishers

New Brunswick (U.S.A.) and London (U.K.)

Library of Congress Catalog Number: 2004046059
ISBN: 0-7658-0252-X
Printed in the United States of America

Library of Congress Cataloging-in-Publication Data

Weidenbaum, Murray L.
    One-armed economist : on the intersection of business and government / Murray Weidenbaum.
        p. cm.
    Includes index.
    ISBN 0-7658-0252-X (cloth : alk. paper)
        1. United States—Economic policy. 2. Public policy. I. Title.

HC106.83.W45   2004
330.973—dc22   2004046059

Contents

Introduction

In assembling this selection of my professional work, I have drawn on publications ranging from scholarly journals to congressional hearings to popular magazines (I frequently have stated that my classroom extends beyond the university).

Rather than presenting any grand vision of the role of economics in dealing with the challenges facing a modern society, these essays are far more eclectic. In effect, they are a form of inductive reasoning, bringing to bear on issues of policymaking the insights that may be gleaned from experience in a variety of public and private sector decision-making positions. Although we each believe that our analyses are carefully balanced, a motivating spirit has been President Harry Truman's famous if not mythical call for a one-armed economist—one who avoids saying, "On the one hand . . . and then on the other hand . . ."

I hope that the reader finds it useful to see how one economist's approach to public policy has been of some value over the years. To a significant degree, the development of the specific topics results from the wide array of career opportunities—in business, government, and academia—that fortune has brought my way. In any event, I have tried to select items that will be of interest to the contemporary reader.

Indeed, as I read over these selections, I find that the questions they deal with still bedevil my fellow citizens: How can we get a stronger economy? How do we reconcile economic growth and environmental quality? How should we simplify the tax system and reduce waste in government? How can we reform corporate governance? How much defense can we afford? Is globalization a boon or a bane?

To enhance readability, I have eliminated tables, charts, and footnotes as well as ephemeral material. I have also updated some terminology such as substituting references to gross national product with gross domestic product. The source notes guide the reader to the full text of each selection. I am grateful to the holders of the copyrights for their kind permission to reprint these writings.

Over the years, I have benefited greatly from association with numerous thoughtful, demanding, and encouraging bosses and colleagues. I learned a great deal about the nuts and bolts of government and policy analysis from I. M. Labovitz and Samuel M. Cohn of the Bureau of the Budget. My mentor at the Boeing Company was Clifford Drown, a modest man of wide ranging interests. Much of my work on the defense industry was encouraged by David Abshire, John Hamre, and Jon Vondracek at the Center for Strategic and International Studies.

My initial research on government regulation was sponsored by William Baroody, Sr., of the American Enterprise Institute, a true think tank pioneer. My writings on public policy generally were supported by the Center for the Study of American Business at Washington University in St. Louis (recently renamed the Weidenbaum Center on the Economy, Government, and Public Policy). My long-term secretary at the Center, Christine Moseley, typed many of the original articles and did so much to prepare the present volume for publication.

I am especially grateful to Irving Louis Horowitz, whose friendship and encouragement have provided an important incentive to continue my various explorations in the development and analysis of public policy. I hope that this volume, which was created at his suggestion, meets his always high expectations.

Over the course of a half century, my wife Phyllis has shared the journey of a truly peripatetic professor, experiencing many moments of joy and disappointment. She should take especial credit for the, perhaps, too few instances of compassion in the work of a hard-nosed economist.

Acknowledgements

The author is indebted to the following publishers and publications for permission to reprint portions of his earlier writings (each selection contains a detailed citation of the original source):

American Economic Review

Astronautics and Aeronautics

Bulletin of the Atomic Scientists

Business and the Contemporary World

Business Economics

Business Horizons

Challenge

Conference Board

Congressional Quarterly, Inc.

Executive Speeches

Finanzarchiv

William S. Hein & Co.

Journal of Economic Issues

Journal of Private Enterprise

Journal of World Trade

Macmillan Publishers

Michigan State University

National Tax Journal

Orbis

Praeger Publishers

Public Interest

Quorum Books

Society

University of Washington

Washington Post

Washington Quarterly

Washington University

Westview Press

Part 1
Innovations in Economic Policy

1

An Ambitious Agenda for Economic Growth

How can we best promote long-term economic growth? Effective policy needs to go beyond conventional monetary and fiscal policy. It requires eliminating the structural defects in the economy that depress productive capacity, productivity, and competitiveness. Tax and budget reform should focus on encouraging saving and investment rather than current consumption. This selection was the Adam Smith Address at the 1996 annual meeting of the National Association for Business Economics.

It has become fashionable to advocate faster economic growth as the elixir to cure all that ails the American society. Surely faster growth produces all sorts of good things, such as lower budget deficits, more new jobs, higher incomes, and rising living standards. Thus, who can object to the general idea of achieving larger economic output?

Economists are destined to bring the wet blanket to the party. We have to raise the question often ignored: How can we not just achieve but maintain a more rapid and more durable pace of economic expansion? The two most popular ways of attaining faster growth fall short of providing a satisfying response. The first simple growth policy is to order the Federal Reserve System (the Fed) to put its collective foot down harder on the monetary gas pedal. The second approach requires Congress just to cut taxes, providing fiscal stimulus for a sluggish economy. Both responses can be useful but they are inadequate.

In recent decades, we have learned that a rapid and sustained expansion of the money supply unaccompanied by substantial change in policy toward the real economy can generate escalating inflation. Rising inflation, later if not sooner, will cause the Fed to shift gears and to pursue a policy of slowing the growth of or even cutting the money supply. In the process, interest rates will rise. More often than not, that sequence of actions will end the economic expansion and precipitate the next recession.

The fiscal alternative, cutting tax rates, can result in a similar sequence of events. However, the process will probably be a bit more indirect. Surely, cutting income taxes alone is not going to energize the economy sufficiently to prevent a rise in the budget deficit. Those deficits can lead to a variety of

Source: Murray Weidenbaum, "The Adam Smith Address: An Ambitious Agenda for Economic Growth," *Business Economics*, January 1997.

negative effects. These range from a diminution of investment capital avail-able for private business expansion to scaring the Fed into tightening the flow of money and credit.

But this is not a counsel of despair. There is a third way of responding to the poor performance of the U.S. economy. It, too, is a supply-side approach but it is more subtle—and avowedly more difficult—than just cutting taxes. It deals with the structural defects in the American economy that depress productive capacity and productivity. Many of these defects arise from the operation of government policies and programs. An example of these struc-tural and institutional shortcomings will provide an inkling of the type of economic cure that is presented here. Although the initial example is regula-tory, the full analysis will cover the gamut of government operations, espe-cially expenditure programs and the tax system.

Dale Jorgensen of Harvard has estimated that, by the year 2005, when the new Clean Air Act is fully in effect, the compliance with that statute and other environmental laws will reduce the nation's capital stock by over 4 percent. It will increase the cost of capital by more than 5 percent, and reduce the economy's growth rate by more than 3 percent a year.

Nevertheless, there is no responsible pressure to dismantle environmental programs. The Manufacturing Institute, for example, suggests that reason-able regulatory and tax reforms can yield technological advances and greater capital investment that could raise the growth rate by a half percentage point. If that number seems small, please remember that compounding it over a decade generates a large cumulative increase in production, income, employ-ment, and living standards.

To clear the air (in more than one sense), this is not a plea to swing the public policy pendulum from the present polar alternative of increasingly tough environmental regulation, regardless of the economic consequences, to the equally undesirable extreme of trying to maximize economic growth while ignoring environment, safety, and other social concerns. Rather, we need to rethink the whole gamut of government regulation of business as part of a comprehensive economic reform strategy.

Similarly, while I can restrain my inherent enthusiasm for simply cutting tax rates, simultaneously altering the fundamental structure of the government's revenue system can contribute in highly desirable ways to strengthening the overall economy. Likewise, substantially shifting the com-position of government expenditures to favor investment over consumption can help quicken the economic growth rate in a sustainable fashion.

The approach presented here will not be an easy strategy to achieve. How-ever, accomplishments along these lines of structural reform will be far more lasting than merely tinkering with the conventional dials of macroeconomic policy.

Shifting the Composition of Government Spending

Let us begin with the opportunities for reforming government spending. Voting to approve the general idea of a balanced budget is only a start on the path of fiscal sensibility. The really tough job is to make the specific spending cuts. Few objective criteria have been developed to guide that effort. The guide suggested here is to concentrate on reducing or eliminating expenditures that hurt the economy. Inefficient public sector programs represent a loss to the economy. They produce lower benefits than if the same funds were invested in private activities that meet the test of the marketplace.

Let us assume that we have the duty of preparing guidelines to assist the Congress in this arduous assignment. The most popular formula—eliminating waste, fraud, and abuse—is not adequate to the task. Of course, there are numerous examples of fraud, waste, and abuse, however those terms are defined. The reports of prisoners who illegally receive social security checks are surely upsetting. So are the stories of companies trying to sell the government shoddy products. These situations should be dealt with severely, but that is just a small start.

Here are five fundamental guidelines for serious budget cutting:

Focus reductions on the large consumption part of the federal budget rather than the small investment component. Such a change would curb the tendency for deficit financing to be a powerful mechanism for converting private saving into public consumption. On occasion, of course, the federal government makes worthwhile investments. Some outlays for education help the recipients achieve careers in which their added incomes generate added tax payments that more than repay the government's original investment.

Alas, such examples of effective federal investments are rare. Virtually the entire increase in federal outlays since 1980 has been in the form of consumption-type spending—aside from interest on the national debt. As a result, consumption outlays dominate the budget. In 1992, federal civilian investment outlays (education and training, research and development, and infrastructure) were only $83 billion, or 6 percent, out of a total budget of $1.4 trillion. Under these circumstances, large reductions in federal spending would be economically beneficial, because they would almost invariably fall on consumption.

By far, the dominant segment of federal consumption outlays consists of transfer payments or, to use the prevailing euphemism, entitlements. Unfortunately, in the largest such program, social security, the recipients have been led (or rather misled) to believe that they have earned the money they receive.

The typical beneficiary has contributed only a portion of the monthly check issued to him or her. A key fact overlooked by most senior citizen groups is that the total of such contributions plus matching employer payments plus interest does not begin to cover the monthly benefit payments. The balance is a gift from the working population.

There is a large but hidden welfare component in the major middle class entitlements. In the long run, privatization may be the most effective response. Meanwhile, reformers need to face the hard fact that recipients have not earned the annual cost-of-living increase (COLAs) that they now expect as a matter of right. The COLAs violate the insurance principle that, on average, you get what you pay for, and they arbitrarily tilt the federal budget even more to consumption expenditures.

If it is not possible to eliminate the annual COLA payments, a "diet COLA" could be limited to the annual inflation in excess of 2 percent. After all, the average working person is not protected completely from the effect of inflation.

Target the many subsidy programs that provide special benefits to limited parts of the population at the expense of the national taxpayer. Such subsidies inherently divert resources away from their most productive uses. Subsidies to agriculture are the largest component of this category. Nevertheless, generous subsidies are also provided to business and labor.

Here, economists can team up with an important interest group with which it is often at loggerheads—environmentalists. Many government programs are both economically wasteful and environmentally undesirable. For example, we continue mining for many metals and minerals at a time that the federal government maintains over $6 billion of these same items in a military stockpile that the Department of Defense now admits is not needed. That surplus should be sold on the open market. Those sales would reduce the need for some mining activity that, even when commercially necessary, is environmentally invasive.

Other economically wasteful activities of the federal government that are also environmentally unsound include selling governmentally produced electricity—as well as water, timber, and grazing rights—at below-market prices. Eliminating these subsidies would simultaneously enhance the efficiency of the economy and reduce environmental pollution.

Avoid funding expenditure programs designed to offset problems created by regulation. A more cost-effective way of dealing with the problem is to change the original regulation that created the problem. To maintain the status quo is to ensure fiscal perpetual motion.

A major example of this shortcoming is regulation of the workplace. For years, economists have written about discouraged workers who drop out of the work force because they do not believe suitable jobs are available for them. Government has created a new category—the discouraged employer, discouraged by the host of government impediments to hiring people.

Regulatory and mandated burdens on the employment process are rarely considered in relationship to the expensive array of government programs that offset their adverse affects by trying to increase the supply of workers. Yet the record of these offsetting programs, such as job training, is not heartening. The society would be far better off with a combination of regulatory reform and expenditure reductions. Such a combined effort would reduce the gap between federal income and outlay and eliminate serious inefficiencies in the American workplace.

Privatize activities that are properly the responsibility of the private sector. We need to go beyond the useful notion of having the private sector produce items under government contract. Although an improvement over relying on government arsenals, this approach to privatization still leaves to the public sector the determination of how much of the nation's resources should be funneled to the designated activity. Many goods and services should no longer be paid for by the taxpayer, no matter who produces them. The extent to which those items are produced should depend on the interaction of market forces.

This is not a simple recipe for cutting services to the public. For example, privatizing the air traffic controller functions of the Federal Aviation Administration would enhance the efficiency of air transportation. The airlines are willing to pay higher fees for a more efficient system than the government now provides. The resultant reductions in congestion and waiting times would more than pay for the private expansion of the air traffic control system.

Use economic efficiency considerations throughout the budget process. The key to success is to enforce this guideline. Benefit-cost analysis has often served to sanctify the pork barrel by overestimating benefits and underestimating costs. The use of basic economic efficiency tests would surely improve the overall effectiveness of government spending and likely lower its aggregate level while contributing to more efficient use of the nation's resources. Here are two examples of what is possible:

1. Charge competitive, market interest rates for all federally provided credit. That one change will quickly reduce the many demands for federally subsidized lending. Under the status quo, numerous borrowers who could obtain credit on their own are given an incentive to seek aid simply because the government charges a lower interest rate than commercial banks and other private lenders. Moreover, the current arrangement encourages the extension of credit to borrowers who do not meet the objective tests of the marketplace.
2. Use the comparable market rates of interest when evaluating proposed federal investment projects. Unrealistically low interest rates result in pulling investment funds from the private sector to lower-yield public projects. By definition, such spending is inefficient and a poor use of the taxpayers' money. Traditionally, these programs are referred to as the "pork barrel," and are an appropriate candidate for a federal diet.

Tax Reform

After years of public debate, it is fair to say that there is no universal agreement on how to reform the tax system. Do we streamline the income tax by shifting to a flat tax? Do we adopt a saver-friendly reform known as the

USA Tax? Or do we replace the income tax with a national sales tax? It will take much more discussion and analysis before a specific tax reform emerges with enough support to be enacted. Nevertheless, progress has been made toward a broad consensus on the direction of change.

The most widely held conclusion is the notion that the tax system is unfair and too complicated. And, when we step back from the mass of specific provisions, it can be seen that the Internal Revenue Code, with its heavy dependence on income taxation, depresses the economy.

There are several key arguments that economists offer for shifting the base of taxation from income to consumption. Consumption-based taxes put the fiscal burden on what people take from society—the goods and services they consume—rather than on what they contribute by working and saving, as do income taxes. Thus, under a consumption-based tax system, saving is encouraged at the expense of current consumption. So is investment. Over a period of time, the society is likely to achieve higher levels of saving and consumption, because the added investment, by generating a faster growing economy, will lead to a bigger income "pie" to be divided among the various participants in economic activity.

A constant theme voiced by tax reformers is the need for increased incentives for saving, capital formation, and economic growth. Under a consumption-based tax, the incentives would be very favorable: the basic way to cut tax payments—legally—would be for individuals and families to save more and for companies to invest more. By increasing the amount that we save and invest, a shift to consumption taxation would augment the forces that create the formation of capital and make possible a more rapidly growing economy.

Combining general tax cuts with comprehensive reform would have special charm. Any reform, no matter how carefully drafted, is bound to generate losers as well as winners, thus reducing the chances of enactment. In contrast, combining reform and rate reductions, for example, will result in more winners and fewer losers, brightening the prospects for the reform being carried out.

The various plans for tax reform are not interchangeable. Each comes with its own set of advantages and disadvantages. Nevertheless, compared to the existing tax structure, any of the three alternatives is simpler, and all of them would encourage saving and investment and result in a faster rate of economic growth. All are variants of consumption taxes, and several would provide immediate expensing of investment. Just as there may be more than one path to salvation, there is more than one approach to tax reform that can achieve the public's expectations.

Reforming Government Regulation

Although no regulatory agency has been given the express mission to depress the economy, many regulatory actions have that undesirable effect. The popular view of regulation is wrong. It is not a contest between the "good guys" (government and the consumer) and the "bad guys" (business). The reality is that the consumer is at the receiving end of the benefits as well as the costs generated by government regulation. Business is the middleman (or woman).

The impact of governmental rulemakers, is in one predictable direction: to increase the firm's costs and reduce the resources available to produce goods and services for the customer. Consider what it takes to locate a new factory. A company must obtain approval from dozens of agencies at three or more levels of government. A single "no" anywhere along the line can halt years of planning and investment.

Even when the regulators say "yes," the paperwork burden alone is staggering. It takes approximately 55 million hours each year just to work up the reports required by federal environmental statutes—at an estimated annual cost of $2.9 billion. To get a feel of the "opportunity cost" of these clerical chores, that sum is more than the annual budget of the National Science Foundation.

Regulation also reduces the flow of innovation because many government regulatory agencies have the power to decide whether or not a new product will go on the market. For example, the major obstacles to the development of a new biotechnology industry are not financial or technological, but regulatory. Higher regulatory costs also erode the competitiveness of American companies struggling in an increasingly global marketplace. Compare the cost of cleaning up a hazardous waste site in the United States and Western Europe. Our average of $30 million per site compares to $1 million in the Netherlands and $1 million to $5 million in the United Kingdom.

The benefits of regulation should not be overlooked. But it is too generous to assume that every regulation is effective. We must ask ourselves three serious questions: What benefits does the regulation produce? Are the benefits worth the costs? Is there a better way?

Regulators tend to forget that competition is usually the most effective way of protecting the consumer. Deregulation of interstate trucking, for example, has resulted in 30,000 new businesses entering the trucking industry. The heightened degree of competition has forced sizable reductions in the cost of trucking, which ultimately shows up in lower prices of all the items that move by truck.

When government does regulate (as in the case of environmental pollution), it should make the maximum use of economic incentives. To an economist, the environmental pollution problem is not the negative task of punishing wrongdoers. Rather, the challenge is the positive one of changing people's incentives so that they voluntarily modify their behavior. People do not pollute because they enjoy messing up the environment, but because it often is cheaper or easier than not polluting.

What about the existing array of command-and-control regulation? Benefit-cost analysis can help to make sure that any given regulation does more good than harm. Of course, many federal agencies already prepare that type of economic analysis before issuing a new regulation.

However, the entire process of executive branch review of proposed regulations is reminiscent of locking the stable after the horse has departed the premises. Frequently, the agency is stuck with trying to come up with the most cost-effective way of writing a regulation that should not be issued in the first place. Each congressional committee should do a benefit-cost analysis before it takes action on a proposed regulatory statute. Those statutes often prohibit the agencies from writing more cost-effective regulations.

Regulation is properly viewed as a hidden tax on production of goods and services in the United States. Given the current estimate of compliance cost of $600 billion a year, if sensible reforms could reduce those outlays by 10 percent, we would have the benefits of a $60 billion tax cut.

Conclusion

Experience teaches us to beware of simple answers to complex questions. There is no quick cure to the slow growth of the American economy. Nevertheless, an extensive array of expenditure, tax, and regulatory reforms could shift the American economy to a sustainable higher growth path. Yet, as we have learned from experience, carrying out needed economic changes requires more than developing attractive new programs. It also means making a continuous stream of hard choices. Aye, there's the rub.

2

How to Buy a Cleaner Environment

This 1970 article was an early attempt to show how economics could contribute to enhancing the quality of the environment. It was written when the author was serving as Assistant Secretary of the Treasury for Economic Policy in the Nixon Administration (a time when environmental policy was a relatively nonpartisan matter).

In any consideration of the environment and how to improve it, there seems to be a division of labor. Ecologists and other scientists are supposed to convey dramatically and vividly the notion that we have a severe pollution problem. Engineers and other more practical types are subsequently charged with coming up with ways of cleaning up the pollution and thus improving the quality of our environment. However, then the economists are expected to fill their unique role. They are supposed to say why we cannot afford to do any of these desirable things. Departing from tradition, let us attempt to see how we can—not necessarily that we will—afford to clean up our environment.

The Federal government currently is embarking on a major increase in expenditures for reducing pollution and otherwise improving the quality of the environment. From a level of $644 million last year, such outlays will reach $1.1 billion in fiscal year 1971. This almost 100 percent expansion during a two-year period is creating undoubtedly one of the major growth areas of the American economy. The 1971 figure represents a more than fivefold increase from a decade ago.

All indications point to a long-term continuation of the growth of government spending in the area of the environment. However, very heavy pressures on the Federal budget are likely to dampen down the growth rate of any government spending program, no matter how worthy. The budget situation is likely to remain relatively tight for some time. Nevertheless, environmental planning is basically a long-term affair. Hence, it would be useful to focus on the period beyond the immediate short run.

Hard Answers

Even though there is room for flexibility in the Federal budget, it is clear that the existing revenue structure—which is not a particularly low one—does not permit too great a variety of ambitious and costly new undertakings

Source: Murray Weidenbaum, "How to Buy a Cleaner Environment," *Bulletin of the Atomic Scientists*, November 1970.

in the years ahead. One rather simple reaction to this type of analysis, of course, is to blithely come up with large new tax programs to cover new expenditure recommendations. New taxes may seem to be an easy financing approach for the proponents of a new spending program. However, in recent years, there has been far from any ground swell of public opinion in favor of raising taxes substantially above their current levels.

Hence, we need to be thinking of some hard answers to the serious question of how we are going to finance the necessary improvements in the quality of our environment. Here an economist has something to say. It may not be pleasant, but it may be useful. As I survey the various estimates of the growing future costs of cleaning up the pollution which has not yet been created, but which is likely to occur on the basis of present practices, the economist in me is greatly stirred.

In a sense, I am offended by the prospect of our having to devote an ever larger share of our national resources to cleaning up an ever faster growing mountain of pollution. Rather, the desirability of adopting methods of producing and consuming which are less polluting than our present practices seems to be required. To an economist, one general approach is particularly appealing—to make the act of polluting more expensive to polluters than not polluting, and sufficiently more expensive that they will change their current ways of doing things.

Far too frequently, polluting is more profitable, or cheaper, or easier, than not polluting. The simple-minded solution that is heard far too often these days is to tear down that capitalistic structure which is doing the polluting. It is certainly hardly necessary for the purpose. No highly advanced noncapitalistic society has been able to avoid polluting on a large scale. Here, the economist does have a way out. The price system really does work to allocate resources efficiently, whether the society is capitalistic or socialistic. Hence, in order to make the price system work in the way that we want it—to discourage pollution—we need to attach some form of economic disincentive to the creation of pollution.

The social cost of pollution now borne by society as a whole—whether in the form of smog or contaminated rivers—needs to be shifted back to the polluters themselves. This is not meant as a form of punishment but, rather, as a direct incentive to change to less polluting ways of doing things. This is a crucial point. If instead we are going the eleemosynary route and have society or the Treasury pick up the cost, we are not introducing an incentive to reduce pollution.

The basic idea is that a product should be valued partly in terms of its burden on the environment. At present, much of the "cost" of pollution is borne by the public at large. To the extent that individuals, business firms or other organizations whose actions contribute to pollution can be forced to absorb some of these hitherto "external costs," the market can be made to work against, rather than for, pollution. Thus, producers will have more incentive to "economize" on pollution, similar to their developing methods of reducing labor and material costs.

Policy Actions

There are several ways of promoting this general approach. For example, a tax could be levied upon the legal act of polluting. Alternatively, regulatory actions could be instituted either separately or perhaps in connection with a related tax payment. At the other end of the spectrum is legal action to make certain types of pollution unlawful. Enforcement could include perhaps levying fines, or taking more drastic action if the polluting continues to be performed.

This does not beg the question as to what level of pollution control or reduction to aim for. Of necessity, we will have to stop substantially short of any simpleminded notion of totally eliminating pollution. To cite a small, personal example: I find that my office generally is cleaned once a day. I am sure that it would be cleaner if that were done hourly; but the inconvenience that it would cause me, plus the added cost, would not be worth it. In the case of environmental pollution, as well as other potential objects of government spending, we are going to have to consider determining where the costs begin to exceed the benefits and even where the margin of benefits over costs is less than that for other claims on our resources.

With reference to taxes as an instrument for reducing pollution, an array of alternatives is available. The tax might well be high enough to cover the cost of cleaning up the pollution. This would bring the social and private costs closer together.

One possible application is to junk automobiles, which are being "produced" in ever growing numbers. The rate of abandonment is increasing rapidly. In New York City, 2,500 cars were towed away as abandoned on the streets a decade ago. In 1964, 25,000 were towed away as abandoned; in 1969 the figure was more than 50,000. The way to provide the needed incentive is to apply to the automobile the principle that its price should include not only the cost of producing it, but also the cost of disposing of it. One method would be a bounty payment (financed by a special tax on auto production) to promote the prompt scrapping of all junk autos.

In many other cases, however, the tax could be sufficiently high that it becomes a type of protective tariff. That is, it does not really bring in any substantial amount of revenue. But, by encouraging less polluting methods, the tax reduces the need for expenditures to clean up the pollution. Even if the budget situation were a happier one—a "birth control" approach to pollution would be desirable to the extent possible.

Although attractive, this approach would not suffice. It is more likely to work on prospective new production and consumption facilities—which have not yet been built and paid for. However, it may be inappropriate or highly inequitable in the case of facilities which are already in existence and which were constructed in good faith under a different set of ground rules. Hence, the case for direct government expenditures and/or substantial tax benefits, particularly during a long transition period, may be strong.

However, it is doubtful whether the tax and expenditure systems by themselves will suffice as devices for achieving the desired level of improvement in the quality of the physical environment. Despite the general distaste for government regulations, pollution control appears to be one of the necessary exceptions.

In many areas, strict standards and strict enforcement will be necessary, not only to insure compliance but also in fairness to those who have voluntarily assumed the often costly burden while their competitors or neighbors have not. Without effective government standards, firms that spend the necessary money for pollution control may find themselves at a serious economic disadvantage as against their less conscientious competitors.

Similarly, without effective Federal standards, states and communities that impose such controls may find themselves at a disadvantage in attracting industry, as against more permissive rivals. Air pollution, particularly, is no respecter of political boundaries. A community that sets and enforces strict standards may still find its air polluted from sources in another community or state.

It is unlikely that we will have available or be willing to devote the resources to clean up all of the pollution that could possibly be generated in the United States in the coming decade, much less in the period beyond that. The approach that is feasible and more economically desirable is to encourage business, government, and consumers alike to so change their ways of producing and consuming as to reduce the amount of pollution that is created in the first place.

3

The Contrast Between Business Planning and Government Planning

Interest in expanding the role of government planning in the economy is a recurring policy issue. This article analyzes the shortcomings of such an expansion of government, drawing heavily on a comparison of business and government planning.

The widespread use of planning techniques in private business has led many observers to draw parallels to government planning. Senator Jacob Javits, a leading advocate of national economic planning, stated that, "if corporations are to take a look at where their companies are heading, it seems appropriate for the government to do the same." Well, yes—and then again, maybe. It all depends on what is meant by doing "planning," which can connote a variety of different things, depending upon the context.

Talk about "corporate planning" and "government planning" in the same breath disregards the fundamental distinction between members of a society forecasting and reacting to the future, and the government of that society trying to regulate or control it. Corporate planning is necessarily based on the business purpose, which is to attempt to persuade consumers to buy a firm's goods or services. Activities aimed at implementing the plan are in the main *internally directed*—for example, toward improving products, sales techniques, investment practices, or other aspects of a company's operations. In striking contrast, the government is sovereign, and its planning ultimately involves the use of its power to achieve the results it desires. Its influence is *externally oriented,* extending its sway over the entire society, including redistributing the resources of that society through taxation, regulation, subsidization, and procurement. Unlike a private organization, government may not only plan, it can also command. While a business firm can set goals only for itself, government can establish goals for society as a whole.

It may be useful to take a closer look at the options open to government to effect a particular goal. If the government decides that the American public is not buying enough cars, several courses of action are available. It can lower the price for the consumer through tax reductions on the automobile industry. Or it can reduce the individual income tax, thereby increasing the consumer's purchasing power. Or it can subsidize the private manufacture of automo-

Source: Murray Weidenbaum and Linda Rockwood, "Corporate Planning versus Government Planning," *Public Interest*, Winter 1977.

biles, or even purchase outright the total output of the automobile industry. In recent years, the government has clearly demonstrated a willingness to involve itself in the production of motor vehicles, at least to the extent of deciding by fiat many aspects of their design and operation, through safety and environmental regulations. Senator Hubert Humphrey, sponsor of the major national planning bills, made the point vividly:

> What can government do about it? Government can do a lot about it. For example, the size of automobiles, and consequently energy consumption, can be influenced a great deal by taxing cubic displacement, horsepower, or weight. A tax will slow down purchases of large cars and give a premium to small car buyers and buyers of cars with high fuel efficiency. Government can also influence industry by giving an investment tax credit to companies that produce fuel-efficient automobiles. These are just two ways in which government policy can influence the private economy.

In contrast, what can Ford, General Motors, or Chrysler do if they are not selling as many automobiles as planned? They can—within their available resources—lower the price, change the nature of their product, or alter their marketing efforts. Or as evidenced by the demise of the Edsel, the LaSalle, and the DeSoto, at times they may be forced simply to abandon the project. The consumer remains the ultimate decision-maker as to both the number and kind of automobiles produced.

Business and government planning are further distinguished by the consequences of errors in planning. If a corporate plan proves inaccurate in its assessments of the future, or inappropriate to changing circumstances, the onus fails on the officers, employees, and shareholders of that company. Government planning, by contrast, focuses on "guiding" or "influencing" the activities of the entire nation. If things go wrong in public sector planning, taxpayers and consumers will bear the brunt of the burden of any adjustments that result.

Another basic difference between business and government planning relates to the intellectual dimensions of the effort. Corporate plans, concentrating in detail on individual sectors of the economy and on factors likely to affect their industry, are relatively succinct. Corporate executives can and do read and understand them. Government planning, on the other hand, necessarily focuses on all economic sectors and their interrelationships. In the words of Wassily Leontief, who has provided much of the intellectual leadership in the current drive for national planning, "A national plan would look like the statistical abstract of the United States." That abstract, published annually by the U.S. Department of Commerce, contains in the neighborhood of 900 pages of fine print and tables. In fact, Professor Leontief was too modest. After Congress completed its deliberations on such a comprehensive plan, it would likely be two or three times as long. And how many members of Congress would then comprehend the overall intent or implications of the plan they were to approve?

But whether they would understand it or not, they would have set in motion powerful forces. Advocates of national planning have denied that they would set specific goals for General Motors, General Electric, or General Foods. But what if the activities of these companies in the aggregate did not further the goals of the plan? Would the results be left to chance or to the market mechanism to resolve? Hardly. Proponents of national planning state that the planning office "would try to induce the relevant industries to act accordingly." As Senator Humphrey described the long-range economic planning section of the Humphrey-Hawkins bill:

> . . . it provides a way for us to look at particular industries and sectors and see what kinds of objectives and policies we ought to establish in those sectors. This will enable us to understand and manage the supply side of the economy much better.

Even a cursory examination of the literature on American business planning shows that private planning is intended to be far more than improved information accumulation and analysis. Although definitions developed by individual scholars vary, most are variations on the theme that the planning process encompasses an evaluation of the future through the determination of desired objectives, the development of alternative courses of action, and the selection from among these options. In *Long-Range Planning for Business,* David Ewing offered perhaps the most terse description of the concept: "Planning it to a large extent the job of making things happen that would not otherwise occur."

The proponents of centralized government planning do not leave the matter in doubt. They clearly state, "The heart of planning is to go from information to action." They go on to indicate, in the words of the Initiative Committee for National Planning, that "in order to be effective and useful, an Office of National Economic Planning must be set up at the center of our most influential institutions."

Planning Experience in Business

Business planning has generally undergone two distinct phases, although many corporations have not yet made the transition to the second phase. The first was essentially an extension of long-range budgeting and sales forecasting. Past and present performance was simply extrapolated into the future on the basis of rather rudimentary techniques. The implicit underlying assumption was essentially passive—that business would respond primarily to current market forces rather than attempt to influence future developments.

The second phase is more activist in outlook. It seeks to identify the major issues and options facing the corporation in the future and to indicate possible new courses of action. It is basically predicated on the belief that the pace of technological and environmental change is more rapid now than in the past, and that information about change is more available.

With the rapid growth of planning staffs, planning documents, and planning personnel, what has been the impact on the companies themselves? In practice how significant have the planning efforts turned out to be? Frankly, there are few objective measurements of this essentially subjective activity, and the experience among companies varies widely. However, we can benefit from the comments and evaluations provided by thoughtful observers of the business planning process. Their analyses have often yielded unfavorable prognoses for corporate planning.

In his classic study of long-range business planning, David Ewing concluded, "The paradox is that the planning movement, despite such strong motives to make it succeed, has not generally been blessed with success. The triumphs have been stunning—but few." In his summary of the state-of-the-art, Robert Mockler concurs with this evaluation, reporting that relatively few companies have developed effective planning operations—although many have tried. These evaluations are in accord with a detailed survey that I made a decade ago of planning in the government-oriented defense industry:

> . . . inquiries were made into the role that formal planning plays in the corporate strategy decisions that determine the future posture of the firm. The responses suggest the limited role that planning does play in corporate decision-making. Corporate executives tend to rely more on their trends and future activities . . . . The executives frequently stated that their decisions are not made from within a detailed planned structure. As one officer put it, they must rely on "taking advantage of opportunities rather than having a deep plot" to achieve successful results in their business.

In specific instances, however, effective and respected planning systems have provided positive contributions to the executive decision-making process in the corporate sector. Their widespread and expanding use provides indirect testimony to the credibility of the planning process. It is difficult, however, to find an unambiguous illustration—to label any specific business planning operation as "successful" on the basis of objective criteria. For example, the establishment and extension of a sophisticated planning operation in a rapidly growing company may primarily reflect the fact that the company operates in a growth market and that its profitability enables it to finance a variety of staff services, of which a planning staff is one among many. Also, the key product and investment decisions may have been made independently of the formal planning process. Thus the success of a specific corporate planning effort cannot be inferred from the overall performance of the organization.

George Steiner has identified four factors that are of especial significance in evaluating the effectiveness of a corporate planning system:

1. The system has improved the quality of management.
2. The company has acquired a larger share of the market in which it does business, and this can be traced to the long-range planning system.

3. The company has had high and rising sales and profits over a period of time that can be attributed to long-range planning.
4. Sales growth, profit margins, return on investment, and per-share earnings are higher than average in the industry, resulting partly from the long-range planning process.

Our review of the literature on business planning has not revealed any systematic attempt to apply these or similar criteria to specific efforts. For example, the planning program of General Electric (GE) is often cited as a model to be followed. The company's Strategic Business Unit produces long-range plans that look ten to fifteen years ahead, with comprehensive predictions of economic, social, and political trends, and evaluations of their implications for the company. Central to the methodology is the concept of "alternative futures." Planning is based on the most probable scenario, but the impact on the plan if one of the "alternatives" occurs is also analyzed.

If accuracy of predictions is a measure of success, then GE has evidence of some accomplishments in specialized areas, such as social trends and developments. For example, early studies allowed the company to get a head start in the areas of minority and women's rights. (GE's guidelines for affirmative action were published a year before the federal government's.) But it is also possible that GE's planning model does not deserve the credit. GE's "success" could simply result from employing shrewd and perceptive individuals in its executive positions.

Corporate Constraints

It may be useful at this point to take a look at factors that have limited the success of business planning. Some of these may be confined to the private sector. Others may be more universal, and overcoming them in the public sector may be even more difficult. The first set of problems encountered in business planning relates to the process itself. The business planner has often been viewed as working in a vacuum, acting more as a sounding board for management than as a participant in the decision-making of the organization. Consider how much more serious the consequence would be if the government planner worked in a vacuum isolated from political reality. However, if the planner became excessively concerned with political realities, then we would cease to have "planning," but rather the political management of the economy.

A second area of difficulty involves integrating the concerns and priorities of the senior executives of the corporation with the planning system itself. Without this integration, the plan will neither be accepted nor utilized by other members of the corporation. Consider then the problems of the government planner, who must try to integrate the goals of 200 million citizens, including tens of thousands of private-sector managers and decision-makers. One finds it hard even to imagine what such "integration" might involve.

Advocates of national economic planning who base their case on an extension of business planning activities overestimate the general state-of-the-art in the private sector. My study of thirteen large, technically oriented manufacturing companies found that most of the output of long-range planning groups was more in the nature of scheduling programs with long lead times, rather than the development of long-range business plans. The study concluded that typical long-range plans contained excessive amounts of trivia, such as monthly delivery schedules, the recruiting budget, square footage of storage space by type, and so on. In part, this may help to explain why business plans often have a limited input into the decision-making process.

Despite these shortcomings, many American business firms continue to engage in formal long-range planning efforts, and they apparently believe that the benefits exceed the costs. A variety of reasons is given, not all of which may be applicable to or desirable in the public sector. Many company managements state that planning is a powerful instrument for tightening organizational discipline and control. Others contend that planning can be used to lend authority and plausibility to the corporate leader—a chief executive officer with a formal plan projects the image of having the enterprise well in hand. His counterpart who still relies on intuition and the proverbial "back of the envelope" may be at a psychological disadvantage.

The corporate planning operation also produces information useful to management, but this involves an important "opportunity cost." The manpower and other resources devoted to the planning effort are unavailable for other purposes. Thus because of the high cost of a planning department and because the output often has not met the expectations of management, many companies have scaled back their planning efforts. To some degree this may have been the natural pattern of reaction and accommodation to the overselling of a new management activity (although certainly one with more durability than a short-term fad). Yet, at least one major corporation no longer uses the word "planning" in any corporate title, or to describe any corporate activity.

Planning Experience in Government

Government experience with formal long-range planning systems appears to be more negative than the experience of the private sector. The most pertinent evidence available on the effectiveness of planning at the federal level is the experience with the process instituted by President Lyndon Johnson. In August 1965, he announced with great fanfare the introduction of "a very new and very revolutionary system of planning and programming and budgeting throughout the vast federal government, so that through the tools of modern management the full promise of a finer life can be brought to every American at the lowest possible cost."

The Planning-Programming-Budgeting System (PPBS) was initially greeted with great enthusiasm. For a while it created a land-office business for the services of economists, statisticians, and program analysts. The August 1965 announcement had a substantial history behind it. Since January 1961, Secretary of Defense Robert McNamara and Assistant Secretary Charles Hitch had been attempting to apply the principles of program budgeting to the Pentagon, notably the five-year projections of force structures and budgets, as well as the review of budget submissions along program, rather than merely organizational, lines.

Some of the enthusiastic overreactions to the implementation of PPBS were perhaps inevitable, and not fundamentally different from private sector experiences. It takes many years, not the mere months of President Johnson's timetable, to establish an effective planning system, public or private. The intent of PPBS was to provide better information for the development of both budgets and legislation, but that was not the initial result. The government was already turning out thousands of analyses, evaluations, and studies every year. It became instead a different, somewhat competitive channel for decision-making; its influence on policy was often negligible. The PPBS apparatus has now been largely dismantled in the federal government. What remains is performed in a more modest manner, as part of the annual budget preparation.

In retrospect, it is quite clear that PPBS—at either the Pentagon or White House level—did not help the federal government avoid fundamental overcommitments, at home or abroad, or an unusual array of "crises." Those who assume that the occasional success of business planning can be readily replicated at the national level should consider the failure of the Edsel in the private sector, and the major federal decisions made at the peak of the PPBS enthusiasm—deeper American involvement in the Vietnam War and the over-promotion of the "Great Society" domestic programs. The point is not that the attempts to introduce organized planning led to these failures, but rather that they clearly did not prevent them. David Ewing offers a stronger conclusion: "For sheer magnitude of fiasco, however, business cannot compete with planners in the military and government."

In view of the impact of more formidable planning systems, such as the one utilized in Great Britain, perhaps we should be pleased that the results of PPBS were mainly paper shuffling and wheel spinning. Many analysts of Britain's experiences with centralized planning have painted a rather dismal picture, characterizing its economic woes as largely the result of giving the State responsibility for so many crucial economic decisions.

Government planning in France also extends beyond forecasts of the economy, at first by indicating directions, following with persuasion, and then resorting to direct action. In his analysis of the French planning experience, John Sheahan cites a different type of problem—the possibility of large private corporations coming to dominate the government planning process. This would be an extension of the widely held "capture" theory, whereby regulated industries increasingly influence the decisions of the government agencies set up to oversee them. Planning by consultation and negotiation in France may be tending to drive the government planners into such a close alliance with business interests that the planning board becomes a champion of the firms that it finds it easiest to deal with. Since these are usually the largest businesses, government planning thus weakens competition and may result in the neglect of social concerns.

Overall economic performance does not appear to have improved under any of these alternative schemes of national economic planning adopted by the primarily market-oriented, non-Communist nations. These planning systems have tended to shift the focus of private enterprise even further away from dealing with market forces and consumer demands, toward reaching an accommodation with an ever more powerful governmental bureaucracy.

Under an American version of centralized economic planning, a company might find it desirable to shift resources from conventional marketing activities to convincing the government to adopt more generous production targets for its industry. Thus there might be less payoff from traditional consumer market research than from new efforts to persuade the government to treat the industry more favorably. In this regard, we could conjure up visions of civilian companies following some of the practices of that branch of American industry, defense production, which is now most closely tied to governmental decision-making. Business-financed hunting lodges and fishing trips for civilian government planners might seem merely to follow an older defense industry tradition, but such public sector "marketing" activities would be a low priority use of business resources. Yet, given the incentive of any organization to grow and prosper in the environment it faces, this result would not be surprising under a system of strong national economic planning and centralized decision-making.

Managing the Government

In a sense, there are two types of government planning that need to be distinguished. The external, national planning discussed above involves numerous extensions of government powers over the private sectors of the economy. A second type of government planning is more internally oriented, and may be more comparable to private sector planning: the management of government's own activities. The advocates of national planning tend to merge the two, using shortcomings in government's management of its affairs as a rationale for extending government power and influence over consumers and business.

In his far-ranging statement advocating national economic planning, Senator Humphrey deals in passing with this second type of government planning: "We don't have any economic impact statement for government decisions. The government goes around willy-nilly making decisions of consequence . . . the manner in which we are presently utilizing government resources and government agencies is a haphazard, helter-skelter enterprise." It would appear, however, that a government conducted on such a haphazard, helter-skelter basis should be reluctant to undertake the extremely ambitious task of managing the entire economy prior to setting its own house in order. This is perhaps an appropriate point to turn to that task.

The federal government presently has an instrument for establishing its priorities and allocating its resources, though it is neither new nor the object of widespread public attention—the budgetary process. To be sure, there are serious limitations to the way it currently works. Despite important reforms, government budgeting rarely addresses itself to the fundamental question of selecting overall priorities. Instead, the major attention of decision-makers focuses on the amount of funds to be allocated to a specific agency, or to an individual project within an agency. Little if any consideration is given to alternative ways of achieving such overall objectives as reducing inflation, increasing employment, and improving living standards.

In striking contrast, the adoption of a government-wide program planning budget would be a useful tool for improving decision-making. Expenditure categories would cut across agencies and would relate to the various programs and activities that serve a given purpose. For example, program budgeting would necessitate making deliberate choices among alternatives: The job training programs of the Labor Department, the tax incentives to employers administered by the Treasury Department, and the economic development subsidies paid out by the Commerce Department would all be viewed as alternative ways of achieving a higher level of employment. In a very real sense, a measure of competition would be introduced into the process of allocating governmental resources.

The underlying rationale for this suggestion for program budgeting is evident in the activities of a well managed company. Such a company would not impulsively decide to devote an increase in earnings to raising the dividend rate. Rather, it would carefully consider the alternative uses of the funds—embarking on a new research program, rebuilding an obsolescent manufacturing plant, or developing a new overseas operation. The basic requirement is the ability to array the pertinent alternatives, each seemingly attractive in its own right, and to choose carefully and intelligently among them.

Although proposals for a national economic planning system may be designed by economists and other technical specialists, it will be politicians and representatives of powerful interest groups who will translate any proposal into reality. They will oversee and perhaps guide the activities of the planning body and subsequently use its output. But as has too often been the case in the past, the results of such an undertaking may not conform to the initial expectations of its proponents.

Most of the public discussion of national planning focuses on the potential contributions to the solution of such macroeconomic problems as inflation and unemployment. However, a centralized planning apparatus could be redirected toward effecting basic changes in, for example, the distribution of income among the various groups of the society. As interest groups recognize a new mechanism for introducing change on a national scale, attempts to make such shifts in economic power would be likely. This may occur even though it was neither a desired nor an expected result of the planning system.

It would not be unusual for economic analysis to be applied to justify politically desirable programs—examples include many Corps of Engineers, Bureau of Reclamation, and other "pork barrel" projects. In each case, detailed economic calculations are made in order to comply with the statutory requirement that measured benefits exceed measured costs. Yet, in practice, many of these projects represent an uneconomical use of the country's resources, resulting mainly in national subsidies to specific regions.

In a different regard, the issue of an unfair distribution of governmental resources is already a major source of debate. There is a growing concern in the Northeastern "frost belt" over the large shares of federal money going to the Southwestern "sun belt." Could a national planning mechanism become an arena for either resolving or intensifying this regional conflict? The latter would be the case if the emphasis in allocating resources shifted from establishing program priorities to altering the regional distribution of those resources.

Possibilities for Planning

Both advocates and opponents of expanding government's role in planning can agree that any effort to deal with the future has built-in limitations. For example, no amount of formalized planning has eliminated any company's uncertainty concerning future technological change, the vagaries of the weather, discoveries of energy or other natural resources, outbreaks of war, assassinations of national leaders, or even shifts in the desires of the fickle consumer. And there seems to be no basis for assuming that government planning efforts would be more accurate or effective than those of business. If anything, national planning introduces a new range of problems. It is certainly conceivable that the bureaucratic process inevitably involved would tend to dilute or possibly redirect the original objectives. Carl Madden has offered cogent words of caution concerning planning efforts: " . . . just as the process of planning stimulates acts of envisioning new possibilities, so the existence and promulgation of a plan constrains such acts. A plan is a device that inhibits further imagining."

The possibilities of using business planning experiences to mold a national planning system are not encouraging. Even disregarding the shortcomings of business plans and planning techniques, the differences between business and government decision-making are fundamental. Business planning is based on the traditionally implicit—and increasingly explicit—assumption that the ultimate decisions on the allocation of society's resources are to be made by individual consumers. The important corollary of this is that if a company's projections are wrong, it will suffer the consequences. National planning by government, implicitly or explicitly, is based on a fundamentally different set of assumptions. Government officials, both appointed and elected, will determine what they consider to be in the overall interest of society. If the public does not respond accordingly, it is not the planners who are considered to be at fault. Rather, new and more effective devices will be employed to induce the public to accommodate the planners' conception of the good society.

Boiled down to its essence, business planning is part of a decentralized decision-making process in which individual consumers make the ultimate choices. National planning is a centralized process in which the key economic decisions are made in the form of governmental edicts. The greatest danger of adopting a form of centralized economic planning is that it will—perhaps unintentionally at first, but inevitably as its initial results prove disappointing—propel the society away from market freedoms and toward greater governmental controls over individual behavior.

But despite the polarized nature of much of the public debate, the controversy over national planning really does not involve choosing between "master" planning and no planning at all. It is apparent that a great deal of planning goes on in the United States, in both the public and private sectors. The crux of the current debate involves deciding who should plan for whom. There is no question about the authority and desirability of General Motors planning its own activities. Likewise, upon reflection, it may be equally desirable for the Department of Transportation to plan its own activities. The point at issue is whether the Transportation Department, or any other federal agency, should plan the activities of General Motors—or its suppliers, employees, and customers.

There may be some high ground—although not necessarily a middle ground—to which the antagonists in the debate can both move, at least for a while: a position related to the need for improving the ability of both government and business to plan—and manage—their own affairs. In *The Road to Serfdom,* Friedrich von Hayek develops this point:

> The dispute between the modern planners and their opponents is . . . not a dispute on whether we ought to employ foresight and systematic thinking in planning our common affairs. It is a dispute about what is the best way of so doing. The question is whether for this purpose it is better that the holder of coercive power should confine himself in general to creating conditions under which the knowledge and initiative of individuals are given the best scope so that *they* can plan most successfully; or whether a rational utilization of our resources requires *central* direction and organization of all our activities according to some consciously constructed "blueprint."

4

The Case for Reaganomics

This article was an early exposition of Reaganomics written when the author chaired the President's Council of Economic Advisers. At the time, it neither pleased supply-side enthusiasts nor traditional Keynesians.

I am reminded of the old saying, "Let him who putteth his armor on not boast like he who taketh it off." Having worn that armor for over a year, I find it useful to look back and examine some of our assumptions and expectations at the time the Reagan administration took office in January 1981.

One overriding point emerges clearly: the fundamental effort to shift resources and decision-making from the government to the private sector is as meritorious as ever. Reducing the burden of taxation and regulation and slowing the growth of government spending and credit are essential steps to achieving stronger economic performance. This ringing endorsement of principles, very frankly, does not encompass each and every economic policy decision or outcome that has occurred, but much of our accumulated knowledge has been reaffirmed.

My first example is the key area of taxes and the relationship between spending and taxes. Despite optimistic claims by some of our friends, from the outset the Reagan administration has proceeded on the assumption that there was no free lunch. In all of our policy documents and statements—beginning with our economic White Paper of February 18, 1981—we associated the desired tax-rate reductions with expenditure cutbacks. To be specific, the published estimates always showed that revenues from the reduced tax rates being proposed would not be as large as the revenues from the preexisting higher tax rates that then were facing the nation. This is precisely why we gave such a high priority, and devoted so much of our efforts, to cutting the outlay side of the budget.

In retrospect, it is clear that there truly is no free lunch, that in the real world a general reduction in income tax rates may yield significant feedback in terms of faster economic growth and a larger tax base, but the total amount of revenue raised will not be as much as it would be in the absence of the tax-rate reductions.

Source: Murray Weidenbaum, "Supply Side Economics," in *Supply-Side Economics in the 1980s: Conference Proceedings* (Westport, CT: Quorum Books, 1982).

Over time, a large tax-rate reduction will have a positive effect on the growth rate of the economy and generate a substantial amount of "feedback" receipts. Recent experience with the capital gains tax reductions suggests that some specific taxes might produce more revenue when the rate is lower. Also, moving the top bracket on personal income from 70 percent to 50 percent may well have a similar positive effect. But, especially in the short run, general tax-rate reductions will increase the budget deficit. This is not presented as new knowledge but merely the reaffirmation of accumulated wisdom.

Earning the Tax Cuts

A bit of unlearning is in order. Let me report from the battlefield bluntly. Cutting taxes provides no assurance that comparable spending offsets will be forthcoming. The nation needs both. But it is demonstrably easier to cut taxes by an estimated $700 billion than to cut government spending by $70 billion. If we want to spend less, Congress has to appropriate less. There is no shortcut. We can be reminded of the old cartoon showing an irate master yelling at his overweight dog for not squeezing into a patently inadequate dog house. That dog house was labeled "Debt Limit," but the basic point is the same.

On the subject of deficits, here, too, experience both ratifies some of our prior knowledge and also raises doubts about some of our preconceptions. For example, economists have not always shared the man in the street's distaste for budget deficits, or at least we have not always attributed the same wide assortment of sinful characteristics to an excess of government outgo over income. As my colleagues and I have pointed out on innumerable occasions, the inflationary consequences that have so often been attributed to past budget deficits have actually been the result of inappropriate monetary policy, which monetized those deficits. We have contended that a policy of monetary restraint—substantial reduction in the growth of the money supply from the rapid pace that characterized much of 1979 and 1980—would contain the inflationary potential of deficit spending.

The current situation is instructive. A rising deficit has been accompanied by a dramatic reduction in inflation. The fiscal 1982 deficit is likely to be in the neighborhood of $100 billion, substantially above the 1981 figure of $58 billion. Concurrently, however, one widely watched indicator of the inflation rate, the consumer price index, has declined from the 12-13 percent range of late 1980 to a 4-6 percent range in recent months. Let us not be so partisan as to contend that the deficits of one political party are inherently less inflationary than those of another, although there may be a germ of truth imbedded in that proposition—namely, that deficits associated with tax reductions are less of a problem for the economy than those arising from a spending increase.

The primary credit for less inflation should be given to the Federal Reserve and its monetary policy, which the Reagan administration consistently supported during the past year. But please note that this statement of support refers to the Federal Reserve's policy and targets. At times, we can wish that their aim would improve, but then again they do too.

It has been clearly demonstrated in the past year that many participants in financial markets are close students of the federal budget and especially of reports of future deficits. The formal economic literature may be ambivalent or equivocal on this point, but at least under present circumstances, investors and their advisers tend to associate larger deficits with higher interest rates. Although econometric substantiation may be less than robust, it would appear that financing budget deficits does decrease—it surely does not increase —the amount of private saving and foreign capital inflow that otherwise would be available for private investment.

Those deficits are a serious problem, but not so serious as to prevent significant declines in market interest rates or to abort the impending recovery. The precise speed and strength of that recovery will be strongly influenced by the further success in bringing down those high interest rates. That is not to discount the severity of the deficit problem. The projected deficits should be a matter of considerable concern, but not national hysteria. It may be of only limited comfort to be informed that the current sizable deficit is largely the temporary product of recession when the expectation is for relatively large deficits in the recovery years that follow.

There is a touch of irony in all of this. It would not be surprising if some people enjoy the prospect of criticizing the large deficits that might be attributed to the political party that traditionally has run against deficit financing. At times, I have expressed my own pleasant surprise that the folks who invented deficit financing have, albeit belatedly, discovered the merits of a closer balance between income and outgo.

A Constitutional Amendment?

Those committed to a smaller public sector see some progress in the growing public concern over large budget deficits. Hopefully, that new interest in sound government finance will be directed primarily to slowing down the continuing rapid growth of expenditures rather than to raising tax burdens.

I have avoided presenting a grand vision, either new or old, of how the economic world works. In this regard, let us recall one of the lesser known statements of Gertrude Stein, to the effect that the trouble with Americans is that they always simplify when they should try to understand complexity. A part of that complexity surely involves the difficulties inherent in quickly changing basic aspects of the structure of the economy.

As an example, we can cite the problem of imbedded expectations, which is a technician's reference to the difficulties of overcoming the legacy of the past. Specifically, we can refer to the inflationary expectations that linger in an environment radically different from the escalating double-digit inflation of 1980.

Although there is no law of free-market economics that precludes immediate private sector adjustment to newly announced government policies, quick or painless adjustment has not been our experience. Part of this rigidity surely reflects institutionalized setting of wages and prices in major sectors of the economy. But part also reflects private sector uncertainty concerning the credibility of new policies. Unfortunately, the legacy of stop-and-go economic policy in the 1970s gives the financial markets and the private sector generally reason to question the longevity of any new set of government policies.

It is heartening to note that the progress in slowing down the current inflation began before the recession and thus is likely to continue during the recovery that follows, as the policy of moderate monetary growth is maintained.

Hidden Progress on Regulation

We also have learned, once again, that undramatic developments are underappreciated. That is the case in the area of regulatory reform. Unlike the tax bill or the budget-reconciliation bill, there is no single piece of legislation embodying the administration's regulatory program to command public attention. Rather, the struggle to reduce the burden of regulation and to introduce economic analysis into the process must be waged on many fronts. Nor have all changes necessarily been victories, even minor ones. Yet dozens of specific actions have been taken that do curtail the often needless burdens of complying with the multitude of federal directives and prohibitions.

We must be aware of—and sensitive to—charges that the Reagan administration has been backtracking on some of the regulatory gains that were achieved in recent years. Frankly, there have been some areas, such as transportation, where proponents of reform have been disappointed. But some of the developments that might interpret as setbacks can be viewed as temporary holding points, pending legislative developments, or a stronger economy.

Nevertheless, the most significant development on the regulatory front may be along the lines of that Sherlock Holmes story where the decisive event was the fact that the dog did not bark. During the past year, not a single major new regulatory law was enacted nor was a major new regulatory program promulgated by a federal agency. It was the first year in several decades that the federal regulatory dog did not bark. The most direct if anecdotal manifestation of the undramatic but changing relationship between business and government is the reported decline in hiring by Washington law firms and the closing rather than opening of Washington offices by private companies. The state is not withering away, but some high-cost resources are being reoriented to more productive pursuits.

Promise and Performance

The more cynical might say that the past year has once again underscored the gap between promise and performance. Of course, it is far too early for anyone to make a definitive evaluation of Reaganomics. But surely it is apparent that great difficulties face any administration attempting to develop and carry out an ambitious and comprehensive new program.

Let us take up the crucial question of budget cuts. The approach was to achieve the budgeteer's goal—the uniform distribution of dissatisfaction. The dissatisfaction has surely been widespread, but it is not accurate to state that it has been as uniform as we would have liked it to be. The realities reveal, at least at the present time, less political opposition to cutting education than to reducing subsidies to business and agriculture. I report this not as a special pleader for student loans and other educational programs but as a budget cutter whose axe is still honed. The reality may not reflect any basic shortcoming in the conceptual basis of the Reagan economic programs. Rather, it demonstrates, once again, the difficulties that are encountered in attempting to change the status quo in a comprehensive manner.

We surely have tried to avoid repeating the mistakes of the past—although no doubt we will produce a full quota of new errors. But this entire process, we can anticipate, will make for both a stronger economy and an improved understanding of the workings of economic policy.

Surely, in the past year we have seen strong evidence of the initial results of the Reagan program, specifically referring to the lower tax burdens and reduced inflation. As details of the program develop, we can anticipate further benefits, especially in terms of economic growth and rising employment, as the economy pulls out of the current recession. The precise timing, strength, and duration of that recovery, it should be acknowledged, will be affected by how quickly interest rates decline from the current high levels. Progress on the budget deficits will play no small part in influencing these interest-rate movements.

All in all, as I look forward as well as back, it remains remarkably clear that carrying out needed economic changes requires more than developing bold new programs; it also means making a continuous stream of hard choices.

5

Shifting from Income to Consumption Taxation

The most fundamental reform of taxation is to shift the basis of government revenue from the incomes that people earn to the expenditures that they make. This radical proposal has strong historical antecedents.

The United States would benefit greatly by reforming the national system of taxation to encourage more saving and investment. Such a transformation would help achieve faster economic growth, higher levels of employment, improved standards of living, and smaller budget deficits. Specifically, a savings-exempt income tax on individuals and families and a companion cash-flow tax on business should replace the existing federal income taxes.

The idea proposed here deals with the missing link in the budget debate. Until now, most proposals to reduce the deficit have focused either on cutting spending or raising taxes. But there is a third alternative: improving the way the tax system functions. The twin proposals made here—the savings-exempt income tax and the business cash-flow tax—would initially raise the same amount of revenue as the existing tax system with far less damage to the economy. This means that over the years the nation would achieve a faster-growing economy. The direct benefits would be threefold: (1) more people at work, (2) lower federal outlays for unemployment payments and so on, and (3) more income to the Treasury from a growing tax base with no future change in tax rates.

All this cannot be attained by tinkering with the details of the Internal Revenue Code. Instead, the present federal income tax system must be overhauled so it exempts saving and investment, which constitute the seedcorn for economic expansion. This is not an argument for an additional tax, but for a sea change in the existing income tax structure.

Going beyond the present array of detailed proposals that would modify the income tax in a piecemeal fashion, let us consider instead making a fundamental transformation in the federal revenue system: abandon the whole idea of taxing income and shift to a consumption-based tax as the primary federal revenue source.

Source: Murray Weidenbaum, "True Tax Reform: Encouraging Saving and Investment," *Business Horizons*, May-June 1995.

Economists have offered several basic arguments for shifting the base of taxation from income to consumption in an effort to achieve greater equity as well as economic efficiency. Consumption-based taxes put the fiscal burden on what people *take* from society—the goods and services they consume— rather than on what they *contribute* by working and saving, as income taxes do. Thus, under a consumption-based tax system, saving—and investment— is encouraged at the expense of current consumption. Over a period of time, the society is likely to achieve higher levels of saving and consumption. This is because the added investment, by generating a faster-growing economy, will lead to a bigger income "pie" to be divided among the various participants in economic activity.

A constant theme voiced by tax reformers is the need for increased incentives for saving, capital formation, and economic growth. It is common knowledge that the United States saves and invests far less than other industrialized countries. In 1990, the U.S. saving rate as a percentage of GDP was only 2.2 percent, the lowest of any member country of the Organization for Economic Cooperation and Development (OECD). In contrast, the OECD average saving rate was 8.3 percent. Standing alone, this fact might not appear terribly harmful. However, among the *major* industrialized nations, there is a clear and positive correlation between the share of GDP going to investment and the pace of economic growth. This is not a transitory or fleeting relationship. The close fit between investment and growth shows up in the data for the past three decades.

In that light, let us examine the ramifications of consumption-based taxation and the major alternative approaches to structuring a new consumption-based tax.

Promoting Investment and Economic Growth

Under a consumption-based tax, the basic way to cut taxes—legally—is for individuals and families to save more and for companies to invest more. To minimize tax liability under the existing tax structure, taxpayers have to earn less. This fundamental fact reduces the incentives for taxpayers to work, save, and invest. By increasing the amount we save and invest, the proposed tax system would augment the forces that create the formation of capital.

To many citizens, any discussion of capital formation immediately brings to mind visions of greedy bankers, wealthy coupon clippers, and—to use what is to many a pejorative word--capitalists. Nevertheless, capital plays a pivotal role in providing the basis for the future standard of living of any society. Capital is essential for increasing productivity and thus providing the basis for rising real incomes. Increased capital formation also enhances our competitiveness in an increasingly global marketplace.

A rising stock of capital is necessary for a growing society. It is a basic matter of how much we want to eat, drink, and be merry today, and how much we want to set aside for tomorrow. Boiled down to its fundamentals, assuring an adequate flow of saving and investment is little more than demonstrating a proper concern for the future.

A slow pace of capital formation in the United States is especially troublesome at a time of heightened global competition, when modern, state-of-the-art machinery and equipment are necessary to match foreign firms with low-wage structures. The increasingly international nature of business competition requires updating the American tax system to face up to these global realities. The current tax code is biased in favor of current consumption and against saving. In effect, the current system taxes saving twice, once when the income is earned and second when the saving generates interest, dividends, and so forth.

Changing the Tax Structure

The United States uses consumption taxes to a far lesser degree than most other developed Western nations. In 1991, the 24 OECD members obtained an average of 30 percent of their revenue from taxes on consumption. For the United States, the ratio was 17 percent.

The U.S. Treasury proposed a "spending tax" in 1942 as a temporary wartime measure to curb inflation. The proposal was rejected by Congress on the grounds that the exemption of saving would favor the rich, since they are better able to save large portions of their incomes. Some believe that this would lead to greater concentrations of wealth in the hands of a few. As we will see, proponents of a consumption tax respond that it can be made as progressive as desired.

Another objection to consumption-based taxation is that it favors the miser over the spendthrift, even when both have similar spending power or ability to pay. The response to this argument is that consumption uses up the resources available to the nation, while saving adds to these resources. Thus, people should be taxed on what they take out of society's pool of resources, not on what they put into it.

Tax experts have devised, and criticized, a variety of specific consumption-based taxes. No consensus has been reached on the details. Three interrelated clusters of issues need increased public attention:

1. The general desirability of a tax on consumption;
2. The specific form it should take ("top-down" or "bottom-up"); and
3. Whether it should replace or augment an existing tax.

There are two major types of consumption-based taxes. One is a "bottom-up" tax on individual purchases of goods and services. The United States provides many examples in the form of state sales taxes. In Western Europe and other industrialized areas, a variation known as a value-added tax (VAT) is customary. Like general sales taxes, a VAT is comprehensive. Essentially, value-added is the difference between a business's sales and its purchases from other companies. The VAT is paid by each enterprise in the chain of production—manufacturer, wholesaler, and retailer. Duplication is avoided by taxing only the added value that the firm contributes to the goods or services it produces.

The second approach to consumption taxation is a "top-down" variation. Over the years, this proposal has been called an expenditure tax and a consumed-income tax; the current nomenclature is a "savings-exempt income tax." Based on the current income tax, it exempts all saving, in effect changing the income tax into a consumption-based tax. As will be shown, this form of taxation avoids many of the negatives associated with the VAT while capturing most of the benefits. Conceptually, the base of the two types of consumption-based taxes is the same (the value of goods and services purchased) and the yields from these taxes could be very similar.

The Value-Added Tax

A value-added tax represents a very different way of collecting a general tax than most Americans are familiar with, focusing on the sales of goods and services to consumers by individual companies. It is, in effect, a sophisticated and comprehensive sales tax that avoids the double counting otherwise inevitable when the same item moves from manufacturer to wholesaler to retailer. In total, a VAT should be equivalent in yield to a single-stage sales tax levied at the retail level.

Essentially, a firm's "value-added" is the difference between its sales and its purchases from other firms. Value-added can also be estimated by adding labor and capital inputs supplied by the firm itself—represented by wages and salaries, rent and interest payments, and profit.

Reasons for Favoring a VAT

Proponents of the VAT maintain it is economically neutral, because ideally it would be levied at a uniform rate on all items of consumption. It would not distort choices among products or methods of production. In that regard, the VAT is indeed superior to the existing array of selective excise taxes.

Advocates of the value-added tax also point out that, in contrast to an income tax, there is no penalty for efficiency—profits are taxed equally as wages—and no subsidy for waste (a dollar of expense saved becomes a dollar of profits and, again, is taxed equally). Moreover, the VAT is neutral between incorporated and unincorporated businesses and, theoretically, between public and private enterprises. By focusing on consumption, it avoids a double tax burden on the returns from capital. This kind of tax starts off with no exclusions or exemptions and thus, at least initially, provides a broader and fairer tax base, one that the underground economy will have more difficulty evading. Consumption taxes such as the VAT are levied on the returns to labor (wages and salaries) equally with the returns on capital (rent, interest, and profits). Thus, shifting to a more capital-intensive and perhaps more profitable method of production would not influence a firm's tax burden.

Another argument in favor of a value-added tax is that many other nations have adopted this form of taxation. It therefore fits in better than conventional taxes with the growing international character of production. Almost every industrialized nation in Europe imposes the VAT, and it has spread throughout the Third World as well. The members of the European Union have used VAT taxation since the late 1960s or early 1970s.

The adoption of a tax on value-added was true reform in Western Europe. The VAT typically replaced an extremely inefficient form of consumption tax that was already in place: a cascading sales or turnover revenue system. Those latter taxes apply to the total amount of a firm's sales rather than only to its value-added. Sales taxes, therefore, would be paid over and over again on the same items as they moved from firm to firm in the various stages of the production and distribution process. Such cascade-type taxes favored integrated firms (that could legally avoid one or more stages of the tax), but they severely discriminated against independent companies that operate at only one phase of the production process.

Reasons for Opposing a VAT

Opponents of a value-added tax offer an extensive list of shortcomings. They contend that a VAT is inherently regressive. Those least able to pay face the highest rates because, on average, the higher your income the smaller proportion you spend on current consumption. Regressivity can be softened by exempting food and medicine or by offering refunds to low-income taxpayers, but such variations make the collection of the tax much more complicated.

Because the VAT is included in the price of purchases, it registers in the various price indices and, hence, exerts an inflationary force on the economy. The counterargument is that any price increase would be only a one-time effect, occurring when the tax is enacted or increased. However, there would be secondary inflation effects resulting from the operation of automatic escalators in wage and price agreements. That inflationary impact could in turn be offset by appropriate changes in monetary policy, albeit at times with an adverse effect on the levels of production and employment.

Opponents also charge that a VAT would invade the area of sales taxation, traditionally reserved for state and local governments. However, most states and some localities have come to rely on income taxes despite heavy use of the same tax base by the federal government.

Turning to the administrative aspects, imposition of a VAT in the United States would require establishing a new tax collection system by the federal government and additional record-keeping on the part of business taxpayers. This would be a vast and expensive undertaking. The Treasury Department, based on European experience, believes it would need 18 months after enactment to begin administering a VAT.

Several different methods have been suggested for collecting a new VAT, the simplest of which is the credit system. The tax is computed initially on a company's total sales and the firm is given credit for the VAT paid by its suppliers. To a substantial degree, such a VAT would be self-enforced. Each company would have a powerful incentive to ensure that its suppliers paid their full share of the tax, because any underpayment would have to be made up by the next firm in the chain of production and distribution.

The Unlimited Savings Account

A new approach to a consumption-based tax has been proposed in the form of a savings-exempt income tax. This is popularly referred to as the Unlimited Savings Account or USA Tax.

Taxes on Individuals and Families

As we have seen, the VAT suffers from a number of possible complications, such as inflation, regressivity, and administrative burden. In contrast, a savings-exempt income tax would be collected much as income taxes currently are. It would be levied directly on the taxpayer. The annual taxpayer return would continue to comprise the heart of the collection system, containing exemptions and deductions, as it does now. However, one fundamental change would be instituted: The portion of income saved would be exempt from taxation. This type of tax has been known by a variety of names. Many prefer to call it a consumption tax, for the intent is to tax what people spend, not what they save. Another frequent name is expenditure tax.

The difficult bookkeeping requirement to tally all consumption outlays could be readily avoided. Because of the notion that income equals consumption plus saving, consumption can thus be readily estimated, indirectly but accurately, merely by deducting saving from income. Taxpayers are used to developing estimates of their incomes. A new schedule of saving during the year would include changes in bank balances and in holdings of bonds, stocks, and similar investment assets.

To a typical taxpayer, a savings-exempt income tax is essentially the equivalent of a universal but simplified Individual Retirement Account (IRA), using an amended rate table. Each taxpayer would decide how much to save and in what form. Many benefits would result. Consider the current tax treatment of housing. A bigger down payment, and thus lower interest payments, gives a homebuyer a smaller tax break. But why should tax policy discourage investing in a home? Under a savings-exempt income tax, down payments and payments of principal would be fully deductible. After all, building equity in a home or business is a form of saving and investment. Home equity loans that tap into this investment would not be rewarded with tax deductions, as they are under current tax law.

The first reaction by many people to exempting all saving from the income tax is that it is unfair because it must be regressive. If this were the case, poorer people would end up paying a larger share of their income in taxes than would wealthier Americans. However, the savings-exempt income tax need not be regressive at all. As with the existing income tax, each taxpayer would face a rate table that could be made as progressive as desired. Under the revenue-neutral shift from the traditional income tax contemplated here, the average taxpayer would experience no change in tax burden. However, at each income level, above-average savers would pay less than they do now and below-average savers would pay more. To deal with the concern over regressivity, lower-income families (those with combined earnings of less than $25,000) would also receive a tax credit for their contributed payroll taxes.

This plan also exempts households with low incomes from the savings-exempt income tax altogether. For example, a family of four might not pay any federal taxes on their first $25,000 of consumption. A graduated rate schedule provides further assurance that the savings-exempt income tax is progressive.

The basic idea is that the new tax structure would raise as much federal revenue as the existing system (this is known as being "revenue neutral"). In the longer run, the reformed income tax could generate more revenue—or permit rate reductions—to the extent that the added savings stimulate economic growth, which in turn increases the tax base while reducing the demand for unemployment benefits and other government spending.

Most important, the reformed income tax is not a new or an added tax; it is a change in the existing IRS tax collection system. Current restrictions on IRAs and other specialized forms of investment would be eliminated. *All* savings would be exempt from taxes. Thus, the savings-exempt income tax does not suffer from the administrative burden associated with a VAT, which would require setting up a new tax-collection system and new record-keeping, causing overhead costs to rise in both the public and private sectors. From the viewpoint of the taxpayer, the current bookkeeping and administrative requirements would actually be reduced under a savings-exempt income tax system.

For example, this fundamental tax reform does not differentiate among different income sources; wages, salaries, interest income, capital gains, and dividends are all treated equally. However, it would eliminate about three-fourths of the current individual tax code that is estimated to cost taxpayers $50 billion in compliance costs annually.

The United States has been moving toward a form of exempting saving from federal taxation, albeit indirectly and in modest steps. The establishment of IRAs enables many federal taxpayers to defer paying taxes on amounts saved and invested in the accounts.

Taxes on Business

Tax incentives to promote saving do not suffice in responding to the desire for more rapid economic growth. A larger amount of new investment is also necessary. To accomplish this, a business counterpart to the savings-exempt income tax should replace the current corporate income tax and provide greater stimulus to investment.

A companion Business Tax would levy a flat 10 percent tax on the cash flow (total sales minus purchases) of most businesses. The earnings of unincorporated businesses would not be taxed until the money was withdrawn for personal use. Export sales would be excluded from the tax base and a tax equal to the Business Tax rate would be levied on imports entering the country. Such a tax treatment is designed to provide a "level playing field" for products sold within the United States.

One important feature of this proposal is its treatment of the current employer payroll tax. All firms would be required to pay a 10 percent tax on their cash flow, including the amounts paid to employees as salaries and wages. However, firms are given a full credit for their payment of the employer payroll tax for social security. This reduction of their payroll tax liability is designed to help offset the new tax on labor costs and other cash flow.

In computing the cash-flow tax, each firm would add up all its sales during the year, then deduct the cost of any purchases it made from other businesses during the year (plant and equipment, outside services, parts). The remaining cash flow would be the tax base, which would then be taxed at the designated rate. Remaining after-tax cash would be available to pay wages, salaries, dividends, and interest, or otherwise to be reinvested in the business.

The key characteristics of the cash-flow tax are:

1. It would apply to all businesses, regardless their legal form: corporation, partnership, individual proprietorship, and so on. Unincorporated firms currently taxed under the individual collection system would instead pay the business cash-flow tax. This would eliminate the incentives for companies to structure themselves in ways that are less productive just to take advantage of tax differentials.
2. Because it is a tax on cash flow, capital purchases would be treated the same as other expenditures: deducted in full at the time of purchase (that is, "expensed"). Because of this, firms would have strong incentives to invest in productivity-enhancing capital equipment. Furthermore, there would be no onerous accounting requirements for depreciation, estimates of an asset's useful life, or any of the other arcane computations required by the current tax system.
3. The current tax advantage afforded to borrowed capital compared to equity—because interest payments are now tax deductible but dividend payments are not—would be eliminated.

A cash-flow tax would simplify the current business tax structure, allowing firms to devote fewer resources to complying with tax regulations (and devising creative methods to minimize their tax burden), and more resources to productivity-increasing investment. For example, the cash-flow tax would eliminate bizarre, complicated tax provisions such as the "amortization of intangible expenditures," a procedure that depreciates purchases of patents, licenses, and other intangibles. Such complicated law contributes to the high costs of tax compliance. The Tax Foundation estimated that business tax compliance costs in 1990 totaled $112 billion, a sum nearly equal to 75 percent of federal corporate income tax collections. The simplifications offered by a cash-flow tax would particularly aid small business.

Conclusion

An Unlimited Savings Account, or savings-exempt income tax, would achieve many of the same budgetary and economic benefits associated with a VAT while avoiding its many shortcomings. Reforming the current income tax to exempt all saving—unlike adopting a new tax on value-added—does not require setting up an additional collection system. Nor is it regressive or inflationary. In contrast, a value-added tax becomes extremely complicated if an effort is made to soften its inherent regressivity by exempting certain categories of expenditures, such as food and medicine, or taxing them at lower rates. Adopting an Unlimited Savings Account does not provide the federal government with a new revenue source. Therefore, the public sector has no special temptation to grow more rapidly.

It is not surprising that politicians in many countries favor sales-type taxation on the assumption that, politically, the best tax is a hidden tax. "Bottom-up" sales taxes such as a VAT are rarely identified separately, because the purchaser merely pays a combined product-plus-tax price.

The combination of a truly reformed personal income tax with an unlimited savings account and a companion business cash-flow tax would initially be revenue neutral, compared to the income tax system it displaces. However, over the years, it would generate more revenue for the U.S. Treasury. This is likely because such a tax system encourages more saving to finance additional investments in a growing economy.

6

Have I Got a Panacea for You!

Carlyle called economics the dismal science. Nevertheless, economists on occasion can laugh, even at themselves.

Tired of slow growth, high unemployment, rising imports, and declining smokestack industries? Relax. Your worries are over. Have I got a remedy for you. Believe me, we can cure all of your economic ailments. How? It's simple. All we have to do is raise taxes, speed up government spending, increase Treasury borrowing, expand government lending and accelerate government regulation.

You say you've been there before? Remember, I told you not to worry. We've got new names for all this. First of all, we're not silly enough to say we're going to raise taxes. But who's against "tax reform" and promoting "tax equity"?

We've got a fascinating way of dealing with the government budget and borrowing situation. We've just reinvented capital budgeting. Remember all the dams and offices and military bases that the government loves to build? We'll simply take them out of the budget and call them "infrastructure." How's that different from the off-budget phony baloney that the federal government has been practicing for years? The title, you dummy. How many citizens have ever seen the federal budget or would be able to read it? Don't get bogged down with the details.

That's why we need to revive the Reconstruction Finance Corp. That big new credit agency will pump up all the distressed smokestack industries. Don't you remember the RFC's role in the 1930s and World War II? You're saying that the RFC made most of its business loans during the boom period after the war, when it was no longer needed? That Congress axed the agency because of all of the scandals that resulted from the goodies it was handing out to its buddies?

Please, I told you not to get bogged down in the details. Anyway, we've also got a sure-fire way of dealing with foreign competition. We'll just keep it out. That sounds too protectionist? It reminds you of the Smoot-Hawley Tariff of the 1930s that worsened the Great Depression? C'mon, that's ancient history. Young people think Smoot-Hawley is a British rock group. Anyway,

---

Source: Murray Weidenbaum, "Have I Got a Panacea for You!" *Washington Post,* September 10, 1983.

we're not protectionist. We just want fair trade, and it's only fair that we protect American industry from foreign competition. A little subsidy can go a long way (except when the "foreign devils" do it!).

You're still not convinced? Remember, I told you not to worry. We've got a new name for this whole approach, this newest economic elixir: we call it industrial policy.

You're against it? How can you oppose it? Industrial policy is the latest buzzword; it's the newest intellectual fad. Do you want to be behind the times? Weren't you for supply-side economics last year? And for Keynesian fine-tuning a few years before that? Of course, we believe in competition and a private enterprise market economy. It's just that adding a lot of government will help it work better.

What are you saying? This approach has failed the last 22 times it was tried? You're such a stick-in-the-mud reactionary. By the way, your bald spot looks like it's getting worse. Do I have a cure for baldness that you wouldn't believe!

7

An Economist in Government:
Views of a Presidential Adviser

It seems appropriate to conclude this chapter on economic policy by drawing on the author's personal experience in these matters.

As the old saw put it, "Economics is what economists do." Judging by both my personal experience and observation of the work of others, the quotation accurately describes the role of economists in government. But, given the great variation possible in the role—and the numerous factors determining that variation—I am content merely to describe the role of one economist during one tour in Washington.

Based on my service as chairman of the President's Council of Economic Advisers from January 1981 to August 1982, 1 would conclude that the role varies substantially over time and that it is a changing blend of participation in policymaking and preaching of economic doctrine, both within the government and to the public.

It would be pleasant to report that those who disagreed with me were generally wrong. If pressed, I might be willing to provide some factual buttressing for that position. Nevertheless, self-serving statements would not be helpful to the reader. Instead, I have tried—albeit likely not with total success—to avoid writing the modern day equivalent of "An Impartial History of the Civil War as Reported by William Tecumseh Sherman."

I attempt to concentrate on the process by which an official economist participates in the policymaking process. Moreover, I write this with the clear knowledge that few if any decisions in government policy—be they labeled economic or social or foreign affairs—are made solely or even primarily on the basis of economic analysis or information from economists. Yet I also came away with the knowledge that most questions of governmental policymaking—especially those labeled "non-economic"—do contain important economic aspects.

The Key Aspects of the Job

At the outset of the Reagan administration, for example, the major role of the CEA chairman was to participate in the development of the President's

Source: Murray Weidenbaum, *An Economist in Government: Views of a Presidential Adviser* (St. Louis: Washington University, Center for the Study of American Business, 1983).

Economic Recovery Program. The initial tax program had been set during the 1980 campaign: across-the-board personal income tax rate reductions plus liberalization of business depreciation allowances. Thus, the emphasis was on developing the initial package of budget cuts. My appointment to the three-man Budget Working Group chaired by Office of Management and Budget (OMB) Director David Stockman meant that a major part of my time and effort was devoted to developing and reviewing proposed expenditure reductions and to convincing the department heads to go along with them.

One Cabinet secretary was quoted as saying that Stockman and I constituted a "good cop—bad cop" routine. As someone who grew up in the old Budget Bureau in the 1950s it was perhaps inevitable that I played the bad cop. But that function was destined to remain with the CEA chairman in many subsequent connections. Surely, I came to advocate rather consistently much larger budget cuts than those approved.

The economic "White Paper" of February 18, 1981, entitled A Program for Economic Recovery, constituted a landmark in the development of President Reagan's economic program. That document announced the four pillars of the program—tax cuts, budget cuts, regulatory relief, and monetary restraint. It also contained the economic assumptions underlying the revenue and expenditure estimates.

As the person who took on the responsibility for the White Paper, I instantly found myself in pitched battles with both supply-siders and monetarists. Without repeating all the doctrinal disputes that occurred, I still vividly recall the fervor of those arguments, which at times bordered on the theological. In any event, I understood the role of the chairman of the CEA not as preaching supply-side economics or monetarism, but rather helping the president develop and carry out his economic program.

Thus, my insistence that a modest period of recession would accompany the imposition of monetary restraint was viewed by the supply-siders as a lack of faith in the instantaneous nature of the economy's response to the tax cuts. Similarly, my unwillingness to include, for the guidance of the independent Federal Reserve System, a set of specific annual targets for monetary growth left the monetarists dismayed.

During this period, I felt a kinship with Lewis Carroll's Alice. In Through the Looking Glass, Alice says, "There's no use trying, we can't believe impossible things." "I daresay you haven't had much practice," replies the Queen. "When I was your age, I always did it for half-an-hour a day. Why, sometimes I've believed as many as six impossible things before breakfast."

After the release of the White Paper, the CEA chairman became one of the three major "salesmen" (along with the Treasury Secretary and the OMB Director) for the president's economic program—aside from the "number one communicator" himself. There followed an almost endless array of joint and individual congressional testimonies and press conferences; White House briefings to the Cabinet, other officials, and numerous visiting interest groups; and speeches to all sorts of organizations—business, consumers, agriculture, ethnic, regional, and religious.

It reached a point that, when I was out for a meal and the waiters began to clear the dishes, I automatically got ready to stand up and speak. At first I referred to the speechifying as economic education and then marketing. Subsequently, however, I found myself using the term "forensic economics" to describe the activity. I was defending the product that I had helped to design, including the inevitable compromises that anyone would reluctantly agree to.

In addition, since there is an important international dimension to economic policy, a wide array of ambassadors and economics and finance ministers from other nations frequently came by for discussions ranging from the courtesy call to the substantive. As chairman of the U.S. delegation to the Economic Policy Committee of the Organization for Economic Cooperation and Development, I carried at times a significant representational load for what was a rather controversial set of policies. As chairman of the Economic Policy Committee, I had a key opportunity to work with my counterparts in other nations to develop positions and draft communiqués with which we felt comfortable and which other nations would accept. Informally, the EPC chairmanship enabled me at key points to unruffle the feathers of foreign representatives who had been upset by earlier, "harder line" American presentations.

I must admit that I felt no reluctance to play the public role the President assigned to me—to serve as a senior representative of his administration at a time when the approval of his economic program by the Congress was an essential step in converting economic ideas to political reality. Thus, I did not see my public role as an economic "oracle" aloof from the foibles of any sitting administration. There is no shortage of that type of expertise in the private sector.

The Day-to-Day Routine

Simultaneously, the development of a host of detailed government programs and policies was taking place inside the administration. An important structural change was the institution of Cabinet Councils to replace the host of interagency committees that typically had been organized by the White House in the past. The CEA chairman was an active member of three of those cabinet-level groups—Economic Affairs, Commerce and Trade, and Natural Resources and Environment—and attended the meetings of the other councils (Human Resources, Food and Agriculture, Legal Policy). Members of the CEA and its senior staff serve on the various working groups and task forces.

The effectiveness of the CEA on any specific issue depends in part on the cogency of its analysis. But that is not always the case. For example, we won the battle to eliminate import restrictions on shoes, but lost the struggle to contain restrictions on imports of textiles. Was it coincidental that the Congressional delegation to the White House urging textile quotas was led by a senior southern Republican who was diligently working for the enactment of the president's program, while the shoe delegation was chaired by a prominent Northeastern liberal Democrat?

The Cabinet Council system ensures that the CEA is represented in the decision-making apparatus that handles a host of issues—social security, foreign trade, regulation of financial institutions, transportation, environment, energy, agriculture, and many other areas. At key points, the president attends a Cabinet Council meeting and, at times, makes a decision on the spot. In this regard, the key role of the CEA was not to develop additional new programs, but to operate a damage limitation mechanism. Thus, the CEA (at least in my time) was expected to, and predictably did, oppose each and every proposal to subsidize some segment of the economy, or to shield a specific industry from competition. At times, a cabinet member proposing an additional form of government intervention in the economy would start off by saying, "Mr. President, Murray will probably give you a different view, but . . ."

In the case of protectionism, we did not win all the battles, but each proponent of additional governmental involvement in the private sector knew that he or she would have to do battle. In certain instances—autos and maritime, for example—we were hampered by presidential campaign commitments. I found myself grudgingly admiring a sitting president who took his campaign oratory seriously.

The Cabinet Council on Economic Affairs was a forum in which I presented analyses of economic developments. Frequently, the president and vice president attended, and my presentation would set off an informal discussion on economic policy generally. One administration wag parodied a presentation of mine in the form of a fictitious memo from "Murray Weidenbomber," who talked about a "slowdown of the downturn." I like to believe, however, that my use of "economicese" was not quite as arcane as this parody might lead one to believe.

Meetings, of course, are the basis—and bane—of a bureaucrat's existence. Surely, a major part of the CEA chairman's time is taken up by participating in meetings with other cabinet-level officials. An important example is the Task Force on Regulatory Relief, chaired by the vice president. Members of this group served as the chief "honchos" of regulatory reform, overseeing the operation of the executive order directing agencies to perform benefit-cost analysis for proposed regulations.

The Task Force also furnished an instance of the need to establish personal priorities. Regulatory relief, for me, was a labor of love. As an academic, I had written on the subject widely. My initial tie to the president was that body of work, which he had drawn upon frequently in his radio broadcasts and columns as a private citizen. Also, I had chaired the task force on regulation during the campaign and the transition period. At key points I was expected to, and did, participate in setting regulatory policy. Yet, I knew that if I participated on a day-to-day basis, the time available for macroeconomic policy would suffer. Thus, I devoted—as does every CEA chairman—most of my time and efforts to macro matters.

One administrative, yet strategic, set of meetings is the daily gathering of the White House senior staff, which the CEA chairman regularly attends. This is an important communication device, providing a ready opportunity to raise issues and policy questions and to push along specific matters. For example, an administration position paper on trade policy had been drafted at one point, emphasizing a strong free trade orientation. Although substantive agreement had been reached by all relevant parties, the document itself was stuck in the administration's paperflow. My merely noting the delay led to an on-the-spot decision to release this important document.

Briefing the President

Of course, the direct contacts with the president are of very special importance. Because I take the role of trusted advisor seriously, there are some matters that I will pass over. I do recall, however, discussing the subject of gold with him on several occasions, a matter that he had studied at some length. During the campaign and earlier, he had indicated strong interest in restoring the gold standard. As a member of the Gold Commission (set up under a 1980 law), I told him that I would pursue the matter with an open mind. Subsequently, I reported that the majority of the Commission opposed a return to gold at this time. That disposed of the matter. I see that episode as another example of the CEA's damage-limitation function or the avoidance of economic harm.

Another important function is to keep the president abreast of current economic developments. In addition to sending out a regular flow of analytic reports, the CEA chairman alerts the president to impending releases of economic news. Thus, the evening before the consumer price index for a given month is issued, the president has on his desk a memo from the CEA chairman setting forth the highlights. At times he will call for amplification. We had a pleasant—but spirited and extended—difference of views on the matter of seasonally adjusted versus unadjusted reports on employment and unemployment. We ultimately resolved this matter by my providing him both sets of data, together with suitable caveats.

An insight into my approach to my job related to that less-than-momentous issue. After hearing me out fully, the president decided that he would use the unadjusted data in a speech. I then suggested a sentence to explain his position: "We do not live in a seasonally adjusted world." He promptly inserted it into his speech.

If the presidency is a bully pulpit, the CEA chairmanship is a most elevated lectureship. As I look back on my experiences in that office, I find that

I used the position to develop four themes: (1) economic freedom is closely intertwined with personal liberty, (2) business-government relations should be characterized by less intervention by government, (3) free trade is the international combination of these two themes, and (4) it is necessary, from time to time, to take a swipe at business' pleas for special privileges.

The View from the Outside

For a teacher, the rewards of service to the president were considerable, albeit psychic. One give-and-take session on national television gave me the chance to explain aspects of the economy to a far larger audience than a college professor normally can generate in a lifetime. I returned to the private sector with no grand lessons. I came away grateful for the opportunity to speak my mind and to know that decision makers in government were listening to at least one economist before making up their minds.

Part 2
Analyzing Government Programs

8

The Timing of the Economic Impact of Government Spending

This article, drawn from my doctoral dissertation—and my first publication in an economics journal—was one of the most professionally influential I ever wrote. It was cited in public finance textbooks and reprinted in books of readings for over a decade. This article changed in various ways how economists measure the impact of the public sector of the economy. Moreover, it provided the theoretical support for my analysis of the economic impact of the Vietnam War that was the basis for an extensive set of congressional hearings and a two-volume compendium on the subject.

The economic impact of a government spending program may occur at the time the disbursements are made or, depending on the nature of the program and the state of the economy, during earlier stages of the governmental spending process. This study indicates the possible effect on economic activity of each major stage of the process.

An Increase in Government Spending: The Simple Case

Four phases of the federal spending process are highlighted: (1) enactment of appropriations, (2) placement of government contracts with the private sector, (3) production in the private sector, and (4) delivery to and payment by the public sector. A number of initial assumptions are made so that the effects on the economy arising directly from an increase in government spending can be readily examined. More complicated situations are dealt with subsequently.

An increase in government spending is assumed which consists entirely of expenditures for goods and services currently produced in the private sector of the economy. These expenditures are financed by borrowing idle funds. It is also assumed that there are sufficient idle resources and mobility in the economy to produce the goods and services without new fixed business investment or price or wage increases and without displacing any private demand. Also postulated is the availability of adequate financing for the government contractors. This increase in government spending generates no indirect effects on consumer or business expectations nor any changes in other government programs.

Source: Murray Weidenbaum, "The Timing of the Economic Impact of Government Spending," *National Tax Journal*, March 1959.

Phase I. Appropriation of funds. The president transmits to the Congress an appropriation request which it enacts after due deliberation. Under the assumed conditions, there is no immediate effect on the economy as measured by any indicators of economic activity, such as the Gross Domestic Product (GDP) or the index of industrial production, or any of the lead series, such as the volume of new orders. Neither is there yet any change registered in any of the measures of government spending. This stage may take one to two quarters of a year, on the average.

Phase II. Placement of contracts. The government agency to which the appropriation is made places contracts with business firms in the private sector of the economy. The following are some of the events that would flow from the receipt by a manufacturer of a government order for items used by the government as well as by private industry.

The firm finds that it cannot fill the new order out of existing inventory. The additional volume of production can be obtained through more intensive utilization of existing capacity, requiring increases in inventories and working capital. On the basis of the company's past performance and the government order, the contractor obtains approval from a bank for a working-capital loan. The contractor begins to place orders for materials, to hire additional workers, and to subcontract parts of the order to other firms.

The first effect on economic activity will now be taking place. As deliveries begin to be made on raw materials and wages are earned by the first of the newly hired workers who are tooling-up, the contractor will be drawing upon the loan authorization and making small amounts of payments to the various factors of production. An increase will be registered in the outstanding loans of the commercial banks and in the total money supply. Also, an increase will occur in gross private domestic investment, the component of GDP that contains the inventory accumulation resulting from the increased amounts of goods in process.

The economic activity represented by contract placements is not reflected in any of the generally used measures of government spending. These contracts are included, but not identified separately, in the reports by the Department of Commerce on new orders received by business firms. The placement of government orders ("obligations incurred" by the federal agencies) is the phase of the government spending process that energizes private production on government account.

Phase III. Production of goods. As quantity production gets under way on the government orders, payments are made by the government contractors for wages to the employees engaged in the work, materials delivered, and the interest due on the working-capital loans. The firms will also be accruing profits on the orders. The costs incurred by the contractors during the entire production period should total the amount of the orders. These outlays of government contractors are not reflected in government purchases of goods and services or in any other government expenditures series at the time they are made. They will currently show up in GDP—in the change in inventory segment of gross private domestic investment. The amount of production on government orders remaining in business inventories during a given period cannot be identified in the available statistics and, hence, the amount of production carried on in the private sector on government account cannot be measured. Only a general idea can be obtained from series on contracts placed and deliveries made.

On the income side, increases will be registered in compensation of employees, corporate profits, rental income and, depending on the legal status of the contractor and subcontractors, earnings of unincorporated enterprises. Increases in consumer expenditures also occur as a result of these income payments. The exact amount of this secondary contribution to the increase of total output would depend on the marginal propensity to consume.

This stage may last from one quarter up to two years or more depending on the production time involved.

Phase IV. Payments for goods. During this phase the contractors deliver to the government the goods that they have produced during Phase III. Following inspection, payment is made by the government. Several economic effects of this activity can be discerned.

The delivery of the equipment shows up as a decline in business inventories and, hence, in gross private domestic investment. It also is recorded as a government purchase of goods and services. These two movements cancel each other out with no net effect on GDP. The government purchases do not represent payments to the factors of production but are in the nature of intersectoral transfers—reimbursements to the government contractors for the outlays during the previous period.

Following the payments by the government, the contractors repay the working-capital loans. These actions reduce the amount of private credit, reduce the government's cash balances, and increase the cash position of the firms doing business with the government. The contractors can now disburse dividends, or set aside funds for tax payments, future expansions, or merely improved cash positions. This is the period during which the government purchase shows up as a budget expenditure and a cash payment to the public.

The following is the sequence in which the various stages of the governmental spending process ordinarily enter into the movements of total economic activity.

1. The enactment of an appropriation indicates the size of a government spending program (for the period for which the funds are appropriated), but is not reflected in any measure of current economic activity.
2. The placing of government contracts and orders with the private sector gives rise to the beginning of production and, hence, furnishes a measure of the early (and potential) impact of government spending (i.e., procurement) on the economy.

3. The actual production in the private sector on government account shows up in GDP as additions to business inventories. This is the stage when government contractors make disbursements for wages and materials. Because of the deficiencies in our knowledge, we cannot measure the magnitude of the private production on government account. Increases in consumer spending also occur during this period as a result of the payments to factors.

4. The completion of production of the goods and services ordered results in deliveries from the private sector to the government. This is the stage where the government spending program shows up as government purchases. With the simultaneous decline in private inventories of a corresponding amount, no net effect on GDP occurs during this period. However, this is the point at which the government generally makes its expenditures for the goods and services delivered to it—when this activity is recorded as a budget expenditure, a cash payment, and a government purchase on national income and product account.

Relaxing the Simplifying Assumptions

Some of the effects on the economy of the various phases of the governmental spending process may be examined under more complicated circumstances.

Anticipatory Effects

The government's act of embarking on a large new program can have a positive expectation effect on consumers and business under certain circumstances. Such was the case in the early stages of the Korean mobilization program when memories of World War II price rises and shortages set off a wave of private ordering and buying in advance of government purchasing. Positive expectations result from the government embarking upon a new spending program.

The anticipatory effect of government spending is too diffuse and elusive to be measurable. We simply do not know what the actions of business and consumers in a given period would have been in the absence of the anticipatory effect of government activity.

Availability of Resources

Unutilized capacity may not always be present. Substantial amounts of new investment may be necessary before production commences. In this case, the production by private business includes additions to private plant and equipment needed to produce the government-ordered goods as well as actual production on the goods destined for government use.

Under a situation of relatively full utilization of resources, the letting of additional government contracts may simply result in accumulations of backlogs. Placing contracts by the government would not immediately energize private production. Attempts by the government to bid away resources from private uses could result in rises in prices. There would not be any real increase in the production of the economy, except that resulting from changes in the product mix. Where the government resorts to material controls and allocation systems, the backlogs may accumulate in the private sector rather than in the work on government contracts. There would be no effect on the aggregate level of economic activity during any part of the government spending program. The authorization of the new spending program could not give rise to any changes in consumer and business outlays (resulting from changes in expectations) nor could the contract letting lead to an expansion in the volume of production. As a result, when production of the government-ordered goods is completed, there would be an increase in government purchases and an equivalent decline in consumer expenditure and/or business fixed investment, depending on which private demands were displaced.

Financing Private Production

It was assumed earlier that the government contractors can obtain financing and thus, once facilities and materials are available, can effectively carry on government-ordered production. It has been observed that the need for borrowing to finance current operations becomes much greater when a contractor embarks upon the performance of government contracts. Borrowings in the performance of government contracts are frequently made necessary because of lags in obtaining payment such as the slow processing of invoices, delays encountered in obtaining definitive contractual instruments authorizing payment, government revisions of schedules which delay or stretch out deliveries over a longer period, thereby prolonging investments in inventories, and other government action.

Both fiscal and monetary tools can affect private finance. In the absence of governmental assistance, there may be substantial financial as well as technological limits to large-scale expansion of production on government orders. As can be seen by the large array of governmental devices designed to ease the financing problems of government contractors and by the performance of the American economy during wartime, these financial limitations have generally not been controlling.

It was assumed earlier that the government payments to contractors would be financed by borrowing idle funds. Other financial techniques could alter the expansive effect of government purchases, but these matters are better treated as separate monetary and fiscal policy issues.

Changes in Rates and Levels of Government Spending

"Follow-on" orders—those which extend and maintain existing production—tend to result in continued stability rather than any net increment in total demand. The permanency of the change in the amount of government procurement is important. Where business and consumers believe that an increase in government spending will be lasting, they may react, particularly in investment decisions, far more fully than if they regard such increases as merely transitory.

Summary

The magnitude of changes in the various phases of the federal spending process can have important economic effects under many circumstances. An awareness of these surrounding circumstances is essential to an adequate analysis of changes in government spending patterns.

The very act of announcing and authorizing a new or increased spending program—the granting of new appropriations—can sometimes give rise, by affecting expectations, to positive or even negative changes in business and consumer spending in advance of the actual letting of contracts or disbursement of government funds.

Placing contracts and incurring other obligations may not always signal the onset of production. The needed production facilities may not be readily available or backlogs of orders may first have to be worked off. Also additional working capital may be required. On the other hand, the government order may be filled out of inventory and no effect on economic activity would take place until some time later. In addition to the direct effects of the government expenditure there will be the accompanying effects of the financing of this outlay.

Although these complications may modify the effect on the economy of a program of government procurement from private industry, the basic relationships generally hold: the primary effect on productive activity (to the extent there is any) occurs in advance of the actual government expenditures. Under most of the circumstances that have been examined, the placing of orders induces (either immediately or after a delay) production on government account and such production remains in the private sector and does not show up as government expenditures until it is completed and the goods involved delivered to the public sector.

9

The Effect of Government Programs
on Price Formation

Commissioned by the Congressional Joint Economic Committee, this article is a comprehensive examination of the wide array of government programs that affect the private economy.

Government can exert an important impact on private price formation through its spending programs. As a major buyer of privately produced goods, it sets or strongly influences prices. As a seller of the goods it produces, the government affects the costs or prices of and demand for privately produced goods. Also, acting as a promoter, the government reduces business costs and increases business demand by subsidizing private production, lending or otherwise making funds available, furnishing facilities, and aiding in the development of new products and new demands.

This paper analyzes the various mechanisms through which federal government programs affect the costs of business firms, the demand for their goods and services, and the prices they charge.

The Government as Buyer

The federal government has become by far the largest single purchaser of the goods and services produced by the private economy. As a result, changes in the aggregate of government expenditures can affect the general price level of the economy. During a situation of relatively full employment, an increase in government procurement would tend to raise prices, as a result of government agencies bidding against private firms and individuals for existing resources. Similarly, government transfers and other payments would tend to increase inflationary pressures by strengthening private demand.

However, a rise in government spending would be expected to have little effect on prices when sufficient idle resources are available to meet the new government demand. The major expansive effect would be on the output of the economy. The precise effects of an increase in government spending on prices and production would depend on the nature of the new government

Source: Murray Weidenbaum, "The Effect of Government Spending Programs on Private Price Formation," in U.S. Congress, Joint Economic Committee, *The Relationship of Prices to Economic Stability and Growth* (Washington, DC: U.S. Government Printing Office, 1958).

disbursements, the composition of competing demands, the structure of the industries affected, and the impact on private expectations.

Often, the mere knowledge that the government is going to increase its spending significantly can set off a wave of private purchasing and an inflationary spiral well in advance of the actual governmental disbursements. The experience immediately after the outbreak of the Korean conflict serves as a case in point. Expectations that sharply expanded defense spending would bring higher prices and shortages led to immediate forward buying. The larger volume of consumer buying contributed to increased demand all along the line. Distributors' orders mounted as they attempted to maintain or build up stocks. Manufacturers' orders for raw and semifinished materials also rose substantially.

As a result, wholesale and retail prices rose sharply during the first few months of the conflict. However, total federal expenditures remained relatively stable during the period and the rate of military orders placed did not rise significantly until the following year.

The price effects of a reduction in government spending would be analogous to those accompanying an increase in public outlays. During a period of relatively full employment, such a decline would tend to reduce general price levels or to dampen the tendencies for further increases, without much effect on total production. Under circumstances of less than full employment, a decline in government expenditures could cause a reduction in total productive activity.

The aggregate approach, however, does not adequately convey the impact of government purchasing on specific industries and firms. The following section of this report attempts to indicate such effects resulting from the operations of individual government programs. In some instances, the government has chosen to set the price at which it will buy specific commodities. In other circumstances, it influences the price because of its strong market position.

Government-Determined Prices

The Department of Agriculture, under the farm price support program, props up the prices of a number of agricultural commodities, notably corn, cotton, peanuts, rice, tobacco, and wheat. The support of farm prices is provided through loans, purchase agreements, and purchases. As the loans are of a nonrecourse type, many analysts view them as merely a preliminary step to the eventual government purchase of the commodities, rather than purely credit transactions. When the market value is less than the amount loaned, the borrowers may choose not to repay the loan; they may surrender the product at the end of the loan period and be free from any obligation to pay the difference between the amount advanced and the market value of the products. Thus the loan is, in effect, a purchase commitment that establishes a price floor for the commodity.

The essential difference between a loan and a direct purchase is that, in the former case, the farmer retains the opportunity to sell the commodities commercially if the market price is higher than the support price. A purchase agreement, on the other hand, provides a convenient form of price insurance for the producer who does not have an immediate need for cash or who is not able to meet the loan storage requirements.

These programs also tend to adjust for seasonal factors in marketing. Farmers are ordinarily inclined to market their crops at harvest time, which sometimes makes for market gluts and lower prices. By giving farmers an opportunity to hold their crops without risk for later marketing, the price-support programs tend to spread marketing over the season, thereby reducing the magnitude of price fluctuations.

The farm price support program is a government spending program with accompanying regulatory features. Farmers desiring to participate must abide by the acreage allotments and marketing quotas in effect for the commodity. When significant numbers of farmers do not participate in the program, the prices of supported commodities may fall below the support level.

Price guaranties probably tend to expand agricultural output of supported items. They permit farmers to plan ahead with greater certainty and may result in increased long-term investment in agriculture. To the extent that price elasticity exists, the program lessens demand; where prices would decline in the absence of the program, price-support payments prevent the rise in demand that would accompany the price reduction.

Under the Defense Production Act and related legislation, the government supports the prices of a number of minerals as a means of encouraging domestic development. The government has entered into contracts with mineral producers to purchase all or part of the entire output from a new source of supply at a specified price for a specified period of time. Generally, producers have the option to sell material on the open market if they can obtain a price equal to or higher than the guaranteed price. However, the government may call for certain quantities during the contract period. Aluminum, copper, nickel, fluorspar, molybdenum, titanium, and zinc purchase programs have operated in this manner.

Titanium furnishes an extreme example of the impact of government procurement on the price level and the very development of an industrial commodity. Government contracts with titanium producers generally provide that the government will underwrite a market at guaranteed prices for the entire production of each contractor.

In addition to executing commitment-to-purchase contracts, the government has advanced funds to contractors to finance the construction of titanium facilities and has underwritten the cost of research designed to improve production, reduce unit costs, and improve utilization of the material. The General Services Administration, the federal agency administering the defense materials program, has stated that titanium "probably could not have been developed except with government assistance."

The Atomic Energy Commission establishes "guaranteed fair" prices for various nuclear materials. Its price guaranty policies for uranium anticipated a transition from a government-controlled to a commercial market. The Commission terminated its guaranteed purchase price for uranium ore on March 31, 1962. Thereafter, until December 31, 1966, it provided a guaranteed market for uranium concentrates produced commercially if from domestic ore. Purchase programs of the AEC are a means of fostering private industrial capacity by creating a base load justifying plant capacity and development effort, which the embryonic atomic energy industry might not support alone.

Government-Influenced Prices

For a number of industries, the federal government is such a large customer that it may exercise an important influence on the price at which the firms sell. Military procurement of weapons is a striking case in point. In 1955, over 95 percent of the total sales of the twelve largest airframe manufacturers were to the federal government. Three-fourths of the firms reported that at least 99 percent of their sales were made to the government. As John Perry Miller has stated:

> the services' purchase policy will inevitably be the principal determinant of the price and profit policies of such industries . . . market experience cannot serve as a guide.

Of necessity, the competition within the defense industry is primarily related to design. By the nature of military requirements, there is maximum pressure upon the armed services to obtain the most advanced weapons. After mission requirements have been established for major weapon systems, engineering design proposals are requested from qualified contractors. Such proposals are evaluated in terms of excellence of design, demonstrated production ability (including both quality and schedule attainment), costs, and other pertinent factors. For any given competition, different weights may be assigned to each factor, depending upon the urgency of the procurement and mission requirements.

Thus, military contracts are negotiated primarily with selected suppliers rather than awarded through public advertisement of bids. During the fiscal years 1951-55, military prime contracts with business firms in the United States totaled $126.8 billion. Of this amount, contracts totaling $111.3 billion were awarded on a negotiated basis.

The initial prime contractor, having already accomplished basic engineering and tooling, has a substantial advantage in pricing the active procurement. Likewise, after producing an initial quantity, the company can take advantage of the savings possible from quantity production. These advantages are so great as to preclude the possibility of meaningful competition for follow-on quantities.

The program of stockpiling strategic and critical materials is another instance of the government buying a significant share of an industry's output and, oftentimes, affecting the general sales price of the commodity. Under this program, the government acquired substantial amounts of seventy-six materials. Contracts for the stockpile have sometimes been above the market price to encourage greater output and, in some cases, have raised the price level of the minerals involved.

During times when the materials being stockpiled are in short supply in the private economy, the government has permitted scheduled deliveries to be diverted to private customers, thus reducing the pressures for price increases. The extent to which similar diversions (and outright sales) could be made in the future may be seen from the fact that sixty-three materials in the stockpile are equal to or in excess of current "priority level" objectives. Items in this category include aluminum, asbestos, cobalt, copper, fluorspar, lead, manganese, mercury, nickel, natural rubber, tin, tungsten, and zinc.

Government-Induced Standards

As an important employer of labor, the government determines the wage rates and working conditions of a sizable part of the labor force. In specific industries, the government is a major factor, while in others it is quite minor. The federal government, at times, has tended to set standards in the labor market. For example, its role in establishing an 8-hour day for its employees tended to make the government a model employer during the nineteenth century.

The government also sets certain labor standards for the work on the contracts it lets. The Walsh-Healey Act requires that every federal supply contract in excess of $10,000 include stipulations calling for (1) the payment of no less than prevailing minimum wages "for persons employed on similar work or in the particular or similar industries or groups of industries currently operating in the locality," as determined by the Secretary of Labor, (2) overtime pay at the rate of time and one-half for hours worked in excess of 8 a day or 40 a week, (3) restrictions on child labor and convict labor, and (4) minimum safety and health standards.

The Government as Seller

Through changes in the volume of goods and services it sells to the public, the government can affect the aggregate level of prices. For example, sales of commodities from government stockpiles during a period of shortages can dampen or prevent price rises. Conversely, the government can support the general price level during a period of surpluses by halting or reducing the level of its sales of commodities to the public. The government may affect the cost of business firms, the prices they charge, and the demand for their output by known pricing policies on the items it sells.

Sales to the Public

Under a large number of programs, the federal government produces or buys goods for sale to private purchasers. For some of these programs, the government establishes unilaterally the prices at which it sells and, hence, determines the cost of these items to private industry. To the extent that these government prices are below comparable commercial rates, an element of subsidy is involved and private sales may be diminished.

Sales to the public of materials and services that the government itself produces are many and diversified. Some of the better known include materials provided by the Atomic Energy Commission, power from Interior Department projects, publications of the Government Printing Office, and mail delivery by the post office. In other cases, the government may sell commodities that it has previously purchased from private firms, such as mineral and agricultural commodities.

The post office is a government monopoly where the price is set unilaterally by the seller. Rates are determined by Congress as a matter of public policy, rather than in direct relation to market factors. An exception exists in the case of parcel post, which is the one major element of postal service competitive with private enterprise.

The Government Printing Office (GPO) is one of the major publishers in the United States, printing and distributing over 100 million books, pamphlets, and other publications a year. The literary output ranges from the perennial best sellers on infant and child care to works on American history and geography, language instruction, home economics, recreational activity, and scientific studies.

The prices of GPO publications generally cover variable or incremental costs only, such as ink and paper, plus a markup. Fixed costs (preparation of copy and setting up of type) are borne by the agency originating the document.

As an adjunct of its surveying activities, the federal government is a major mapmaker. The Geological Survey, the Coast and Geodetic Survey, and many other agencies prepare various types of maps and charts that are used by the general public, by scientific and professional personnel, and by private mapmaking establishments. In this area, also, the prices charged do not cover the full cost of preparation but are usually limited to incremental costs.

Some governmental sales are designed to make the results of research and development available to the public. Radioisotopes are sold by the Atomic Energy Commission to private business firms. These radioactive byproducts of atomic energy activities are used in the cigarette, oil, paper, and other industries, primarily as density, thickness, and related gages.

In addition to affecting the costs of the private purchasers of goods and services from the government, governmental pricing policies may influence the pricing policies of private firms producing the same or similar goods and services. Such an effect is provided by the operations of the Tennessee Valley Authority. A former chairman of the TVA has pointed out that a short time after TVA announced low rates for the power it sold, the neighboring private utilities of the Southeast followed suit by making large reductions in their own rates. Use of electricity in the area increased significantly.

There has been considerable controversy over whether TVA's power rates involve an element of subsidy, inasmuch as part of its facilities can be charged off to flood control. When governmental production is supported by tax revenues, there may occur, in addition to any displacement or curtailment of private enterprise, an increase in business costs resulting from taxation to cover the subsidy.

Federal power programs also involve an element of choice among prospective buyers. Preference clauses on federal power projects require that states, counties, municipalities, and cooperative organizations be given first choice. As a result, the bulk of federally produced power available to non-federal users is purchased by publicly owned power systems.

Moreover, under its "sole-supplier" clause, TVA requires all of its regular utility customers to take their entire supply from its facilities. Such requirements prevent the distributors from constructing generating facilities of their own. As a result, only two small privately owned utilities distribute TVA power; the bulk is handled by local public agencies.

Government Provision for Government Use

Government itself produces much of the goods and services that it requires for its own operations. To the extent that these requirements could be met from private sources, the demand for private production is reduced. A recent inventory of commercial-industrial activities which the federal government conducts to provide goods and services for its own use reported that 19,321 installations were being operated with capital assets estimated at $3 billion and 266,000 employees.

The Government as Promoter

Governmental expenditures for subsidies, loans, facilities for use by business firms, and developmental purposes all can reduce costs of business firms, increase the demand for their output, or otherwise affect their price policies.

Subsidies and Related Payments

Federal subsidy programs include payments to marginal high-cost producers to obtain increased production as well as across-the-board payments to all producers of the subsidized commodity.

A major category of federal subsidies is in the form of payments to farmers for following a prescribed course of action, often one that they would not pursue in the absence of the government payments. The agricultural conservation program (ACP), the disposal of surplus agricultural products, the Sugar Act program, the wheat agreement program, and the soil bank are representative programs in this category.

Under the ACP, the Agriculture Department pays a cooperating farmer a portion of the cost of various types of conservation practices. A major part of the funds has been spent for materials and practices that raise current production, such as fertilizers and cover crops. Some of the payments also cover reforestation, reseeding of depleted ranges, and building storage dams and reservoirs. To the extent that the participating farmers would not engage in conservation practices in the absence of these payments, the ACP program affects investment and production patterns of agriculture.

The Agriculture Department encourages the export of wheat by paying exporters the difference between the selling prices prevailing under the International Wheat Agreement and the domestic market price of wheat.

The Sugar Act Program is another instance of government spending being utilized to effectuate regulatory activity. Payments are made to producers who abide by the marketing allotments established for sugar beets and sugarcane. Qualifying farmers must also pay wage rates no less than those determined by the Secretary of Agriculture to be fair and reasonable and must abide by restrictions on the use of child labor.

The program for the disposal of surplus agriculture commodities is devoted principally to perishable farm products not receiving direct price support. Subsidy payments are utilized to encourage the sale of these surplus commodities. Export subsidies are paid to cover the difference between the domestic prices and lower world prices. Diversion payments enable processors to purchase surplus commodities on the domestic market, direct them to byproducts and new uses, and sell them at lower prices comparable to those of competing products.

Under the soil bank program, farmers are paid to reduce agricultural production. Farmers who enter into contracts with the Agriculture Department for removing cropland from production and establishing long-range conservation practices receive payments for instituting the practice and annual payments for the duration of the contract. Farmers who reduce their acreages of the basic commodities below acreage allotments are compensated under the acreage reserve program.

Another area of private production subsidized by federal payments is mining. Under the Defense Production Act, the federal government made subsidy payments to producers of aluminum, copper, and zinc. Copper and zinc subsidies were paid to keep in production those marginal mines that would have gone out of production as a result of increased costs and fixed ceiling prices.

Subsidy contracts were terminated on removal of copper and zinc from price regulation in 1953. The aluminum subsidies covered the high cost of supplying power to the marginal facilities reactivated during the mobilization period.

Governmental subsidies are also paid to private firms in the transportation field. The Federal Maritime Board encourages the maintenance and development of the American merchant marine by subsidizing domestic ship construction and ship operation. Construction and operating-differential subsidies are paid to cover the differences in the relative costs of building and operating ships in the United States and in foreign countries. For many years, the Civil Aeronautics Board fixed rates for the transportation of airmail to promote the development of air transportation. These rates included an element of subsidy.

Loans and Loan Guaranties

Government may affect business costs and the allocation of resources through its credit programs. Where federal credit is provided to business firms at less than commercial rates, the interest expense of the recipients is reduced. To the extent that the government provides credit to firms that would otherwise be unable to obtain credit, the recipients may be enabled to undertake various investment or operating activities they would otherwise have to forego.

The Rural Electrification Administration (REA) lends to cooperatives at 2 percent, considerably below commercial rates for money of comparable term. In reducing the cost of loanable funds, the REA encourages investment in agriculture. The Farmers Home Administration (FHA) makes loans to farmers who otherwise would be unable to obtain credit. By law, emergency crop and feed loans by the FHA are limited to marginal borrowers—farmers "who cannot obtain loans from any other source."

In contrast, the Farm Credit System was organized to set standards for interest rates, terms, and credit services for farmers generally. The federal land banks, one of the constituent agencies, introduced long-term amortized loans to farmers on a nationwide basis. This did away with frequent, costly, and uncertain renewals that had characterized most farm mortgage lending previously. At times, the land banks have led the field in adjusting interest rates downward. One observer claims that long-term interest rates to farmers are at one-half of 1 percent lower than would be the case in the absence of the land banks.

Federal credit programs have also been important in the residential housing area. Primary emphasis has been placed on guaranties of private loans rather than on direct lending of federal funds. Although it can be more liberal with guaranties than with direct loans, the government has more control over the timing and volume of direct lending than over guaranteed private lending.

Programs of federal guaranties of private lending can have important leverage effects on the economy beyond the direct influence on the flow of funds. The guaranties of residential mortgages by the Veterans Administration and the insurance of residential mortgages by the Federal Housing Administration have had such effects.

These programs have stimulated the construction industry, increasing the willingness of builders to undertake construction by reducing the equity required to invest in projects and by raising their expectations as to the salability of the final product. These programs also have increased the willingness of lenders to invest in mortgages and thus to supply investment funds and have helped to increase the demand for housing loans. Federal housing credit programs may thus be interpreted as efforts to raise the proportion of resources devoted to housing construction above the level that would be obtained from the interplay of market forces.

In expanding the demand for housing, these programs often resulted in increases in prices of building materials and existing houses. Possibly more important has been the effect on the nature of the mortgage instrument. As government has assumed much of the risk involved, short-term, nonamortized first mortgages have given way to relatively long-term mortgages with high loan-to-value ratios and regular amortization payments.

Federal guaranty programs can also be accompanied by regulatory aspects. Veterans loan guaranties, for instance, are only made in those cases where the purchase price does not exceed the value of the property as fixed by the approved appraiser. Thus, the guaranty activity has had a direct effect on the pricing of a substantial portion of the output of the housing industry.

For some specialized housing programs, primary emphasis has been given to direct lending. The Housing and Home Finance Agency provides loans at 2-3/4 percent to colleges for the construction of dormitories and related facilities. The ready availability of federal funds has encouraged this form of construction. However, the low interest rate virtually has eliminated all private investors from the college housing field, an area where private funds had been available to the larger educational institutions.

Most government loan programs to private businesses have been noncompetitive with commercial lenders. The Small Business Administration makes no loans unless the financial assistance applied for is not otherwise available on reasonable terms. No direct loan may be made if participation with a bank is available.

Provision of Facilities

The federal government provides and maintains a considerable array of facilities used by private business firms at nominal or no charge. The largest of these programs are in the transportation field. No tolls or other charges are made for the use of domestic waterways improved and maintained at government expense. The rates charged by common and contract carriers using these facilities do not reflect the entire cost involved. In some instances, water transportation appears to be less expensive than other forms of transportation. This tends to place it at a competitive advantage and to result in an allocation of traffic not based on real differences in costs.

The federal-aid highway program, operated on a grant basis to State governments, is another example of government expenditures for transportation facilities for private business and other uses. It is open to question whether the federal excises on gasoline and related products paid by the specific categories of users cover the cost incurred on the behalf of each group, such as truckers. It is clear, however, that improved transportation facilities result in savings to business from reductions in time of haul and in the operating costs of vehicles. Moreover, new transportation facilities open areas formerly inaccessible or not readily accessible, increasing property values and industrial development.

Typically, one of the first effects of highway construction is an increase in adjacent property values. The value of some typical areas adjacent to the New York Thruway rose from $700 an acre before construction to $6,000 an acre after construction. Plants representing a total investment of $150 million were erected adjacent to the throughway even before the highway was finished.

In the case of air transportation, the federal government maintains airways at no charge to the user. The Civil Aeronautics Administration operates air traffic control centers, airport control towers, domestic and international aeronautical communications stations, and other aids to air navigation.

The federal government also provides facilities to private businesses engaged in production on government contracts. The bulk of the production facilities of the aircraft industry, for example, is furnished by the government. This government investment has a number of effects. It enables the private firms to engage in a much larger volume of production than would be possible without the government-provided facilities. In turn, the prices charged the government for production at facilities it provides are lower than would be the case if they were to cover the amortization of an equivalent amount of private investment.

Research and Assistance

By developing new products, sources, and demands government can reduce costs or increase production of private business firms. Such programs of research and assistance are numerous. The Department of Commerce and the Small Business Administration offer many services to business. These aids include scientific information, arranging for free use of government-owned patents, assistance in developing new products, counsel on how to expand markets, advice on efficient methods of management, and information about federal procurement and surplus disposal plans.

The Department of Agriculture conducts a variety of education, demonstration, and technical assistance activities designed to reduce farm costs and improve farm methods. Terracing and contour farming have been introduced into some hilly areas where they are appropriate for conservation. Cover crops and crop rotations are used more widely.

Although military research and development programs are not undertaken because of their civilian applications, many of the results have been used commercially. New or improved civilian products resulting from these programs include high data capacity machine records systems (Minicard), dry photographic processes (Kalfax, Electrofax), anti-motion-sickness drugs, advanced electronic components such as silicon transistors, thin-flat television display tubes, mechanical smoke generators for crop protection from frost, radiation preservation of food, and jet engines.

In a broader sense, the developing atomic energy industry is a result of military research and development. The Atomic Energy Commission has made available to private industry much of the information required for the peaceful application of nuclear power. In addition to support through purchase and sales programs, the Commission has provided fundamental cost and technological data for corporate planning.

Conclusion

A vast array of government spending and related mechanism can influence private price formation. Many government programs, directly and indirectly, intentionally and unintentionally, affect the price levels of the economy.

As a purchaser of goods and services, the federal government can affect price levels in varied ways:

1. It can establish a floor under the prices of specific commodities by guaranteeing a market at the support price.
2. It can strongly influence the prices of many commodities through its dominant position as the major customer.
3. It can affect the labor costs of business firms by setting wage and other working standards in its contracts and through its position as a major employer of many types of skills and professions.
4. Under conditions of relatively full employment, it can cause general price increases through bidding against business firms and consumers for available goods and services or even through "announcing" that it intends to increase its volume of purchasing.

Similarly, the federal government can affect price levels as a seller of goods and services.

1. It can set the price at which it sells specific commodities, often thus establishing a ceiling on their prices. When combined with purchase programs, government thus can determine the prices for these items charged by all sellers.
2. When it is in a monopoly position, government can set the price unilaterally and, hence, determine the cost to private firms.

3. It can sell to certain classes of buyers at less than market prices, thus reducing their costs compared to buyers who obtain the items from commercial sources.
4. It can produce and sell goods and services for government use thus reducing markets for private business firms.

The federal government, through its expenditure programs, can affect private price policies in other ways:

1. It can lend funds at lower than commercial rates, thus reducing the interest costs of the recipients.
2. It can lend to recipients who otherwise would be unable to obtain funds, thus enabling them to engage in various investment and production programs.
3. It can subsidize the private production or sale of goods and services that private firms would not otherwise produce.
4. It can provide facilities to private firms to enable them to engage in production. These facilities may not be provided commercially or only at higher rates.
5. It can make available to business firms the result of the research it conducts and it may provide other information and assistance to reduce costs and increase efficiency.
6. It can encourage the public to purchase certain types of goods and, services, thereby altering the structure of demand.

In some basic sectors of the economy, notably agriculture and mining, government programs often exercise a decisive influence on prices. In contrast, government-spending programs exercise insignificant impact on retail and wholesale trade.

In other sectors, such as manufacturing, government programs have varied impacts on prices. In the aircraft and shipbuilding segments, government is a major factor; however, neither government purchases nor sales are an important factor in the manufacture of apparel or furniture. Similarly, while government programs have an important influence on the demand for medical and educational services, they have little impact on other service areas, such as personal services, repair services, and business services.

If any single conclusion emerges, it is that the price effects of government's combined role as buyer, seller, and promoter need to be considered in formulating broader government programs designed to promote economic growth and stability.

10

Economic Analysis and Government Expenditure Decisions

This article examines an ambitious effort to apply economic analysis to the decision-making of the federal government. Although the specific structure has not endured, useful concepts were developed which, with modification, are now in use. Specifically, benefit/cost analysis, which was originally employed in connection with government spending programs, is now routinely used in reviewing proposed government regulations.

A fundamental shift is occurring in the focus of that branch of economics traditionally described as public finance. As recently as the late 1940s or early 1950s, the textbooks in the field primarily dealt with taxation. A few chapters were devoted to public debt and fiscal policy and perhaps a section described the mechanics of governmental budgeting.

The pendulum now appears to be swinging sharply. Recently the emphasis in public finance, certainly so much of the new work, has been on the expenditure side, in attempting to apply economic analysis to governmental expenditure decisions. Benefit/cost comparisons and cost/effectiveness analysis have become important manifestations of this shift in emphasis. The most recent and ambitious operational effort along these lines is the Planning-Programming-Budgeting System of the federal government.

Before evaluating this governmental innovation, it may be useful to see how earlier developments in the economic analysis of governmental expenditure decisions relate to it. We may then be in a better position to evaluate the Planning-Programming-Budgeting System, or PPBS, as the effort is commonly called.

Antecedents of PPBS

Economists have long been interested in identifying policies that would promote economic welfare, specifically by improving the efficiency with which a society uses its resources. Governmental budgeting provides one important example of this concern.

At the theoretical level, economists have wrestled with the question, what are the necessary and sufficient conditions for achieving the optimum level of welfare? Under the most ideal conditions, and using a most general ap-

Source: Murray Weidenbaum, "Economic Analysis and Government Expenditure Decisions," *Finanzarchiv*, November 1966.

proach, this ideal state has been defined. However, what started as an attempt to determine economically superior public policies concluded at one point that economists have little basis for making any policy recommendations at all. This leads, of course, to what Charles Hitch and Roland McKean refer to as ". . . a whole branch of economic theory unfortunately labeled welfare economics . . ."

In the welfare economics literature, the optimum level of welfare is most rigorously defined by what is termed Pareto Optimality—where it is impossible to make anyone better off without making anyone else worse off, or technically, when the marginal rate of substitution is equal for all consumers and is also equal to the marginal rate of transformation for all products. Certainly, as anyone who has examined the theory underlying these statements will quickly attest, formal welfare economics is rather elegant. The identification of the actual movements to Pareto Optimality—the translation into operational usefulness—may be another matter.

For example, because of the difficulty of making interpersonal utility comparisons, at one point it appeared that economists could not recommend a policy which, although it will benefit many people, will also hurt a few. The question was raised, "on what objective basis can we say that the people who are benefited are more important than those who are hurt?" Strictly speaking, this approach would have prevented government from implementing antirecession policies, because some people on fixed incomes benefit from the low prices that often accompany depressed conditions.

Ingeniously the so-called New Welfare Economics developed the concept of compensation tests: would those who benefit from a change be able to compensate the losers fully and still have some net benefit left over? If the answer is in the affirmative, it is reasoned that the change would improve welfare. There are all sorts of subsidiary questions as to the need for compensation actually to be paid, but we can ignore them for the present inquiry. It has been said that the progressive income tax may be looked upon as a built-in compensatory or income redistributive device helping society achieve that state of distributional equity that is socially desired.

Where does that leave us? We can argue that changes that would raise the level of allocative efficiency of the economy—that is, increase the amount of economic production available to the nation—may be deemed to improve economic welfare. Hence, in appraising a specific action—a government project or program—we are, from this point of view, asking the double question: do the gains to the beneficiaries outweigh the losses to the rest of the community and, hence, do the benefits exceed the costs to the economy as a whole? The benefits are in the form of increased production of goods and services and the costs are in terms of the foregone benefits that would have been obtained by using the resources in some other activity.

Benefit/cost analysis has been applied by several federal agencies, particularly the Corps of Engineers and the Bureau of Reclamation, to the evaluation of prospective projects for many years. Despite important operational difficulties, such as choosing an appropriate discount rate that would correspond to a realistic estimate of the social cost of capital, the use of benefit/cost analysis has yielded several gains in improving the allocation of government resources. It has served as a partial screening device to eliminate obviously uneconomical projects, that is, those whose prospective gains are less than estimated costs. It also has provided some basis for ranking and comparing projects, that is, a means of choosing among alternatives. Perhaps the overriding value of benefit/cost analysis has been demonstrating the importance of making fairly objective economic analyses of proposed essentially political actions and perhaps narrowing the area in which political forces may operate.

A related development has been the application of *cost/effectiveness analysis* to military budget decision-making. For military programs, ordinarily the benefits or results cannot be expressed in dollar terms. However, the end objective, such as the capability to destroy X number of enemy targets under stipulated conditions, can be expressed in quantitative terms and, more important, the alternative methods of achieving the objective—Y bombers versus Z missiles or some combination—can be priced out and a least cost solution arrived at. This approach has been at the heart of the Planning-Programming-Budgeting System introduced in the Pentagon by Secretary Robert McNamara and economists Charles Hitch, Alan Enthoven, and their associates. The McNamara approach led to the adoption of a government-wide PPBS effort. A fundamental shift has occurred in military resource allocation. Under the old system, each service competed for a larger share of the defense budget and, within the service totals, strategic weapons such as ICBMs competed for funds with tactical programs such as fighter aircraft. Under the new system, close substitutes for performing the same or similar mission are compared with each other, such as ICBMs and submarine-launched strategic missiles, although different services are involved.

It will be recognized that the ingredients of the concerns of welfare economics are here: how to attain a higher level of economic performance with the resources at hand and thus increase the welfare of society.

One other development needs to be acknowledged in sketching out the origin of the current program budgeting effort and that is the work on performance budgeting encouraged by the two Hoover Commissions and implemented in part by the U.S. Bureau of the Budget. By a *performance budget*, the Commission meant ". . . a budget based upon functions, activities, and projects . . ."

Such an approach, it was contended, would focus attention on the general character and relative importance of the work to be done, rather than upon the things to be acquired. Although it may not sound it, this was a fundamental shift in budgetary thinking at the federal level. Less of the budgetary details was to be devoted to changes in numbers and types of clerical personnel and office supply usage and more attention was to be given to the activities to be performed. However, the implementation was slow and only partial. The current emphasis on program budgeting may represent the delayed fulfillment of the Hoover Commission recommendation. As we will see, cost/benefit and cost/effectiveness analysis also play important parts in this new budgetary approach.

The Essence of PPBS

The Planning-Programming-Budgeting System, which each major federal government department and agency is now setting up in response to the directive from President Johnson, is patterned on the approach which has been instituted at the Pentagon. The entire system is new and its structure has barely been developed or put into operation to any significant degree. Hence, it is hazardous to attempt an evaluation at this early point.

PPBS is based on the introduction of three major concepts into federal government operations:

1. *The development in each government agency of* an analytical *capability to* examine in *depth both agency objectives and the various programs to meet these objectives.* This is hardly the traditional "green eye shade" type of approach to financial management and may be far more difficult to accomplish. However, it widens the frame of reference of governmental management officials and sets the stage for the next steps.
2. *The formation of a five-year planning and programming process coupled with a sophisticated management information system.* This should yield an improved basis for decision-making by department heads and the president in that it is designed to provide a comprehensive framework for acting on the myriad of questions that face the management of an organization, public or private.
3. *The last and perhaps fundamental concept to be introduced is the creation of* an improved *budgeting mechanism which can take broad program decisions, translate them into more refined decisions in a budgetary context, and present the results for presidential and congressional action.* This may be more of a statement of ultimate desire and long-term objective to be achieved.

Through the combined planning and budgeting process, it is hoped that broad national goals will be reduced to specific program operations and the most economical method of carrying them out will be identified. *Four major steps* have been identified which will need to be taken in order to accomplish this rather tall order:

1. *Identifying national goals.* The specific goals that are deemed proper and appropriate for the federal government to be seeking will somehow have to be selected in the light of an evaluation of national needs and objectives. This is now beginning to get underway in each major department and agency.
2. *Relating broad goals to specific programs.* Specific alternative programs that may help to achieve the broad national goals and objectives will then be examined. The ones that appear to be most promising, given the various constraints under which the federal government operates, are to be selected. The subject of constraints is not one to be passed over quickly. The typical government agency may find itself with little discretion in selecting the optimum combination of programs that can assist in achieving broad national goals in its area of operations. They may very well find that there is little or vague or conflicting congressional guidance as to the goals to be attained. However, there may be a very clear and precise congressional directive as to which specific programs are to be conducted—and in what amounts and particulars. The task here may well be both to infer the goals from the specific programs that have been authorized by Congress and then to conjure up new or improved means (other programs) to achieve these goals or objectives.
3. *Relating programs to resource requirements.* The specific costs of alternative programs will then need to be estimated (in terms of total resources they would require) in order to compare their efficiency in achieving the goals. This will be no mean achievement in many illusive program areas. All sorts of specific techniques come to mind here, including such formal ones as benefit/cost and cost/utility analysis, as well as more informal examinations with less quantification. In view of the many theoretical and operational shortcomings of these tools, the user will need to keep in mind that the basic purpose of any of these techniques is carrying out broad systems analyses in which alternative program are compared with respect to both the costs to be incurred and the gains to be achieved. Recent attempts to apply benefit/cost analysis to fields other than water resources (such as health, education, transportation, research, etc.) reveal the host of pitfalls and shortcomings of available techniques and methodology.
4. *Relating the resource inputs to budget dollars.* Finally, the manpower, facilities, and other resource requirements will need to be translated into budget dollars so that the costs of the programs can be analyzed over a meaningful period into the future and decisions made to implement the results. This sounds much easier than it is likely to be in practice. To cite one among numerous possibilities, one may wonder as to how the externalities involved—especially non-federal costs—will be handled.

Perhaps the most essential ingredient is the acceptance, at each line and staff level, of the value of and need for the tremendous amount of detail and effort being imposed. To some degree this is inherently both subjective and circular. The better the quality of input into the system, the greater the likelihood of good results. But it will be the value of the results that will justify the substantial expenditure of the time and effort involved.

The Framework of the System

The main product of PPBS is designed to be a comprehensive multi-year Program and Financial Plan for each government agency, which will be updated periodically and systematically. An early and essential step is determining, for each agency or department, the output-oriented categories that cover its area of responsibility. Such a mission-oriented or objectives-oriented program format would be in sharp contrast with present practice which focuses on the increase in funds over the previous year's budget required to meet rises in the annual expenses of the agency, that is, a budget review which is oriented to organizational units and to inputs such as wages, travel costs, office equipment, and so forth.

The first level of detail or breakdown in preparing the Program and Financial Plan is termed Program Categories, which are groupings of a department's activities serving the same broad objective or mission. For example, one broad program objective may be improvement of higher education. This program category might contain such federal programs as aid to undergraduate, graduate, and vocational education, as well as such auxiliary activities as library support and research assistance.

The second level of information is the Program Subcategories. These combine activities on the basis of somewhat narrower objectives contributing directly to the broad purposes of the program category as a whole. Thus, expansion of engineering and science training could be a program subcategory within the program category "improvement of higher education."

The third level of detail is the Program Element, which is the basic building block of the PPBS structure. An element may be a specific product that contributes to the program's objectives. An element could include personnel as well as equipment and facilities. An example of a program element expressed in terms of the objectives served would be the number of teachers to be trained in using the New Math as a part of "improvement of elementary education."

There are many difficulties involved in selecting the measurement of the output or performance of a program. Conceptually, only the end product should be measured rather than intermediate outputs. For example, in the Post Office, the end product might reflect the number of letters delivered, and not the number of times these letters were handled at the various stages of their journey.

Similarly, in the case of hospital programs, it may be possible to look at output in terms of patient-days. However, the mission of a hospital might be described better as proper treatment of patients. Therefore, the number of patients treated may be a better unit for measuring hospital output. However, within a broader framework, the mission of a health program might be viewed as promotion and maintenance of good health and the output measure might reflect prevention of diseases as well as their treatment. Legend has it that in better days Chinese patients paid their doctors in times of health and not of illness—a high mark of output rather than input orientation.

The agencies are encouraged to consider comparisons and possible trade-offs among program elements that are close substitutes, even though the activities may be conducted in different bureaus. This attempt to introduce some element of competition is designed to achieve greater effectiveness from the limited budgetary resources utilized for a given program category or subcategory.

In sharp contrast to the historical focus of federal budgeting on the next twelve-month fiscal period, PPBS is intended to extend usually five years into the future. In some cases, such as timber production and multiple-purpose water resource projects, longer time spans may be more appropriate.

Transportation is a good example of a major federal program category which consists of a variety of activities or program subcategories carried on in different departments, with little attention to gaps, overlapping functions, or conflicting objectives. The major agencies involved are the Bureau of Public Roads and the Maritime Administration in the Department of Commerce, the Federal Aviation Agency, the Corps of Engineers in the Department of the Army, the Forest Service in the Department of Agriculture, the National Park Service in the Department of the Interior, the mass transit assistance program in the Department of Housing and Urban Development, plus a number of regulatory operations, such as the ICC, CAB, Federal Maritime Board, and the Coast Guard. Only a few of these agencies are scheduled to be absorbed by the new Department of Transportation.

Specific elements might comprise one of the transportation subcategories: urban commuter transportation. These elements may vary from the number of miles of way placed under construction (a measure of capital investment) to the number of ton-miles of freight carried (a measure of operation or utilization).

It is doubtful whether, in the initial stages, the Planning-Programming-Budgeting System is able to do much toward rationalizing the whole gamut of federal transportation programs. Presumably, the current emphasis is on improving the "building blocks," the difficult task of evaluating the individual components. Nevertheless, all this is indicative of the broader horizons of the new breed of governmental budgeteers and may represent an initial small step along a relatively new path in governmental resource allocation.

Long-Term Impacts

Assuming that some aspects of PPBS do increasingly become operational at the departmental, then bureau, and then program level, the decision-making process in the federal government ultimately may undergo substantial change. With the introduction of sophisticated managerial tools such as benefit/cost, cost/utility, and systems analysis generally, there will be a reduced tendency for decisions on authorizing and financing individual government programs to be made in isolation and solely on the basis of subjective, intuitive judgments. Of course, computers will not replace managers in making decisions, nor will staff analysts replace the functions of line management.

It is possible that the composition of the federal budget will shift as a result of the implementation of the PPBS approach. On the basis of the work that has been done to date, it appears that benefit/cost and similar analyses will show that certain government programs yield a greater economic return (dollar benefit to the nation) than do others.

Federal expenditures for education and training—investments in "human" resources—are likely to yield estimated benefits substantially in excess of total costs. In contrast, some of the more traditional construction-oriented activities, notably irrigation and other multipurpose water resource projects, are likely to show up far less favorably in this regard. Hence, some shifts from "physical" to "human" capital investment may take place.

The Prospects for PPBS

As almost every examination of the federal budgetary process has concluded, major shortcomings are apparent and fundamental improvements are needed. There has been little interest in focusing on the goals and objectives of government spending programs or, as a result, on alternative and more effective ways of achieving them. The future costs of present decisions are often ignored. Hence, it is not surprising that formal planning and systems analysis have had limited effect on budget decisions to date.

The PPBS approach is designed to help remedy these shortcomings. If it succeeds in only a limited way, it will represent a major advance in the application of economic analysis to the allocation of public resources. It is premature, however, for any judgment as to the likelihood of PPBS succeeding. Will the vast system of reports generate into a wheel-spinning operation, or will the results become a significant factor in public policy formulation? From one viewpoint, PPBS is too ambitious, in that it is attempting to apply economic and systems analysis to the vast gamut of civilian government operations simultaneously. Perhaps some pilot studies or a few test cases in civilian agencies work would have provided a sounder basis on which to proceed.

From another viewpoint, however, the PPBS approach may be failing to come to grips with the larger choices in allocating federal funds among different agencies and programs. "Would a dollar be more wisely spent for Education or for Public Works?" This fundamental question implicit in the allocation of budget funds is not raised anywhere in the budgetary process at the present time nor is it likely to be answered or even raised under the suboptimizing approach of PPBS as it is being implemented.

11

The Modern Public Sector

When we think of government activities, the first image that comes to mind typically is a vision of government employees designing forms and filing reports. In contrast, the contemporary public sector devotes most of its resources to financing private sector production and consumption.

If there is anything that can get virtually unanimous agreement—on the part of liberals and conservatives alike, young and old, Republicans and Democrats—it is that we are all dissatisfied with the way in which government operates. We do not like the way in which public functions, military or civilian, are performed. There is no shortage of advice on how to improve the situation. In particular, two polar alternatives have received considerable attention.

The first, suggested by Peter Drucker in his recent book, *Age of Discontinuity,* may be called the private sector solution. Drucker tells us that government really can only make policy. It cannot carry on programs of its own, at least not with any degree of competence. Drucker reaches a striking conclusion: The main lesson of the last 50 years is that "Government is not a 'doer.'"

It is hard to fault his next conclusion—the purpose of government is "to govern." Drucker concludes that, "This [governing] as we have learned in other institutions, is incompatible with 'doing.' Any attempt to combine government with doing on a large scale paralyzes the decision-making capacity." Drucker is led to the conclusion that the execution of public programs should be turned over to the private sector.

Nationalization versus Privatization

The second polar alternative, best exemplified by John Kenneth Galbraith, may be called the nationalization solution. Galbraith, in his *New Industrial State,* tells us that government and industry are going to be working more closely together in the future. He contends that the large modern corporation is becoming part of the governmental administrative complex. As he puts it so decisively, "The mature corporation, as it develops, becomes part of the larger administrative complex associated with the state. In time, the line between the two will disappear." In the case of defense, he would hasten this trend by nationalizing the major corporate contractors.

Source: Murray Weidenbaum, "Toward A Modern Public Sector," *Conference Board Record,* September 1970.

In deriving his inferences, Galbraith draws on the present author's work. Yet, contrary to Galbraith's line of reasoning, I was led to conclude that the defense contractors are drawing away from commercial enterprise so fundamentally, and are embracing the Pentagon so closely, that they are losing some of the basic characteristics of commercially-oriented private business. Examples of this semi-nationalization of the defense industry include General Dynamics and General Atomics, not General Foods or General Motors or General Mills or even General Electric. In fact, the data tend to show a growing cleavage between the defense contractors and the rest of American industry.

Where does all this lead us? It would seem to suggest that we search for a more general theory—one which is a little more complex and offers more alternatives than either Professor Drucker or Professor Galbraith envisioned —but one which draws on both views.

Such an approach is based on an analysis of fundamental changes which have been occurring in the structure of governmental institutions. The transcending development is the intermingling between public and private activities, and between federal government and state and local government operations. In a rising number of cases, the dividing line between the federal government's sphere of operations and the rest of the economy has become increasingly blurred. To cite just a few examples: Is the antipoverty Community Action Organization public or private? What about the Federal National Mortgage Association (Fanny Mae)?

Drucker is right in stressing the growing division of labor in the functions of the federal government between policy formulation and supervision on the one hand, and actual program execution on the other. However, the relationships are considerably more complex than a simple public-private dichotomy.

The tendency of the federal government to become primarily a policy formulator and overseer can be clearly seen when we compare traditional federal departments and activities with the most recently established departments and programs. The older agencies typically devote the great bulk of their resources to their own payrolls and direct operations, to the direct delivery to the individual citizen of whatever service they are supposed to perform. Key examples of these old-line agencies are the Departments of State, Justice, and Treasury (aside from interest on the national debt).

In contrast, most of the newer agencies established by the federal government devote the great bulk of their resources to payments to individuals and organizations outside of the federal government, but not just to private industry. The Department of Health, Education, and Welfare (created in 1953) makes over nine-tenths of its expenditures in the form of grants-in-aid to state and local governments and transfer payments to individuals. The Department of Transportation (set up in 1965) spends three-fourths of its money on grants-in-aid to state and local governments. NASA (established in 1958) spends nine-tenths of its budget on contracts with private industry, universities, and nonprofit research institutes. In the military, the newest service, the Air Force, depends more heavily than either the Army or Navy on a variety of contractors, public and private, profit-making and otherwise.

Specifically, the area in which the federal government already depends most heavily on private industry—the design, development, and production of weapon systems—appears to be a poor precedent for a massive contracting out to private industry of other federal programs. In national defense procurement, the nation is not obtaining the advantages which are normally associated with the private business firm. The Lockheeds, North Americans, McDonnell-Douglases, and Boeings are behaving less like other corporations and more like government agencies or arsenals. In these cases, the Pentagon, in good measure, is taking on the traditional role of the private entrepreneur and the decision-making functions which are normally the prerogatives of business management.

This assumption of, or active participation in, private business decision-making by the federal government takes three major forms: (1) influencing, if not determining, the choice of products the government-oriented firm produces, through the customer funding the R&D (quite unlike the case in the commercial sector); (2) providing the bulk of the working capital used by defense contractors and the bulk of the fixed capital (plant and equipment) in the case of the large contractors; and (3) through the mechanism of the procurement contract, taking on many powers over the internal operations of the contractors.

These unilaterally determined grants of authority (the so-called boilerplate language in military contracts which is presented on a "take-it-or-leave-it" basis) vary from matters of considerable substance to items so minor that they border on the ludicrous. For example, the governmental "customer" enjoys the power to review and veto company decisions concerning which activities to perform in-house and which to subcontract, which firms to use as subcontractors, which products to buy domestically rather than import, what minimum as well as average wage rates to pay, and how much overtime work to authorize.

In effect, the quasi-public nature of the contracting firm is given implicit recognition by inserting language in the government contract that requires the firm to conduct itself in much the same way that a federal agency does — favoring so-called depressed areas, small businesses, and so on. One of the more striking examples of the minor matters covered is the prescription that the safety rules followed in the offices and factories of the defense contractors must be consistent with the latest edition of the Corps of Engineers safety manual.

Looking at what may be called government-oriented (as opposed to market-oriented) companies, one finds numerous indications that their entrepreneurial abilities have become attenuated. The dependence of shipbuilding companies on government contracts and subsidies has led to that industry's failure to undertake new product development on its own or otherwise to compete effectively in world markets. Few purchase American-built ships unless forced to by law—and then they are heavily subsidized. Similarly, the aerospace industry has had many more failures than even mild successes in attempting to utilize its much vaunted systems analysis capability to penetrate commercial markets.

The defense industry is not unique in this respect. The numerous attempts to involve state and local governments in national programs via grants-in-aid also have yielded mixed results. The dictionary may define a grant as a gift, but that is hardly true in the case of this gift horse. From the recipient's viewpoint, federal grant funds come with many strings attached. In a wide variety of cases, federal departments must approve, in advance of giving out the grant, the state operating plan for the program as well as the specific expenditure plan. Very substantial shares of state and local budgets come under strong control of federal departments such as Health, Education, and Welfare; Housing and Urban Development; and Transportation. The effective power of elected officials is curtailed; the road commission looks not to the governor or the state legislator but to the Federal Bureau of Public Roads. The local health departments may be more concerned with the U.S. Public Health Service than with the mayor or city council.

In contrast, from the viewpoint of the cognizant federal agencies the problem frequently may be the reverse—how to get these other units of government to spend the federal money in accord with national priorities.

When other mechanisms are used which are ostensibly lodged in the private sector —e.g., nonprofit research institutions—we find that they present another set of problems. They circumvent civil service and related federal operating requirements. Yet, those which rely almost entirely on federal financing may not necessarily provide the objectivity expected of a not-for-profit private research institute.

Suggested Changes

Specific ways suggest themselves for improving federal use of each of these individual mechanisms. The answer to the close relationship between the Pentagon and the defense industry may not be, *á la* Galbraith, to bring them even closer together. Rather, a more capitalistic solution might be tried —to wean the major contractors away from overdependence on the protective governmental environment and to make them behave more like the competitive private enterprises that we think they are. This may involve such specific steps as reducing the free provision of working capital, cutting down on the host of procurement regulations, and broadening the base of companies which serve as the major defense contractors.

Let defense companies develop their own safety rules to discourage employees from skidding on factory floors. We seem to forget why, in the first place, we prefer to use private enterprise rather than government arsenals to develop and produce weapon systems. It is not because private corporations are better than government agencies at following rules and regulations. It is precisely for the opposite reason. We hope that they are more creative and innovative.

Similarly, the improvement of federal-state-local relationships may not require even more grant-in-aid programs—but the lessening of federal domination and control. The new federal revenue-sharing proposals point the way; they attempt to give state and local governments a portion of the rising federal revenue base without any strings.

These specific suggestions, of course, all set the stage for a more basic and general suggestion on how better to manage a modern public sector. Basically, the idea of competition should be extended to the public sector itself.

There exists a wide spectrum of alternative mechanisms which the federal government can utilize in carrying out its functions. These include direct employment of civil servants, transfer payments to individuals, contracts with business firms and nonprofit organizations, and grants to state and local governments. A careful examination of each of these alternative methods of conducting the government's business is revealing. Each has advantages as well as disadvantages.

Direct federal operations can be subject to close congressional as well as departmental control, but the ability to respond quickly, particularly to new problems requiring new skills, may be quite limited. In contrast, private industry may more readily be able to marshal rapidly a wide variety of physical and human resources—but at the expense of attenuation of public control over publicly financed programs. Similarly, state and local governments may constitute an already-present network of delivery agencies for a wide variety of social programs, but a host of publicly elected or appointed local officials may have their own ideas as to the future direction of these programs.

Increasing Competition

A more effective form of competition among alternative recipients of federal funds is my approach for improving the future structure and performance of the public sector. If revenue sharing so strengthens the states and localities that they can effectively carry on a growing array of programs with a national interest, then we would be wise to increase the resources available to them. If that does not prove to be the case, then perhaps some new pattern of contracting with the private sector needs to be developed. On the other hand, if some form of negative income tax reduces the need for an administrative bureaucracy, public or private, then let it be used.

In choosing among the array of alternative mechanisms available, federal policy-makers should not be oblivious of their own impacts on the fundamental structure of these mechanisms. One basic approach is to reduce federal dependence on any single mechanism. Perhaps a more fundamental answer is to shift the solution of some of these national problems to other segments of society. Tax incentives to private industry, untied transfer payments, tax sharing, and lowering the level of federal taxes all represent ways of channeling more resources to other segments of society.

If this idea of competition within the public sector sounds a little far-fetched, consider possible application in the "war on pollution." At each antipollution meeting, speakers are prone to throw out a variety of relatively untested suggestions. Some want the federal government to mount a major effort to clean up the landscape; others want the states to take the lead; still others want the local community to be in the vanguard. A large contingent would foist the responsibility on business in a variety of different ways: subsidies, regulations, and taxation.

How are we to determine which approach is likely to be most effective? That is precisely where the idea of competition comes in. At this comparatively early, developmental stage of national concern with improving our physical environment, there is real merit in trying out a few approaches simultaneously, rather than relying entirely on one method.

For example, is it sensible to devote an even larger share of our national resources to cleaning up an even faster growing mountain of pollution? Is it not imperative to adopt methods of production and consumption which are less polluting than present practices? If so, one approach would require that via taxation the act of polluting be made more expensive to the polluter than not polluting—and sufficiently so to induce the polluters to change their ways of doing things.

This approach may not suffice. It is likely to work on new production and consumption facilities, but it may be inappropriate and highly inequitable for facilities which are already in existence and which are constructed in good faith under a different set of ground rules. Hence, there may be a case for some direct government expenditures, or at least tax benefits—particularly during a transition period. The choice among different levels of government would still have to be made.

Thus, we may have an opportunity to compare the effectiveness of a variety of governmental mechanisms, each of which represents an alternative approach to the same basic problem of cleaning up the environment. That prospect of competition within the public sector seems attractive and worth trying.

Toward the Future

The prospect is for a mixed economy in the United States, but a far more intricate mixture than has been experienced thus far. In the past, most discussions of the role of government have simplistically assumed a clean dividing line between public and private. The very phrase "mixed economy" has mainly indicated that the line was not being drawn at either extreme, that both public and private production occurred in a given industry. For example, the Tennessee Valley Authority and the Pacific Gas and Electric Company both produce and distribute electric power, the former being a government agency and the latter a private corporation. The Post Office Department and the Railway Express Agency both deliver parcels; again, one is public and the other private.

The mixed economy that is now developing is more complex. It is characterized by mixed organizations, each of which possesses characteristics of both public institutions and private organizations. The most obvious examples are the large defense contractors and the not-for-profit research laboratories that do most of their business with the federal government.

The modern public sector that is developing is hardly something aloof and entirely separate from the private sector. Rather, in its usual pragmatic fashion, the United States is fashioning policy tools not for the sake of their intrinsic beauty, but to achieve a growing variety of difficult and far-reaching national objectives.

It would appear likely that in coming years increasing proportions of federal funds will be disbursed via state and local governments, intergovernmental agencies, government-oriented corporations, quasi-private institutions, and perhaps even newer organizations possessing both public and private characteristics. The typical federal agency indeed will probably be a policy formulator and overseer of programs dealing with operations which have been decentralized in a variety of ways and over a wide span of the American economy. This will provide a very considerable strength and resiliency to American institutions during a period of substantial stress and change.

12

Government Encouragement of Innovation

This survey of the different ways that government can encourage innovation emphasizes incentives for private sector initiatives in new research and development (R&D) activities. A federal tax credit for business R&D is proposed, an approach that in modified form was later enacted into public policy.

The shift in emphasis in the federal budget from defense programs to domestic and welfare types of expenditure has also meant a relative decline in federal support of research and development. The adverse impact on R&D has not been by conscious plan because, in the main, the Congress does not vote billions of dollars for R&D in order to promote science and technology per se. Rather, with the exception of an agency such as the National Science Foundation (NSF), the Congress typically appropriates money for defense or to land a man on the moon or to build roads or to reduce poverty. And these programs may, or may not, have a high R&D content.

Because of changing priorities, the relative importance of these areas has been shifting, as well as the role of the mechanisms used to carry out these programs. Thus, spending more money on civilian programs also means a relative shift from direct purchases to transfer payments, grants to state and local governments, and credit programs—because there is a fairly consistent pattern in the use of mechanisms to achieve a given national purpose (e.g., purchases for defense and transfer payments for welfare). Likewise, as relative priorities change among the different functions, there are concomitant shifts in the extent to which the different expenditure mechanisms are relied upon. The impact on R&D occurs because the R&D intensity of priority programs and the various expenditure mechanisms varies by orders of magnitude.

Thus, without even making such a decision consciously, this nation has tended to curtail federal support of R&D as a consequence of updating its priorities. The reductions in military spending over the last several years have not been accompanied by increases in federal civilian spending with an equivalent content of R&D.

Why should the government be interested in funding R&D per se? Basically because the civilian areas that have recently received greater priority have not been, at least in the past, large users of R&D. The major civilian

Source: Murray Weidenbaum, "Government Spending and Innovation," *Astronautics and Aeronautics*, November 1973.

program expansion of the past decade has been in transfer payments, notably Social Security pensions. As would be expected in the case of an income-redistribution program, the income-security function devotes a miniscule part of its budget to R&D—$62 million out of $65 billion in 1972. This stands in striking contrast to national defense, which devoted $9 billion to R&D out of $78 billion in 1972.

The second area of major expansion in federal spending in recent years has been grants to states and localities, and the pattern of R&D usage has been similar to the case of transfer payments. Of the more than $18 billion of grants-in-aid expenditure in 1968, only about $100 million was devoted to R&D. The propensity of states and localities to spend their own revenue on R&D is even less than their modest commitments out of federal grants. In 1968 states and localities spent less than $100 million out of their own funds for R&D, a year when their total revenues from their own sources (excluding federal grants) came to $113 billion.

In the case of government credit programs, the bulk of the activity is currently devoted to banking-type operations, such as providing funds to farmers and financing home mortgages. The impact on R&D appears to be nil.

These changes in basic budget priorities have had striking implications for R&D. As long as the high-R&D-intensity programs were also the high-priority areas, science and technology implicitly were given a high priority in the budget. But the shift to low-R&D-intensity programs requires a re-thinking of the role of science and technology in national priorities. Perhaps "R&D" or "technological innovation" should be elevated to the status of an end-purpose.

Should that course of action be taken, attention would need to be given to the various expenditure mechanisms that could be relied upon in using government resources to promote research, development, and innovation. The remainder of this article arrays the various federal expenditure approaches that could be drawn upon.

Even though the non-purchase mechanisms do not now have a significant R&D content, nothing inherent in their characteristics prevents a greater technological emphasis in the future. Several such future possibilities are therefore presented for consideration, with emphasis on ways of encouraging the private sector to undertake R&D and to increase the rate of innovation of new products and processes.

Characteristics of Alternative Mechanisms

The federal government can use a great variety of methods to influence technological invention and innovation by the private sector. These include direct support of R&D, federal procurement of goods and services, tax and credit subsidies, and more indirect mechanisms. Only two mechanisms—federal employees and government purchases—now have a substantial impact on the objective of fostering R&D and innovation. These, also, are the expenditure categories involving the largest proportion of federal funds, the greatest degree of federal control, and the smallest extent of private initiative.

Federal Employee Activities and Innovation

Traditionally, much federal support of R&D has taken the form of making available to potential producers the results of the efforts of employees working in government laboratories. Much of the developmental work on commercial air transports was performed in the laboratories of the National Advisory Committee on Aeronautics, the forerunner of NASA. Similarly, throughout the nineteenth century and during the early years of the twentieth century, the military establishment relied on government-owned and -operated arsenals and shipyards to design and develop its specialized equipment.

Since World War II, the role of government installations has declined, and dependence increased on the private sector for the design, development, and production of the highly sophisticated systems and equipment that the government requires. Nevertheless, a considerable number of outstanding laboratories continue to be operated and staffed by government agencies. Federal employees can and are employed in other ways to foster R&D, but on a much smaller scale, and with varying effectiveness. These technology transfer mechanisms include providing scientific and other technical documents and publications, maintaining computerized data banks, and sharing federal laboratories and test facilities.

Among the most publicized efforts have been those of NASA, the Small Business Administration (SBA), and the Department of Commerce. The technology-utilization program of NASA provides the results of government work in science and technology to prospective users in the private sector. The Department of Commerce and the SBA provide technical and managerial assistance to entrepreneurs.

Government Purchases and Innovation

The major financial support by the federal government to R&D now takes the form of contracts with the private sector. A wide array of contractual arrangements are utilized, and their characteristics vary substantially. Contracts for R&D per se have the largest direct and positive impact, of course, on the level and composition of private R&D. In the process, the bulk of the financial risk is shifted from the private sector to the taxpayer.

The effects of many of the specific contractual arrangements depend on the formulation. For example, cost sharing of 80 percent or more by the private entrepreneur may result in little federal control or financing, and in practice border on a modest subsidy. In contrast, cost sharing of 20 percent or less approaches a federal grant or contract for R&D, and its impacts may be quite similar.

Although there are important differences between contracts and grants, both are generally included in data and reports on federal purchases from the private sector. Unlike contracts, grants usually do not require the recipient to deliver any tangible object, other than administrative reports. Much of the specific detail normally contained in government contracts is not included in grants to scientific investigators.

The method of administering the contract form can strongly influence its characteristics. For example, a rule that all unsolicited projects must provide for some cost-sharing constitutes a deterrent to private initiative. Indirectly, it provides further encouragement to the prospective government contractor to respond to the leadership of government agencies in identifying promising R&D work rather than to apply its own innovative resources.

The bulk of the federal government's civilian purchases has been devoted to fairly standard and conventional low-technology items available from commercial sources. In order to use the government's vast purchasing power to foster a greater degree of technological innovation, it has been suggested that the General Services Administration (GSA) set up an Experimental Procurement Service (EPS). Innovation here is viewed as a worthy objective in its own right, in terms of its contribution to economic growth and productivity. Established alongside the existing Federal Supply Service, the EPS would have a modest budget—say $15-20 million—to purchase new and relatively unproven products. As it gained experience, the new bureau also would develop performance standards for government procurement.

Supporters of an EPS contend that the federal government's existing procurement practices inhibit its role as a leader in purchasing new and improved products. The use of physical instead of performance specifications often precludes the introduction of new products. Product diversity is also discouraged by the tendency to reduce the number of different catalogue items in any one category. Moreover, a simpleminded emphasis on price competition ignores the better performance (such as lower operating costs) that may be achieved by new products.

GSA now takes too literally the requirement to seek the lowest priced items. In the case of air conditioners, for instance, the present approach focuses exclusively on cooling ability (as measured by BTU rating), and ignores such other factors as power consumption and noise levels. An air conditioner offering improved power or noise features would presumably only be purchased if it was cheaper than other units with the same BTU rating.

In this respect, the federal government already uses its massive role as purchaser to require its contractors to adhere to many "socioeconomic" objectives. The government insists that firms doing business with it maintain "fair" employment practices, provide "safe" and "healthy" working conditions, pay "prevailing" wages, refrain from polluting the air and water, give preference to U.S. products in their purchases, and promote the rehabilitation of prisoners and the severely handicapped.

The benefit of using government contracts to promote basic national policies is clear. Important objectives can be fostered without the need for an additional expenditure by the Treasury. Yet these special provisions do constitute burdens on the procurement process. They are not costless insofar as they increase overhead expenses of private contractors and federal procurement offices.

Government Subsidies and R&D

Few federal expenditure programs are formally designated as subsidies. Aid to agriculture, airlines, shipbuilders, and ship operators are the major examples. In most other cases, there is a subsidy element in some other program, such as a purchase, loan, or tax incentive. The overt subsidy programs do not appear to have much effect on the desire or capability to perform R&D and to innovate. In effect, the government support insulates the industry from the effects of competition from other sources. In the shipbuilding case, U.S. industry has the reputation of being one of the least progressive and least efficient. The airline subsidies are received by the local feeder, or regional airlines, which usually follow rather than lead the major trunk lines in the selection of new types of equipment.

From time to time, suggestions are made for new types of subsidies, more oriented to R&D. Some of the Western European governments share the cost of developing, producing, and marketing new products and processes. Others offer, for approved projects, "launching aid" in the form of sharing the losses that might arise during the first year or two after the introduction of a new product. More limited aid is provided in the form of grants to cover the salaries of scientists and engineers assigned to approved R&D projects. Some of these government subsidies are accompanied by a requirement that they would be recoverable to the extent that they generated successful and profitable products. Thus, royalty payments to the government can be required equal to some percentage of gross sales or net profits.

Such subsidies involve substantial degrees of government control and influence, as well as financial risk-bearing. As the Department of Commerce noted in an analysis of various foreign efforts: "A high level of funding provided for the implementation of a specific technology enhancement program does not necessarily ensure success or accomplishment of objectives." Fear of governmental interference or excessive red tape were cited as principal reasons for lack of success of these governmental promotional efforts. There is a tradeoff, of course, between government support and control, on the one hand, and the extent of private initiative and risk-bearing, on the other.

Transfer Payments and Innovation

As pointed out earlier, existing transfer payments do not have a significant R&D content. From time to time, however, the suggestion has been made to tailor a specific income transfer payment to scientists and engineers. During the recent extensive cutbacks in defense and space employment, numerous proposals were advanced to provide unemployed scientists and engineers with sufficient income so that they could retrain or retool for comparable civilian work, rather than be forced to take jobs pumping gas or other employment not utilizing their technical skills.

Thus far, little public support has been generated for giving scientists and engineers more liberal income transfers than others who lose employment. There appears to be less resistance to devoting federal funds to activities with a high R&D content that, indirectly, would provide income to those obtaining jobs from the resultant disbursement of funds.

Grants-in-Aid and Innovation

Existing grants-in-aid to state and local governments, as pointed out, provide very little support to R&D. A state and particularly a local government is similar to an individual firm in its inability to recapture the external benefits of the R&D that it may finance or perform.

A number of possible ways of encouraging states and their subdivisions to do more along these lines can be developed. The federal government could award special grants-in-aid for R&D in general, for high-priority areas or projects, or for technical assistance to local entrepreneurs. During this period of restraint on federal spending, the prospects are not very bright for such a new undertaking.

An alternative would be to add some R&D "strings" on existing grants-in-aid; that is, the federal government could impose another condition on the states and localities receiving these funds—to devote some minimum portion to pertinent R&D. This approach would go against the current thrust in reforming and rationalizing federal aid to state and local governments to reduce the extent of federal control and influence over state and local decision-making and to increase the discretion exercised by these levels of government.

In one of the few grants-in-aid which have been used purposively to foster innovation, the Capital Grants Program of DOT's Urban Mass Transit Administration, the federal government will underwrite two-thirds of the cost of buses purchased by urban transit authorities if the purchases conform to the federal specifications for a "new generation" bus. The federal role includes financing the development of the specification, as well as the production of prototype buses.

Tax Incentives and R&D

In the other industrialized nations, tax benefits are the most frequently used method of government encouragement of private-sector research, development, and innovation. Although the U.S. tax system does not rival them in scope and variety, it hardly lacks tax incentives either. The largest of the tax incentives relate to the manufacturing stage—the provision of liberalized depreciation allowances and tax credits in the case of investment in new plant and equipment.

Only a few tax provisions of significance are expressly designed to encourage R&D per se. One provides for the current deductibility from taxable income of the total value of equipment purchased for R&D work. This constitutes a more powerful incentive than the traditional capital recovery systems that require the taxpayer to write off the investment over a period of years. Another provision of the Internal Revenue Code allows sale of patents to be taxed at the lower capital gains rate.

Additional tax incentives to promote R&D have been suggested from time to time, often patterned after the Western European experiences. The most frequently encountered suggestion, a partial tax credit for R&D, resembles the existing partial tax credit for the purchase of new equipment. It has been estimated that a 25 percent tax credit for R&D would cost the Treasury about $2-3 billion annually in lost revenue. Other proposals involve an extra tax credit or deduction for incremental R&D—that performed by a company above the amount in some base period. One difficulty with such a proposal: it may be a reward for the company on a rapid growth path and increasing its R&D outlays anyway. Also, it would not benefit the lagging firm, which might particularly require some outside assistance.

Federal Credit and Innovation

The federal government makes credit available to a large array of borrowers, usually at a subsidized rate. Existing federal loan programs generally do not involve activities with a significant R&D content, although some of the recipients of SBA loans have been technically oriented enterprises. The mechanism of federal credit does lend itself to adaptation for purposes of encouraging R&D and product innovation. For example, loans could be provided to medium-sized and larger enterprises when conventional credit sources prove inadequate to finance new products or processes.

As with federal loan programs, federal guarantees of private loans do not involve significant R&D activity. Yet the loan guarantee mechanism may merit attention because it does not directly require any substantial amount of expenditure commitment or revenue loss. The administrative costs are typically small and covered by user fees. The guarantee does generate a contingent liability on the Treasury should the private borrower default.

Governmental loan guarantees are not costless to society. Although they may not involve the use of government spending, the guarantees constitute a lien on available private investment funds. Particularly in a period of credit stringency, government guarantees for the borrowing of some groups of the population inevitably "crowd" out the unprotected borrowers. Loan guarantees do not add to the investment funds available to a nation, but they rearrange the preferential order of different classes of borrowers.

Over the years, the federal government has embarked upon a number of credit programs which gradually have been converted in whole or part to private ownership. Various methods have been used. Initial private users of the federal National Mortgage Association (FNMA) were required to buy stock in the Association. After a time, the private capital enabled the original Treasury advance to be repaid, and the Association became a privately held corporation. As with other government-sponsored enterprises (such as the Federal Land Banks and the Federal Home Loan Banks), various degrees of special federal regulation and financial support continue.

The federal government might consider following the Western European example of fostering cooperative technical association within a given industry. To a limited extent such associations are now in existence. However, antitrust and tax considerations generally require that the results of their R&D be put into the public domain and thus made available to those who did not support the undertaking. Changes in legislation might encourage greater use of this cooperative device, particularly if there was some federal support and sponsorship. The federal role might encourage more companies to participate, particularly the smaller ones, while protecting the public interest.

One method of encouragement of such cooperative R&D ventures would be to require any patents to be made available free of charge to all of the industrial participants. To assure that the benefits would be widely transmitted, other companies could be allowed to use the patents after payment of reasonable royalties.

Government Assets and Innovation

In a modest way, existing government assets promote private-sector R&D. Such activities do not constitute any current charge on the federal budget (although, alternative uses might produce greater revenue for the government). Surplus assets are often donated to educational institutions that may perform some R&D. Government-owned R&D and production facilities are leased to private concerns for commercial work (the practice usually being limited to contractors who may be using part of the facility for work on government contracts).

Both of these methods lend themselves to promoting technological innovation in the private sector. Surplus federal assets might be donated to organizations other than educational institutions for scientific and technological exploration. Dormant federal R&D facilities might be rented to private users who are not government contractors. The rental payments could be made especially low if the federal government wishes to encourage a particular technological application, such as the design of low-cost mass transportation systems.

Other Factors in the Stimulation of R&D

It is possible to provide a favorable context for R&D without any specific incentive. General measures to stimulate business activity and consumer demand may create a favorable climate for technological innovation. For example, government policies to stimulate greater consumer demand may encourage the research effort by providing the basic incentive of rapidly rising markets. Efforts to promote higher levels of business investment in plant and equipment might aid in a variety of ways. The incentives would apply to laboratories, office buildings, and other relatively durable facilities directly related to the R&D effort.

More indirectly and perhaps more important, such incentives may have a more powerful effect on the research effort at the innovation stage by easing the burden of financing the capital equipment needed to produce and market any successful products emerging from the R&D effort. Rising levels of business generally would increase the amount of internal R&D investment funds available to industry. Such a favorable business environment would also reenforce the more specific governmental expenditure measures that may be undertaken to increase private sponsorship and financing of R&D.

Conclusion

The policymaker has little formal methodology to draw upon in choosing among the alternative ways in which the government can encourage R&D and the introduction of new products and processes into the American economy. The type of comparative analysis presented here may carry policymakers a part of the way; but they may find little substitute for the lengthy and expensive processes of trial and error.

Examining the relevant experiences of other industrialized nations, it can be seen that many have substantial programs to encourage R&D in both the public and private sectors. The justification for the government aid rests on the belief that business firms tend to underinvest in R&D and hence to innovate very little—simply because much of the return on such outlay takes the form of benefits to society as a whole, rather than to the firm financing the work.

In reacting to that problem, the federal government should avoid taking on the bulk of the responsibility for proposing the areas of R&D to be emphasized, as well as deciding which specific projects and performers should be chosen, and at what precise level the activity should be funded, and thus assuming virtually all of the risk-bearing and other attributes of the entrepreneurial function.

But the federal government should not accept the opposite set of alternatives either. Because so much of the benefits of R&D may not be captured by the individual firm doing the work, the free-market solution does not yield a level of research, development, and innovation adequate to meet national goals. Policy instruments should permit a judicious balancing of these two inherently conflicting sets of concerns.

Considerable weight should be given to the tax alternative because, in contrast to the other approaches, it relies primarily on market forces and normal business incentives to allocate resources, including R&D resources. Thus, R&D does not become a "free good," but merely a bit cheaper than it would be in the absence of the governmental assistance. There is still pressure on the business firm to make sure that it is getting a favorable return on its R&D investment.

In the design of expenditure programs, great pains should be taken to avoid the situation where the firm doing the work need not concern itself much with the economic feasibility or profitability of the project, so long as it fulfills the terms of the R&D contract. Cost-sharing does reintroduce some market forces. Moreover, private laboratories possess important advantages over government facilities—not necessarily in terms of technical competence, but rather the likelihood of applying results. There are great problems in having R&D conducted by organizations not in close touch with the production and marketing of the product. The likelihood is that R&D will be misdirected or neglected or resisted by potential users.

No single mechanism should be relied on exclusively in designing a program to enhance technological innovation. A combination of methods should be used. We should experiment with alternative approaches so as to be in a better position to identify the most attractive combination of alternatives. There is no substitute for a variety of trials and efforts—and a modicum of good luck.

13

The Use of the Government's Credit Power

Federal credit programs are perhaps the least well understood mechanism of public policy. This article examines the nature of these programs, illuminating their hidden costs and their off-budget nature.

The arsenal of government power over the economy is extensive, including the authority to tax, the ability to spend the proceeds of that taxation, and the capability of issuing rules and regulations determining or influencing private behavior. One of the lesser known components of that arsenal is the government's power to provide credit to various individuals and organizations.

Most credit activities do not appear in the federal budget. Many do not involve any direct federal expenditure. Hence, they seem to be a painless way of achieving national objectives. In the main, the federal government is "merely" guaranteeing private borrowing or sponsoring ostensibly private institutions. Is this use of the government's credit power a variation of the proverbial "free lunch?" In this context, the costs as well as the benefits that may flow from this often overlooked aspect of government interaction with the private sector will be examined.

The Variety of Government Credit Programs

Over the years, substantial numbers of credit programs have made their way through the legislative process of the federal government. These programs emerged on an ad hoc basis, with each program directed toward providing assistance in overcoming a specific problem at hand. As a result of this gradual but very substantial accretion, federal credit program subsidies are now provided to a great many sectors of the U.S. economy—housing, agriculture, transportation, health, education, state and local governments, small business—as well as to foreigners. The total amount of credit provided under federal auspices has risen substantially.

There are three major uses of the federal government's credit power.

Direct Loans

Direct loans extended by federal agencies generally involve significant subsidies because the loans are made at interest rates below those available in

Source: Murray Weidenbaum, "The Use of the Government's Credit Power," in Kenneth Boulding and Thomas Wilson, eds., *Redistribution Through the Financial System* (New York: Praeger Publishers, 1978).

the private sector. In many cases, the government also absorbs the administrative expenses and losses arising from loan defaults, thus further increasing the amount of the subsidy. Although not formally considered a federal credit program, the generous progress payments made by the Department of Defense represent interest-free provision of working capital to government contractors on a very large scale. Direct loans are an important form of federal credit. However, in recent years, they have been exceeded in size by the various guarantee programs and lending activities of government-sponsored but privately owned credit agencies.

Loan Guarantees

The attractiveness of loan guarantees to government policymakers stems largely from the fact that the loans themselves are made by private lenders and thus are excluded from the federal budget. Technically, all the government does is to assume a contingent liability to pay the private lender if the private borrower defaults. Loans made under some housing subsidy programs have experienced very high default rates in spite of their being backed by the security of real property. Other new programs generate higher risks because there has been a tendency to move toward the guarantee of loans that require little or no collateral in connection with the guarantee.

Loans by Federally Sponsored Agencies

Ostensibly private institutions such as the Federal National Mortgage Association, the Federal Home Loan Banks, and the farm credit agencies are not included in the total of federal spending. They raise their funds primarily through borrowing in the nation's capital markets. However, these agencies possess various tax advantages and are able to borrow funds in the market at low interest rates because of the implicit government backing of their debentures. Loans made by these sponsored agencies have increased sharply. They now comprise the largest single form of federal credit assistance to the private sector.

Impact on Saving and Investment

The impacts of federal credit programs on the total flow of saving and investment in the U.S. economy are clear. These programs do little if anything to increase the total flow of saving or investment. They mainly change the share of investment funds going to a given industry or sector of the economy and, in the process of doing so, exert upward pressures on interest rates as investment funds are bid away from other sectors.

In commenting on existing programs of federally assisted credit to the private sector, Henry Kaufman has written: "Federal agency financing does not do anything directly to enlarge the supply of savings. . . . In contrast, as agency financing bids for the limited supply of savings with other credit demanders, it helps to bid up the price of money."

In a comprehensive study of federal credit programs for the Commission on Money and Credit, Warren Law concluded that they have created inflationary pressures in every year since World War II. One cost of federal credit programs arises from the fact that, given the availability of funds, an increase in credit for housing means lesser amounts for other borrowers. The two borrowing groups most adversely affected by tight credit are state and local governments and small businesses. A further cost is that the operations of the federal credit agencies tend to increase the level of interest rates above the level that would have prevailed if they had not entered the credit markets.

This phenomenon occurs for a variety of reasons. The total supply of funds is broadly determined by household and business saving and the ability of banks to increase the money supply. The normal response of financial markets to an increase in the demand for funds by a borrower, such as is represented by a federal credit program, is an increase in interest rates so as to balance out the demand for funds with the supply of saving. But the federal government's demand for funds is "interest inelastic" (the Treasury will generally raise the money that it requires regardless of the interest rate) and the interest elasticity of saving is relatively modest. Thus, weak and marginal borrowers will be rationed out of financial markets in the process, while the Treasury and other borrowers pay higher rates of interest.

Important insight into the effects of federal credit programs on capital markets has been provided by Bruce MacLaury, a former deputy undersecretary of the Treasury:

> The more or less unfettered expansion of federal credit programs and the accompanying deluge of agency direct and guaranteed securities to be financed in the credit markets has undoubtedly permitted Congress and the Administration to claim that wonder of wonders—something for nothing, or almost nothing. But as with all such sleight-of-hand feats, the truth is somewhat different.

MacLaury goes on to point out that there are extra costs associated with introducing new government credit agencies to the capital markets. These costs involve selling issues that are smaller than some minimum efficiently tradable size and selling securities that only in varying degree approximate the characteristics of direct government debt in terms of perfection of guarantee, flexibility of timing and maturities, and "cleanness" of instrument. As a result of such considerations, the market charges a premium over the interest cost on direct government debt of comparable maturity. That premium ranges from one-fourth of 1 percent on the well-known federally sponsored agencies, such as the Federal National Mortgage Association, to more than 0.5 percent on such exotics as New Community Bonds. In general, if cost of financing were the only consideration, it would be most efficient to have the Treasury itself provide the financing for direct loans by issuing government debt in the market.

Reduced efficiency occurs in the economy by providing a federal "umbrella" over many credit activities without distinguishing their relative credit risks. A basic function that credit markets are supposed to perform is that of distinguishing different credit risks and assigning appropriate risk premiums. This is the essence of the ultimate resource-allocation function of credit markets. As an increasing proportion of issues coming to the credit markets bears the guarantee of the federal government, the ability of the market to differentiate credit risks inevitably diminishes. Theoretically, the federal agencies issuing or guaranteeing debt would perform this role, charging as costs of the programs differing rates of insurance premiums. In practice, all of the pressures are against such differential pricing of risks. This is a hidden cost of federal credit programs.

The very nature of federal credit assistance is to create advantages for some groups of borrowers and disadvantages for others. The literature provides clear answers on who will tend to be rationed out in the process. It is unlikely to be the large well-known corporations or the U.S. government. It is more likely to be state and local governments, medium-sized businesses, private mortgage borrowers not under the federal umbrella, and consumers, thereby contributing to additional economic and financial concentration in the United States. The competition for funds by the rapidly expanding federal credit programs also increases the cost to the taxpayer by raising the interest rate at which the Treasury borrows its own funds. There has been a massive expansion in the public borrowings that have been undertaken to finance federal government credit programs.

Virtually every session of the Congress in recent years has enacted additional federal credit programs. Since 1960, the Federal National Mortgage Association (Fannie Mae) has been joined by the Government National Mortgage Association (Ginnie Mae), the Student Loan Marketing Association (Sally Mae), and the U. S. Railway Association.

Subsidies in Credit Programs

Substantial subsidy elements exist in most federal credit programs, which, of course, make these activities especially attractive to the recipients of the benefits. The subsidy element typically is fundamental, in that the basic purpose of the government's involvement is to provide certain categories of borrowers with credit on terms that are more favorable than those available in private markets.

To the extent that social goals are achieved regarding preferred expenditure flows and resource uses, subsidies can be regarded as beneficial. At the heart of a subsidy is a political decision to favor some at the expense of others. Because a credit subsidy involves a balancing of interests, it would be useful to have fairly well-developed notions regarding the incidence of benefits and costs of any specific program. In light of the variety of credit programs, it simply is not possible to make firm statements with broad applicability.

In a study of the home mortgage purchase program of the Government National Mortgage Association, George von Furstenberg has shown that the principal result of that government credit program has not been to increase the volume of resources going into housing. Rather, the credit programs have mainly provided arbitrary subsidies to many homeowners who otherwise would have had to pay more for their home mortgages. Many of them could have obtained the private financing in the absence of the government subsidy.

Most frequently the improved terms take the form of an interest rate that is lower than the rate charged to private borrowers. Also, the length of the loan and the loan-to-value ratio may be more favorable. In addition, subsidies may result from inadequate fees or premiums that do not cover administrative costs and losses on credit guarantees. At the heart of a subsidy is a political decision to favor some at the expense of others.

Credit program subsidies may be discussed in terms of (1) the benefit to the borrowers, (2) the "opportunity cost" to the government, or (3) the out-of-pocket or "cash cost" to the government. The benefit-to-borrower concept is the most attractive to the economist as a measure of the impact of federal credit aid on demand and on the allocation of resources. Yet the benefit concept poses formidable measurement problems. Some lenders may use the insurance and guarantee programs simply because they are there, making loans that they would have made in any case, though on somewhat more stringent terms. In contrast, guaranteed loans to submarginal borrowers, for example, may be in principle at least as income generating as government transfer payments. In practice, however, it is difficult to identify these benefits unequivocally.

There is no conclusive method of measuring the extent to which loans under some guarantee programs might have been made without the government guarantee. This is particularly true of guaranteed loans at market rates of interest, such as the regular mortgage insurance program of the Federal Housing Administration and the Export-Import Bank guarantees. It is not clear in such self-supporting programs whether there is a substantial benefit to the borrower or whether in many cases the borrower would have been able to obtain nonguaranteed credit on essentially similar terms.

On the other hand, many loans clearly would not have been made without the government guarantee. An extreme example is the loan guarantee program for public housing, where virtually all of the principal and interest payments are made by the federal government. That is, the rental income from public housing projects barely covers current operating and maintenance expenses, and in some projects not even those expenses are covered. Thus, the public housing bonds are ultimately retired almost entirely from annual contributions by the federal government.

The proportion of subsidy to total amount of the loan varies substantially from program to program. Unlike subsidies in other federal spending programs, credit subsidies tend to be hidden. Hence, their magnitude remains generally unknown to either the public or to most government decision makers.

The Foreseeable Trend

The upward trend in the size and number of federal credit programs shows no signs of slowing down. During the last few years, the Congress has approved a new loan guarantee program to assist industry in the commercial development of energy from geothermal resources (the Geothermal Energy Research, Development, and Demonstration Act), voted credit to the nation's largest city (the New York City Seasonal Financing Act), and authorized guarantees of loans for new underground coal mines (the Energy Policy and Conservation Act).

In December 1975, the Farmers Home Administration (an agency of the U.S. Department of Agriculture) expanded its credit operations to provide up to a 90 percent guarantee on private loans that companies obtain for use on plants in rural areas. There have been little if any offsetting reductions during recent years in the scope of existing federal credit activities.

Summary

Contrary to the popular view, government credit programs are not costless, either to the Treasury or to citizens in general. Three distinct costs of these government programs can be identified:

1. *The economic cost.* As they do little if anything to increase the total supply of investment funds in the economy, government credit programs take credit away from other potential borrowers. These unsubsidized borrowers might have contributed more to society than the recipients of the government-supported credit. This can be the situation where the presence of federal credit encourages individuals or organizations to incur expenditures that they would forego in the absence of the federal subsidy.
2. *The initial fiscal cost.* To the extent that government credit programs increase the total size of government-related credit, they cause an increase in the interest rates that are paid in order to channel these funds away from the private sector. Some increase, therefore, results in the interest rates paid on the public debt, which is a direct cost to the taxpayer.
3. *The ultimate fiscal cost.* When defaults occur on the part of the borrowers whose credit is guaranteed by the federal government, the Treasury winds up bearing the ultimate cost of the credit. In such cases, government credit programs become a form of backdoor spending, whereby federal expenditures are incurred in the absence of direct appropriations for the purpose.

Several ways have been suggested to deal with the various problems that arise from the expansion of federal credit programs. One general approach is to require that all proposals to create new federal credit programs or to broaden existing ones be accompanied by an appraisal of the relation among the interest rate charged in the program, the rate that would be charged by competitive and efficient private lenders, and the rate necessary to cover the government's costs.

A more detailed method is to establish controls over the total volume of federally assisted credit. Even though no immediate impact on the federal budget may be visible in most cases, the influence on the allocation of resources, and on the composition of income and employment, may be very considerable. At present, many of these federal credit programs tend to have virtually a blank check on the nation's credit resources. Under this second method, they would no longer be treated as a "free good."

One way of controlling federal credit programs is to impose a ceiling on the total borrowing of federal and federally sponsored credit agencies, both those "in" and those "out" of the budget. In addition, the Congress could enact a ceiling on the overall volume of debt created under federal loan guarantees. It would be important to establish procedures to permit review of commitments far enough in advance to permit evaluation of their likely impact when the commitments become actual loans.

A third method of controlling federal credit programs more effectively is to require these credit programs to be reviewed and coordinated along with other federal programs in the preparation of the government's annual budget. At the present time, numerous federal credit programs—guaranteed and insured loans and loans by federally sponsored enterprises—escape regular budget and program review.

Perhaps the most fundamental proposal does not deal with federal credit programs at all, but with the underlying conditions of which they are symptoms. Hence, if an economic climate more conducive to private saving and investment can be created, that will reduce the need for private borrowers to seek federal credit assistance. The creation of that climate may require a tax system that tilts in favor of saving rather than consumption and a fiscal policy that avoids the large Treasury deficits whose financing competes with private borrowers. Until these fundamental changes are achieved, continued expansion of federal credit programs seems likely.

14

A New Look at Health Care Reform

A greater reliance on competition and the marketplace is suggested in this rather unconventional response to the shortcomings of the existing health care system.

The time is ripe for taking a new look at health care reform. Conventional approaches have bogged down in the legislative process. A fresh start is necessary. Truly reforming the health care delivery system of the United States requires developing a sensible and sensitive mechanism to balance the demand for health care with its supply. That is the only effective way of dealing simultaneously with the powerful demand for medical services, the limited resources available, and the pressures of rising costs and prices.

I put aside the question of lack of universal health insurance coverage. The justification for doing so is that most public discussions erroneously equate lack of insurance with lack of medical care. A large array of health care providers gives medical services—at low or no cost—to those without insurance. To be sure, often the result is inefficient, such as the excessive use of emergency rooms. But, that is just a special case of a problem that I will be dealing with—people demanding expensive health care without paying the full cost.

One complication is curable. At present, employees—or employers acting in their behalf—cannot buy a modest health care plan. State insurance commissions dictate the composition of these plans and they are very amenable to lobbying by special interests. In many states, the plans must include hair transplants, acupuncture, and other optional items. In effect, the purchaser of health insurance cannot buy a Ford. It must be a Lincoln—or nothing. As Voltaire said it, the best is the enemy of the good. Each state insurance commission should shift its focus from serving the special interests among health care providers to meeting the needs of the patients.

Alternative Health Care Reforms

There is a spectrum of possible responses to the health care dilemma, each with its own set of advantages and disadvantages. At the free market end of the policy spectrum is an approach based on each family or unattached individual making their own choices on what type of medical outlays they will

---

Source: Murray L. Weidenbaum, "A New Look at Health Care Reform," in William R. Frey, ed., Cross *National Perspectives* on *Health Care Reform* (Buffalo, N.Y.: William S. Hein & Co., 1995).

request—and pay for. This means a general elimination of third-party payments and a restoration of the traditional producer consumer relationship which is found in most other product and service markets.

The primary reliance on third party payments is a relatively recent phenomenon—which reminds us that the present pattern can be changed. Third party payments have become important only in the last several decades. Back in 1960, people paid 49 percent of their health care costs, while government agencies paid 24 percent and insurance companies paid 22 percent. A complete reversal has occurred in the intervening years. By 1993, people paid less than 18 percent of their medical costs. The lion's share was borne by government (44 percent) and insurance (34 percent). For hospital service, the patient now pays only 3 percent. For doctor bills, the average patient payment is 15 percent of the total.

The implication of the shift to "third party" financing of health care cannot be overestimated. Important evidence comes from an experiment by the nonprofit Rand Corporation. Thousands of families were given one of four health insurance plans. The difference between the plans was the co-payment rate, the portion of health expenses paid by the family. The co-payment rate varied from 0 to 95 percent. Under all the plans, if a family's out-of-pocket expenses reached $1,000, the insurance paid for all additional expenses.

The main finding was that the higher a family's co-payment rate, the less often members of that family went to a doctor and the less often they incurred medical expenses generally. In the words of David R. Henderson, "people do consume more health care when they are spending other people's money." Rand found no substantial improvement in health outcomes for the higher spending by the families with low co-payment rates.

Relying on the marketplace is the self-policing way to control medical costs. When patients pay the bills directly, they become cost conscious— and so do the people and organizations serving them. The market approach differs fundamentally from the typical "third- party" payments so widely used in the United States. Under this latter method, patients usually do not know the prices and costs of their medical care beforehand, if ever.

Third parties that pay the bills have effectively removed the patient from the traditional consumer role of watchdog. Rarely are prices of physician and hospital services or goods such as prescription drugs advertised to consumers.

Of course, there always were exceptions to the operation of the free market in health care. Modem society has never been willing to accept the full consequences of allocating medical care solely on the desire and ability to pay. However, in this approach, market forces are supplemented, not supplanted. Poor people receive free or low-cost medical treatment, although sometimes of a lower quality than the rest of the society and usually at greater inconvenience.

Primary reliance on the market means that the price system rations the amount of health care produced and consumed. That amount is likely to be less than the results of current policy. A sensible step toward the free-market approach is to reduce the governmental subsidies which increase people's demand for the "best" health-care service. A good place to begin is to eliminate the tax advantage now given to health care over other consumer expenditures. Employer-financed health insurance should be included in taxable employee compensation along with direct payments of wages and salaries. Employer-financed insurance plans became popular during World War II as a loophole to get around wage controls. The special tax treatment is not justified by any canon of efficiency or fairness and should be eliminated.

Much of the formal effort to "economize" on health care costs by departing from marketplace competition is illusory. A major example is the cost shifting under Medicaid and Medicare. That does little to reduce the nation's total medical outlays. That procedure forces other patients to pay for a portion of health care for the poor and the elderly.

To some significant extent, private health plans—goaded by employers who are unhappy at the steady stream of premium increases —can try to weed out high-cost providers, to limit the use of expensive specialists, to monitor closely the performance of health care providers, and to emphasize preventative care. Such pressures can be reinforced by giving employees a similar stake in controlling health insurance premiums.

At the other end ofthe policy spectrum is the notion that the society should finance whatever level of health care is required by each citizen. This general notion is embodied in the "single payer" plan, whereby government simply pays everyone's health bills. Practical problems abound. When health care becomes a free good, the individual response quickly becomes, "Nothing's too good for me if I don't have to pay for it."

Because human wants are insatiable, the notion that each of us is entitled to all the medical care that we ask for exhausts the ability of even the most generous source of financing. Therefore, in practice, each single player plan adopts some form of rationing. One of the most widely used means of limiting care is indirect. It is the bureaucratic technique of delay and inconvenience —forcing people to wait longer than they now do before they receive medical services, including having to go through a variety of reviews or "gatekeeper" approvals. It has been said of some high-risk surgical procedures under the Canadian system that the patient is more likely to die while waiting than on the operating table.

Rationing by delay appeals to the bureaucratic instinct. It does not require making many difficult decisions. It is easy to administer. The queue even sounds fair: first come, first served. But rationing by delay distributes the benefits of limited care arbitrarily. A safety valve often accompanies the queue approach. It favors upper income individuals or at least people who value health care highly enough to pay for it. Wealthy Canadians, for example, come to the United States for serious surgery when they are not content with the quality or the time availability of the health care provided in Canada.

One of the claimed benefits of the single payer approach could be achieved without resorting to a massive expansion of the government's role. A standard medical card for each person with the vital personal and insurance information would avoid the repetitious collection of the same data by each health-care provider. The transcription errors that occur so frequently would be avoided, as well as the delays bedeviling patients and medical offices alike.

Surely, in this electronic age, the paperwork burden could be reduced substantially. Voluntary cooperation on the part of key private associations— the American Medical Association, the American Hospital Association, the American Pharmaceutical Association, etc.—should be able to accomplish this useful change.

Along these lines, the Quincy Foundation for Medical Research has proposed the establishment of a network of computer terminals located at care delivery sites. All participants in the program would receive coded cards containing their social security numbers and basic personal and medical data. We can endorse this proposal without embracing the notion of using the card to administer eligibility for a variety of governmentally imposed benefits.

All in all, it seems unlikely that public policy will adopt either of the two extremes. Yet it is useful to view the various individual proposals in terms of whether they move the health care system toward the governmental pole or toward the individual choice pole. It is pertinent to acknowledge a separate and noteworthy development. While Congress has been debating inconclusively how to provide and finance better health care, the institutions that actually provide medical care have been undergoing an unprecedented but voluntary restructuring. The health care delivery system is being reformed. The marketplace is transforming itself and is delivering health care at reduced costs or at a slower rate of price increase. The voluntary changes being made in health care are taking many forms. By the end of 1994, a majority of privately insured Americans were enrolled in managed-care plans that limit choice of doctors and treatments. In California, three-fourths of all privately insured patients are now in Health Maintenance Organizations. Three-fourths of all physicians had signed contracts, covering at least some of their patients, to reduce their fees and to accept oversight of their medical decisions. About nine out of every ten doctors who work in group practices have agreed to managed care arrangements.

The Michigan health care network is an example of the voluntary changes taking place. The network is vertically integrating the Henry Ford Health System, Mercy Health Services, and Michigan Blue Cross/Blue Shield. The network of hospitals offers health care to groups of 100 employees or more. It requires a fixed monthly payment for an individual or a family. New York Hospital has established a regional alliance with seven other non-profit hospitals, two nursing homes, and four walk-in clinics. Three large hospital alliances, created in the last two years, now care for three-fourths of the hospital patients in the St. Louis area. Each alliance is actively buying up the practices of primary care physicians.

In many communities, hospitals have been hiring or buying out the practices of primary care doctors—family practitioners, general internists, and pediatricians—to assure a stream of patient referrals and to increase their bargaining power with insurance companies. The South Carolina Medical Association has been developing an alternative approach. It is forming a statewide network of doctors to negotiate contracts with employers and take responsibility for controlling their health costs. Health care networks already dominate Southern California. Hospitals, physicians, and insurance companies all have established health care networks. Solo practitioners are becoming rare.

On a national scale, an unprecedented wave of mergers and acquisitions is occurring among major health care providers. Columbia/NCA Healthcare, the country's largest for-profit hospital chain, has bought out Medical Care America, the largest chain of surgery centers. In contrast, Surgical Care Affiliates, which operates a chain of outpatient surgery centers, is luring patients away from hospitals. These centers provide a lower-cost setting for many of the less critical operations, such as removal of cataracts, tonsillectomies, and laproscopic gallbladder removals.

Meanwhile, many individually owned pharmacies are finding that they lack the resources to compete for managed care business and are becoming members of chains, franchises, and other group efforts. In the future, perhaps insurance companies and hospitals will get together. Between them, they have the large organizational skills and record keeping that are necessary. Hospitals have the patients and insurance companies have the market—the willingness of employers to pay for the health care of the employees. Ultimately, these conglomerates may include, in addition to insurance companies and hospitals, some of the following: outpatient clinics, doctors' offices, nursing homes, hospices, home health care services, pharmacies, drug treatment centers, and medical equipment suppliers.

Suggestions for Reform

The operation of market forces often proceeds more rapidly and more effectively in responding to serious problems than do the more ponderous decision making mechanisms of the public sector. Often the reduction of governmental impediments to competition represents the most efficient and least costly solution. The most effective driving force to slow the rapid rise in health care costs is now the business firms who find that this special expense reduces their competitiveness in an increasingly global marketplace. The pressure they exert on their health insurance carriers, in turn, is transmitted to health care providers. As we have seen, hospitals, physicians, and pharmaceutical firms have been engaged in an unprecedented effort to restructure, streamline, diversify, and otherwise reduce their costs—while they maintain or expand their share of a rapidly and radically changing marketplace for health care.

There is an important role for public policy in this important adjustment process, but it is not the role usually envisioned. To continue the movement to greater efficiency while meeting the needs of the patient, it is necessary to further reduce the impediments to the fuller operation of competitive market forces.

The most fundamental change needed is to reduce the dependence on third-party reimbursements. To the extent that patients view medical care as a "free" or low-cost good to them, the ability to contain costs will be greatly limited.

For the typical middle-class patient/consumer, it makes no sense to go through an insurance/reimbursement system for routine office and out-patient hospital visits and procedures. What is required is to cease regarding health insurance as a benefit or, worse yet, as an entitlement. Rather, each of us must consider health insurance as a form of insurance protecting us from chance but potentially devastating circumstances. The implication of that seemingly simplistic change is profound.

Take automobile insurance as a basis for comparison. Each vehicle owner chooses a form of deductible. This means that many fender benders or paint scratches (the equivalent of the routine office visit) are not covered by insurance. There is no massive outcry that this approach is "unfair" to poor people. Motorists generally understand that a deductible is necessary to avoid swamping the insurance system with the paperwork that would push up premiums very sharply. As a result, of course, many paint scratches and dented fenders go unfixed—but that is the considered choice of the owners who would rather spend their money on something else.

Indeed, one company in Virginia has moved in this direction. It treats its health program like true insurance, reimbursing for insurable events rather than for routine medical expenditures. The plan is structured so that employees are reimbursed for a small number of large claims rather than a large number of small claims. Savings from shifting away from traditional health care coverage are shared equally between the employer and the employees.

Under the present array of public policies, primary reliance on third-party reimbursement strikes most taxpayers as highly desirable. Not many citizens are sophisticated enough to understand that such fringe benefits as employer-paid health insurance are a substitute for wages in the employee's compensation package. But even among the growing minority that comprehend the process, the status quo is still considered to be a good deal because wages and salaries are taxable income, while fringe benefits are not.

The answer is to make the entire compensation package taxable, including employer-paid health insurance premiums. That will not eliminate the demand for such fringes for a variety of reasons. Some of these are eminently sensible, such as the desire to obtain the economies of scale that result in lower group rates. A level playing field in the taxation of compensation would not constitute a panacea but it surely will help.

Increasing the knowledge available to consumers will enable them to make more informed choices. In the purchase of pharmaceutical products, government policy now restricts or prevents the patient from acquiring information concerning the prices charged by different providers for the same or similar products. Many states prohibit advertising the price of prescription drugs. Such restrictions make it difficult for consumers to shop for the best price. States that have enacted such anti-consumer legislation should promptly repeal it.

At the federal level, the Food and Drug Administration should reduce the barriers that inhibit advertising prescription medicines. Because consumers must obtain a prescription from a physician in order to acquire prescription drugs, there is little reason to fear deception in advertising in this market. Experience shows that direct advertising can reduce the prices that consumers pay. Such evidence was cited by the Supreme Court in the decision overturning state bans on advertising of eyeglasses.

The current FDA rules on advertising are needlessly bureaucratic. The agency should reconsider the requirement for the misnamed "brief summary" which must accompany any ad that both mentions a health condition and the name of a drug which can be used for the condition. The "brief summary" is actually a lengthy statement in small print listing side effects and contraindications associated with a prescription drug.

Such information is essential for physicians, for whom the brief summaries were originally designed. But, for the average patient, the technical language is incomprehensible.

The FDA also discourages prescription drug ads from being shown on television, a major source of information for many consumers. The high cost of ads in the print media—resulting from the FDA requirements—also reduces their use. Like so much government regulation, the result is the opposite of what the FDA says it wants. Due to the restraint on advertising, consumers may not be aware that a treatment exists for a certain condition and so they will not consult a physician. In other circumstances, consumers may suffer some symptoms (e.g., thirst) without realizing that these are symptoms of a treatable disease (e.g., diabetes). Alternatively, a new remedy with reduced side effects may become available, but patients are not aware of it and do not visit their physicians to obtain a prescription.

If there is any single conclusion that emerges from this analysis, it is that no single solution—no silver bullet—is available to cure all the ailments besetting the American health care system. What will help in a fundamental way is to acknowledge that difficult choices have to be made among imperfect alternatives.

Part 3
Applying Economics to Business

15

The Role of Economics in Business Planning

This article draws on the author's experience as the corporate economist for the Boeing Company as well as an extensive study of business planning he subsequently performed at the Stanford Research Institute. The state-of-the-art has advanced since the time of writing (1960s).

An economist may make a number of contributions to business planning, particularly in relating the external economic environment to company decision making. This article briefly describes the business planning process and then discusses how economics and economists can contribute to that process. It is a synthesis of available information on industrial economics and is not limited to the experience of a single company.

The literature on business planning is sufficiently voluminous without adding to the available descriptions of techniques to be used in preparing planning documents or in organizing the planning operation. However, the repetition of a few fundamentals of planning may be beneficial both to those who participate in the process and those outside of it who wish to understand it.

Fundamentally, business planning is not, or at least should not be, merely a collection of estimates of future sales, profits, manpower, or other statistical forecasts. To cite the obvious, Webster's *New International Dictionary* informs us that to plan is "to devise or project as a method or course of action." Here we have the essence of business planning: it is a process that is designed to provide a course of action for a business enterprise. The statistical data merely furnish a basis for decisions. The present article is primarily concerned with the overall planning of a diversified business enterprise rather than the planning performed by an individual division or department. Much of the approach and methodology is equally pertinent.

Economics and business planning certainly are not synonymous, although many people may take them to be so or would like them to be so. Business planning properly is a multidisciplinary field, utilizing economics, accounting, engineering, marketing, and many other specialties.

It should be acknowledged, perhaps with some pride, that a goodly number of directors of business planning are economists. By rough count, ap-

Source: Murray Weidenbaum, "The Role of Economics in Business Planning," *Michigan State University Business Topics*, Summer 1962.

proximately a dozen members of the National Association of Business Economics are planning directors. Their titles range from the simple Director of Planning to Economist and Director of Planning and Coordination. In many other instances, the planning directors have come up through the financial or marketing routes. In any event, the planning organization must contain or draw upon people with all of these capabilities as well as others.

The following are some of the major phases of the business planning process, especially those to which economists may contribute. Each phase will be discussed in turn.

- Setting forth the external environment in which the business enterprise will be operating during the planning period.
- Establishing goals and objectives for the enterprise.
- Analyzing the capability and resource availability of the enterprise.
- Developing the specific programs to be undertaken.
- Evaluating the projected performance of the enterprise.

Forecasting the External Environment

Most business plans, particularly those of a long-range nature, begin with or are prepared on the basis of an evaluation of the external environment in which the company will be operating. This is the area in which business economists may make their most important contribution. All available surveys of the role of company economists indicate that forecasting is the predominant activity that they have in common.

A survey of economic staffs of American industry conducted by the Conference Board revealed that "periodic forecasting is reported by respondents to be the most important single activity of staff economists." A similar survey conducted by the Mobil Oil Company concluded,

> If there is a single activity common to all the company economists surveyed . . . it is forecasting long- and short-term trends in the national economy and relating them to sales and profits.

It was reported that such forecasts are of value to management in preparing sales objectives and planning inventories, procurement, production, and capital expenditures for periods from five to twenty years in the future.

Methodology for Forecasting

Company planning may utilize different types of economic forecasting. These vary from sophisticated models of the gross domestic product (and other items in the national income and product accounts) to a naive assumption à la Sewell Avery of Sears that the storm cellar is the most likely symbol of the economic outlook.

Almost all of the long-term economic forecasts used by business firms that have come to the attention of the writer in recent years are based, with varying degrees of sophistication, on the following simple formula:

$$G = E \times H \times P$$

G stands for the gross domestic product; E is the average number of persons employed during the period; H is the average hours worked per employee; and P represents the output per worker-hour or productivity. This, of course, is the projection of potential supply of gross domestic product.

Employment Estimates

The employment estimates are generally based on Census Bureau and Labor Department projections of population and labor force. Given the population forecast—and the Census Bureau obligingly provides several alternatives, based primarily on different assumed fertility rates—the estimate of the labor force primarily is a question of determining participation rates among the groups of working age. For forecasts up to about fifteen years in the future, the relevant population distributions involve little guesswork, except for in- and out-migration and mortality rates, which are factors of lesser order of magnitude than fertility.

Assumptions are then necessary as to the portions of the labor force not involved in civilian employment: the members of the armed forces and the unemployed. A 4 percent unemployment ratio seems to be the most popular assumption. The estimate of hours is generally based on the historical experience of a declining secular trend in the average work week—usually a reduction of less than 1 percent a year.

Productivity

Productivity is estimated to increase as the result of expanded research and development, new business investment, and increasing application of new technologies such as those spawned by the entire field of electronics. The differences in assumed rates of productivity can be crucial to the GDP figures finally obtained. As would be expected, the various estimates of GDP obtained by different forecasters cover a broad range, although there is virtual unanimity that the trend is upward sloping.

Models of the Economy

Many long-term forecasters crosscheck these projections of supply of GDP against a more complete model of the economy. Such a model may show, on the one hand, the demand for output by consumers and others, and, on the other hand, the cost of producing the output (national income, by component, plus the adjustment factors between national income and GDP). Such a model provides a useful cross-check of the internal consistency of the estimates used.

In many cases, much detailed analysis of economic history and a very considerable amount of judgment and insight goes into the preparation of these forecasts. Also, the spelling out of the basic assumptions underlying the forecast serves as a description of much of the external environment in which the enterprise will be operating. Typical assumptions include the following:

- The current state of international tensions—the cold war—will continue. No major war will occur during the forecast period, nor will a workable disarmament program be adopted.
- Scientific and technological advances will continue at the current rate or higher.
- The federal government will take necessary action to avoid major depressions or runaway inflations.
- Prices will rise at the average rate recently experienced (or, alternatively, all estimates are prepared in "constant" dollars).

Projections of the overall performance of the economy are in the nature of a starting point and need to be related to specific industries and geographical areas. For military producers, for example, the forecast of GDP is used in projecting the military budget, which is the basic market research task for that industry and central to its long-range planning.

A widely used methodology for military market forecasts is based on a three-fold process:

1. A long-term projection of GDP.
2. A projection of the military budget on the basis of the economic forecast.
3. A statistical analysis of the composition of the military budget.

The simplest method is to take military expenditures as a constant percentage of GDP. A slightly more sophisticated approach, somewhat in line with recent experience, is to estimate the military expenditure level as a declining percentage of GDP.

Reality is more complex than that. In the post-World War II period, military expenditures have been a major part, but only a part, of the federal budget and certainly a much smaller proportion of GDP. Within the constraint of a budget that is approximately in balance over the cycle, the GDP, and its growth, is far more of a limitation on federal revenues than on military spending directly. A model of the federal budget is needed, which is built up from both the revenue side and the expenditure side, which encompasses the various non-defense programs as well as defense programs, and possibly, tax and debt reductions over the period.

The contribution of economists to projecting the future composition of defense spending is two-fold: Through even the simplest of statistical analyses of historical data, they may bring to light emerging trends in military procurement and research and development which may have escaped others in the planning process who are less familiar with economic and budgetary statistics. Changes in the product mix of military R&D provide a "leading" indicator. The shifts in R&D from aircraft to missiles, for example, herald future shifts in the same direction in the larger category of procurement. An emerging shift to astronautics presages future expenditures for military space programs in the procurement statistics.

Goals and Objectives

The second phase of the business planning process relates to goals and objectives. It is problematical whether, in this area, economic theory may necessarily make a practical contribution. Economists have generally been nurtured on the doctrine of profit maximization as the rational mode of conduct for entrepreneurs. The transition is almost instinctive from the belief that profit maximization should be the desired goal to the certainty that it must "obviously" be the accepted goal of entrepreneurs. Profit maximization may be the dominant goal of a business enterprise, but that is not necessarily the situation. A large business organization may have a diversity of goals.

William Baumol, an economist with a substantial amount of business consulting experience, has concluded:

> ... most oligopolistic firms aim to maximize not profits, but sales volume (measured in money terms; sales are what the economist in his jargon calls "total revenue"). So long as profits remain at a satisfactory rate, management will devote further effort to increasing its sales rather than its profits.

In practice, there are many forms that the goals and objectives of an enterprise may take. Management may wish to maintain—or increase—the historical growth in sales or earnings. It may wish to attain a given percentage rate of return on investment. A certain diversification of the product line or market served may be desired. Some or all of these objectives may be aimed at. In fact, they may be interrelated and many of them may be derivatives of an explicit or implicit profit maximization goal. The economist may aid both in selecting the type of goal to be followed and especially in providing statistical measuring sticks for gauging attainment.

In the case of sales goals, the economist can point out the historical and projected rates of growth in the economy as a whole, in the industry or industries in which the company is operating, and for other companies of comparable size or market position. Similar data can be obtained for profit rates.

Sales objectives can be set in the form of maintaining or improving market shares. Here, knowledge of the historical trend of the pertinent industries and markets, as well as usable economic forecasts can play an important role. In some cases, the identification and measurement of the market or industry may be no simple task. The electronics "industry," to cite an important example, still has not come into its own in the Standard Industrial Classification (SIC), which underlies the data of the Census Bureau and many other governmental agencies. Bits and pieces of electronics production are contained in a dozen or more SIC codes. The case of missile production would be even more difficult, were it not for the fact that the customer is in position to make comprehensive reports available.

Resources and Capabilities

The economist can make a contribution to the analysis of an enterprise's resources and capabilities during the planning period by stressing the element of futurity. For example, financial and engineering personnel may be in the best position to estimate the basic costs of future programs. Yet, they may or may not need to be reminded that price levels may change, and possibly at different rates than those that obtained in the recent past. Some simple analyses of overall supply and demand factors for the commodities involved may prove to be quite helpful. This is illustrative of a general function of the industrial economist, to relate the activities of the individual company to broader trends in the national and increasingly the international economy.

Personnel management may perform the basic projections of manpower requirements. Yet, they may or may not need to be advised concerning future trends in national or regional labor force availability. In this connection, the U.S. Department of Labor's studies of the future composition of national employment can be useful to management in relating the problems that a company may consider peculiar to its operations to fundamental developments in the national economy. The anticipated shift from relatively unskilled workers to professional and technical personnel is striking.

In the short run, the analyses of the external business environment may be required by treasury officials concerned with estimating the cost and availability of corporate funds and the preferences among stock issues, bonded indebtedness, and bank debt. In some cases, the proposed capital asset portion of the business plan may usefully be related to the outlook for business investment generally and to sales-investment ratios for specific industries. Types of economic data and guidance required in developing the resource aspects of business planning vary with the individual firm.

Development of Programs

The development of specific programs to utilize the enterprise's resources in meeting established goals is generally a function of line or divisional management. Here, too, the role of the economist is essentially that of advice or review.

The most apparent utilization of economic analysis is in connection with sales forecasting. Forecasts of the sales of specific products need to be checked against appraisals of the market potential. Hopefully, the sales estimates were prepared on the basis of a comprehensive market research job in the first place, which included use of the analyses and forecasts of the national economy and of the specific industries in which the firm is operating.

In a more fundamental way, continuing analysis of the various segments of the national economy may yield selected growth markets which the enterprise might wish to penetrate with new products or adaptations of existing products. Conversely, information on differential growth and profit rates can be useful in selecting, among the various possibilities, products to be developed and marketed.

Evaluating Performance

A critical aspect of business planning is the evaluation of the adequacy of the individual divisional and departmental plans as well as that of the company total. The evaluation itself is a proper function of management. The economist and other staff specialists mainly provide the materials for making the evaluation, such as the quantifications of the performance of the larger group of which the enterprise is a part: the industry or the economy as a whole. The goals and objectives described earlier can play a crucial role in evaluating performance.

Here we close the loop. The reasonableness of the goals and targets set earlier are checked against the likely accomplishments of the enterprise in view of its resources and capabilities in the expected environment. Necessary modifications may then be made in the goals and targets as well as in the programs to accomplish them.

Conclusions

In planning, as in the other phases of business operations, the economist must be guided by the special problems being faced by the company, its particular history and outlook, and the stated needs of its management for staff work. The role of the economist, or of any staff specialist, is not to identify the most intellectually stimulating problems to work on or necessarily to use the most advanced and sophisticated techniques. That function is to make, on the basis of special training and capability, the most useful contribution to the management. This contribution certainly is not to talk down to management or to put some intellectual window dressing on the most fashionable current opinion.

This contribution consists of bringing to bear on business problems the tools of economic analysis, the results of economic research, the findings from economic statistics and, in a generalized way, the value of professional objectivity. The role of the business economist might be considered to be furnishing a window through which the firm can see aspects of the outer world it may otherwise ignore or not fully comprehend. Perhaps Sir Dennis Robertson, in an address to the Royal Economic Society entitled, "On Sticking to One's Last," said it best:

> I do not want the economist to mount the pulpit or expect him to fit himself to handle the keys of Heaven and Hell . . . I want him to be rather humble . . . I like to think of him as a sort of Good Dog Tray. . .

16

Shortcomings of Business Planning

This is an antidote to the excessive enthusiasm often displayed by newcomers to the business planning function.

Conceptually, business firms deliberately and systematically make their plans for the future. It is assumed that they establish goals and objectives for the enterprise, identify opportunities that are likely to exist in the foreseeable environment, choose from among the alternative opportunities that may help them achieve their objectives, and then evaluate the likely performance, in a feedback or loop-closing fashion.

The writer has little quarrel with the need to conceptualize or to prepare an adequate framework for business planning. This is clearly a necessary, but possibly not sufficient, condition for successful forward thinking by a business firm. A recent study of a significant segment of American industry reveals some fundamental shortcomings in the actual execution of business planning.

The following are highlights of a study conducted by the writer and his associates. The study covered a sample of thirteen large, technically oriented manufacturing companies, primarily in the aerospace and electronics industries. It would appear, from informal crosschecking of the results with colleagues acquainted with other industries, that many of the findings are not limited to the two industries studied, but may indicate some of the problems often encountered in applying principles of planning to actual cases. The material presented is a distillate and not intended to refer to specific companies in the industries sampled.

True Long Range Business Plans are Rarities

Most of the output of long-range planning groups was found to be more in the nature of scheduling current programs with long leadtimes, rather than in the development of true long-range business plans—courses of action to deal with the future. The qualification for determining what was a business plan was no more rigorous than the dictionary definition that to plan is "to devise, or project as a method or course of action."

In practice, "planning" documents usually were focused on analyzing future potentials and requirements of *existing* product lines and programs— expected sales and profits, projected manpower and facilities, and so forth.

Source: Murray Weidenbaum, "Shortcomings of Business Planning," *University of Washington Business Review,* October 1964.

Some of these estimates also covered the future potentials and requirements of the new products on which the company already was *currently* working, in either the preliminary design or prototype stage. George Steiner defines planning as "the conscious determination of courses of action to achieve preconceived objectives." However, there appeared to be few business plans which attempted to bridge the gap between current programs and long-term targets. Even fewer business planning efforts involved an explicit choice among alternatives. Certainly, there are exceptions to these findings.

Top Management is Rarely Involved

In discussing their long-range problems with the senior executives of the companies studied, there was little, if any, mention of the actual use of their long-range plans for decision-making. Often, some reference was added indicating that this sort of activity was going on—somewhat akin to hiring a proper quota of sales representatives from a given minority group.

Some of the more thoughtful executives quickly pointed out that the data in the formal planning documents were useful to them in their planning. The divorce of the formalized planning process from the actual planning and, more important, the decision making is made even clearer when it is realized that many chief executives are supposedly charged with long-range planning as their primary responsibility and have delegated the operating responsibilities to an executive vice president, or some other number two official. Even in this case, we customarily found that the formal planning organization is somewhere down in the bowels of the corporate staff, possessing a rather tenuous relationship to the supposedly planning-minded chief executive.

The usual business firm's long-range plan informed the reader in wearying detail of monthly delivery schedules, the recruiting budget, square footage of storage space by type, and so forth. This may—in a small way—help to explain why business plans are so infrequently used as real decision-making tools. A mark of the more sophisticated business plan may be the absence of computations of overhead rates to four-decimal places. As one industry planner has written:

> There are documented long-range plans in most of the large and medium defense concerns today, but usually they tend to become annual routine. Most of these plans are documents of projections or compilations of business data. They must be supplemented by action plans which specify objectives, milestones, resources. . .

Formal Planning Rarely Comes to Grips with Key Problems

The failure of so much of business long-range planning efforts to come to grips with the key problems facing the organization and/or its industry may be the inevitable result of what can be termed a major planning "dogma": planning must be done by the line departments; the headquarters organization should mainly concern itself with aggregating divisional or departmental submissions—"the direction of the planning process should be upward, not downward."

Although the decentralization of planning has merit as a general proposition, some negative side effects may have been overlooked. As a result, we found occasions where a headquarters organization did do some developmental long-range planning—such as examining those new or potential areas that do not fall within the current jurisdiction of, or have been overlooked by, the operating divisions. However, the headquarters staff generally was careful not to inject such "extraneous" material into the formal business planning process.

The headquarters staff often was looked upon merely to add some polish to the planning process, such as a broad brush evaluation of the external environment or an analysis of the public relations image of the corporation.

Asking the chief executive of a large, technically oriented manufacturing company what alternatives have been developed in the event that current programs or product lines do not work out as expected can be an illuminating experience. Typically, little if any contingency planning exists for such eventualities. For example, asking officers of large defense contractors about contingency planning they have done to cover the possibility of arms control or disarmament yields answers such as the following:

"We don't plan on going out of business."
"You can't plan for catastrophe."
"Why waste time on hypothetical questions."

The fact that some obscure market analysis or operations research group in one department of the company had done some exploratory work in a new market or product area did not qualify, by the standards used in the study, as contingency planning for the corporation. This sort of "soft" staff study was sharply distinguished from "hard" planning involving preparation of detailed alternative courses of action, especially with the personal participation of one or more members of top management.

Avenues for Improvement

It may be easier to cite the shortcomings of what has become the traditional approach to long-range business planning in many companies, than to suggest possible remedies. There should be some hesitancy in using the term "traditional"; perhaps this is rather a "new orthodoxy" in view of the relatively recent development of the formal business planning function.

In effect, it appeared in our survey that much of business long-range planning had fallen into a mold or, worse yet, a routine. The costing out, simplified or elaborate, of the status quo or the current outlook just may not suffice. It may not ruffle the feathers of line management, but neither is it likely to yield a creative product in the company's decision making process.

Perhaps, if long-range planning is to avoid complete preoccupation with technique and methodology, the planning process must take up the major substantive problems and challenges facing the company and its industry, and not avoid them because they do not fit neatly into the format.

In the case of the large, science-oriented corporations, there seems to be an increasing availability of such basic problems. For example, the unprecedented growth market in defense/ space systems and research and development is slowing down noticeably. The military customer in particular is curtailing what many have taken to be an almost insatiable demand for systems engineering and technological advancement.

To compound the problem, the companies that have been most successful in meeting the federal government's requirements for advanced technology generally have been unable to penetrate commercial markets to a significant degree. The numerous attempts to utilize the technological capabilities developed in the course of their government work have ranged from aluminum sport boats to welding equipment to cargo handling systems. In the aggregate, however, such commercial diversification efforts have produced little in the way of sales, and usually marginal or negative profit results.

Yet, in view of emerging developments in the government market, the challenge of transferring the unique defense/space R&D and systems capability to civilian pursuits may very well be one of the major planning tasks for American industry. Unless a significant improvement occurs in the state of the art of business planning, it is likely that corporate decisions on fundamental questions such as this one will be made more frequently by default than by design.

17

Learning to Compete

The mid-1980s were characterized by laments over the industrial heartland of the United States becoming a "rust belt." Some economists had declared that "the engines of growth had closed down." This article was prepared as a response, demonstrating how American business was taking important steps to improve productivity and competitiveness.

The time has come to sound an upbeat note for the future role of American business. It is not a matter of wishful thinking, but of realistically assessing the positive responses to the adversities experienced by many companies in recent years.

During hard times, organizations often take steps that provide the basis for future recovery. These include cost-cutting, product and process innovations, and other productivity-raising and market development moves that help to turn the tide. The United States is experiencing such a period of adjustment right now. Three forces are emerging that make a period of sustained prosperity more likely in the years ahead:

1. Numerous company actions are reducing the cost of producing goods and services in the United States.
2. Workers and managers are becoming aware of their personal responsibility for the quality of what Americans produce.
3. Investments in research and development, which are the basic fuel for innovation and technical progress, are growing rapidly.

Let us examine the growing importance of each of these factors.

Reducing the Cost of Production

For a variety of reasons—most notably to keep up with foreign competition—many American business firms have been reducing their costs of production. Manufacturers of automobiles, steel, chemicals, textiles, and machinery have taken actions that range from simple changes in production methods to a basic restructuring of the business firm.

Reducing Labor Costs

Because compensation of employees constitutes about two-thirds of the cost of producing the nation's output, labor costs are a natural starting point for cost cutting. The measurable improvements that are occurring in the labor

Source: Murray Weidenbaum, "Learning to Compete," Business Horizons, October 1986.

market are dramatic. For example, the fifty-four major strikes in the U.S. during 1985 were the fewest since the Labor Department first began compiling such statistics. In addition, the 324,000 workers involved in the strikes represent the lowest number of strikers on record.

More fundamentally, competitiveness has been enhanced by the substantial slowing of the rise in wage costs. In 1980, the average U.S. worker in the private sector received a 9 percent wage increase. By 1985, the average annual increase was down to less than 4 percent. In some industries workers actually "gave back" prior wage and benefit increases. While management negotiations with unions are stabilizing labor costs, import penetration has sparked a war on other costs. By improving productivity, firms are attempting to get more for their labor dollars. They are accomplishing this goal with more flexible work rules and improved worker attitudes.

Flexible work rules generate important savings in the production process. The traditional way was to have narrow job classifications, with each employee performing one task. With new agreements to perform several different tasks, however, fewer workers are required or the same number of workers can produce more. Downtime is reduced when it is no longer necessary to wait for a worker with the right classification.

For example, a Chrysler plant in Indiana reduced labor costs 30 percent by getting workers to agree to perform tasks outside their crafts. Goodyear has signed a pact that allows the 429 craftsmen at its Alabama plant to work outside their trade as much as 25 percent of the time. General Motors successfully negotiated with its Mansfield, Ohio, union to eliminate jobs such as machinists' "tool chasers." Having machinists get their own tools, combined with other changes, raised productivity in one stamping plant by 26 percent.

Work-rule changes also saved money in the petroleum industry, where refiners report that output per worker increased by more than 10 percent in recent years. At one refinery an oil company merged six classifications into two, cutting the work force by 25 percent.

On the reasonable assumption that motivated workers do better work, some companies have attempted to improve worker attitudes. At Jones & Laughlin, a major steel maker in Aliquippa, Pennsylvania, a labor-management participation team analyzes production problems and suggests ways of improving efficiency. In one recent year the company saved $75 million, largely because of employee suggestions and work force cutbacks that resulted in the remaining workers being assigned more duties.

Changing Production Approaches

Several American companies have adopted the Japanese just-in-time inventory system, which provides components as needed instead of having large batches made in advance and stored. Harley-Davidson reports that at one plant alone the system freed $22 million previously tied up in inventory and dramatically reduced reorder lead times.

The Chrysler plant in Fenton, Missouri, also is using the just-in-time approach. The system cut its inventory from $29 million to $20 million, resulting in savings of $1 million a year in interest costs. Reduced inventory also has meant less damage to parts from overcrowded storage conditions.

One of the most ambitious production improvement efforts to date is the General Motors Flint Assembly project, which is converting a sixty-year-old complex of unrelated component manufacturing and auto assembly plants into a 500-acre integrated production facility. The Flint Assembly complex builds under one roof the major components needed for GM's front-wheel-drive vehicles. The work performed includes engines, transmission components, and complete bodies. Steel blanks for body construction enter at one end of the plant and finished cars leave at the other. Previously, automobile bodies were partially built at a body plant on the other side of town and shipped to the final assembly location.

The complex operates without the usual inventory safety net in a conscious effort to force discipline into a manufacturing system that formerly operated with convenient, but expensive, fallback positions. Each of the major auto producers is pursuing joint ventures with Japanese and South Korean companies as a long-term way of cutting costs on small cars.

Adopting Realistic Pricing Strategies

Price reductions forcing cost containment are the dominant response American firms make to import pressures. But they rely simultaneously on other approaches. In addition, there are many variations on the price or economizing approach to meeting foreign competition.

For example, in the automobile manufacturing industry, for many years operations had been based on achieving economies of scale through high-volume, long-running production with fairly rigid production specifications. Because economies of scale emphasized large factories and standard product design, changes in the product could become expensive. Today, as a result of a shift to computer-based manufacturing, production can be based on economies of scope. This newer approach allows for low-cost, flexible production of a variety of products on the same automated equipment.

An extension of this economizing strategy is leading to important structural changes in many American corporations. The horizontally integrated firm, which produces virtually every product in the markets in which it operates, is less prevalent. Many companies prefer to specialize, focusing on specific product niches that are secure against foreign competition. This is to be expected as U.S. firms find themselves competing more fully in a global economy. Surely, far fewer of our domestic markets can be properly thought of as part of a closed economy.

In an ambitious restructuring effort, General Electric has raised about $5 billion since 1981 by selling off 155 divisions. Among them were GE's small-appliance operation, which manufactures toasters and irons, and Utah International, a natural-resource subsidiary. The company's new strategy is to gradually move away from traditional manufacturing and to focus instead on growth industries, such as electronics and financial services. The proceeds from its restructuring activities helped to finance its acquisition of RCA, a move strengthening GE's position in electronics and services.

The Union Carbide Corporation, a firm under severe pressure for many reasons in addition to foreign competition, also has undergone extensive restructuring. It has divested more than $500 million in what it now views as "nonstrategic" assets and businesses, including its commodity-metals business, its European bulk-chemical, plastics, and polyethylene businesses, and its battery division.

Product innovation also has been emphasized. To ward off foreign competition, American shoe firms such as Timberland Company, Reebok International, and Rockport Company have responded with stylish footwear. Even apparel manufacturing, one of the most import-affected industries, is using style to compete with low-cost foreign products. Companies such as RJMJ Inc. continue to make a profit selling women's pants and shorts through improved timing and greater flexibility of production.

While foreign apparel makers need at least six months' lead time to coordinate manufacturing with retail sales, Robert Shipman, RJMJ's president, says his company "can turn on a dime. We can get piece goods to [our plants] in a day or two and produce products for the shelves in three to four weeks. That enables us to catch a trend."

Improving the Quality of U.S. Products

An important lesson that American companies have learned in recent years is that "Made in Japan" (or South Korea or Taiwan) is not synonymous with shoddy quality, as it sometimes was before World War II. In fact, the inroads of foreign competition into U.S. domestic markets have frequently been caused by the superior quality of the import rather than simply by lower cost. As a result, unprecedented pressure has been generated for improving the quality of products that American businesses manufacture.

Meeting Domestic Quality Requirements

Many U.S. firms are responding positively to the consumer preference for quality. For example, Steinway & Sons, facing rising competition from Yamaha, has improved the quality of its pianos, which remain popular with concert pianists. The well-known piano manufacturer proudly notes that thirty-five of the thiety-seven Asian contestants performed on Steinway grands at a recent international competition.

The key payoff of higher quality comes from avoiding the costs of reworking defective products or replacing defective parts. Failures are much more expensive to fix after a unit has been assembled than before. In addition, complaints about products—even when the items are subsequently replaced—often result in the long-term erosion of a company's customer base.

Westinghouse Electric is an example of a corporation that can show benefits from emphasizing quality. It has established 2,000 quality circles involving 20,000 employees and a Quality College to foster participative management and quality training. The result has been that Westinghouse has averaged real productivity gains of 7 percent a year for three years in a row.

Harley-Davidson has also profited from emphasizing quality. All employees receive 40 hours of training in statistics so that they better understand how to measure the quality of their output and improvements in it. The moves have resulted in a greater number of defect-free motorcycles coming off the assembly line. Where five years ago half the motorcycles contained defects, 99 percent are now reported to be flawless.

Ford Motor Company provides another example of progress. The company reduced its rejection rate of sheet steel from its domestic suppliers from as much as 9 percent in 1979-81 to under 2 percent in 1985. In comparison, rejection of imports for failure to meet Ford's quality standards averaged 2.5 percent from Japanese suppliers and 3 percent from European suppliers.

Another way to improve quality is to iron out the bugs in the assembly process before shipping the product. GM took this step in its new Wentzville, Missouri, facility. The announcement was unusual because previous practice in the company—and the industry—was to iron out these problems while continuing production. To avoid the huge costs of halting production, quality problems were thus passed on to the dealers and customers.

A similar experience occurred in Ford's automotive operations in Dearborn, Michigan. Production was delayed because the rear doors were not meeting the rear fenders correctly. One Ford executive said, "Ten years ago, confronted with the same problem, we would have built on the appointed day. Today we start when we meet the standard."

Quality is important not only to Americans but to foreign consumers as well. Capitalizing on the Japanese consumers' characteristic concern for higher-quality products, Ocean Foods of Astoria, Oregon, has made Japan one of its principal markets. "They'll pay top dollar for your product, but only if it's of absolute top quality," says a vice-president of Ocean Foods.

Making a Commitment to Quality

The enhanced concern with improving quality in American industry has not been primarily a matter of setting up new quality control departments or even expanding existing ones. Companies in the U.S. traditionally devoted far more resources to quality-control efforts than did their foreign counterparts. Moreover, quality assurance is more than just a collection of expensive scientific and professional personnel who check, review, and improve production practices. Producing quality requires emphasizing this aspect of the production process throughout the firm.

A study of the air-conditioner industry confirms this point. By means of such innovations as internal consumer review boards to evaluate products, Japanese companies pay more attention to quality than many of their American competitors. The Japanese also foster quality by having top management hold daily review meetings about quality. In contrast, American firms with the lowest assembly defect rates met ten times a month; the worst-quality U.S. companies averaged four such meetings a month.

Management's message was reflected on the front lines of production. First-line supervisors at four of six Japanese air-conditioner manufacturers surveyed said quality was most important to management; their counterparts at nine of eleven U.S. companies surveyed said meeting the production schedule was the highest priority.

Management can communicate its emphasis on quality by paying attention to details. For instance, National Steel now requires workers to clean their work stations instead of leaving the task for janitors. The Japanese co-owners, who suggested the policy, reasoned that if workers have enough pride to take care of their work stations, they might also care more for their product.

Thus, the most effective quality controls involve a shift in the locus of responsibility—from the inspectors in the quality control department to the employees who actually do the work. Pushed by foreign competition, many U.S. companies are discovering this way to achieve higher quality production. A recent survey by the American Society for Quality Control shows that many U.S. industries are more than holding their own against foreign competition when it comes to consumer views of product quality.

The Acceleration of Research and Development

Spurred by a felicitous change in tax policy in 1981, the private sector is emerging as a more important channel than the federal government for financing and promoting research and development. Both the private and public trends in R&D spending have pointed sharply upward in recent years. The huge buildup of U.S. defense spending in the 1980s has reinforced this upward movement in the sponsorship and performance of scientific applications and high technology.

The massive buildup in U.S. defense spending begun in 1981 has ended the slowdown of federal R&D outlays that occurred in the 1970s. Now the largest dollar increases in federal expenditures are budgeted for the Pentagon, a part of the government that spends more than twice the proportion of its budget on R&D than does the typical civilian agency.

When the Department of Defense devotes an additional $100 billion to applications of science and engineering in a half-decade, there is an excellent chance that a larger stream of product and process innovation will occur in the years ahead. That possibility is reinforced by the Pentagon's current tendency to support technological advancement in areas having civilian applications—computers, for example. The Department of Defense recently awarded Carnegie-Mellon University a $103 million contract to develop and operate a Software Engineering Institute. The bulk of the Institute's work will be unclassified research, including development of better education processes for teaching software. Although the main customers will be defense contractors, a second tier will include companies that build such commercial items as telecommunications and air traffic control systems.

Some indicators show the effects of the stepped-up investments in R&D. More than 15,000 companies make high-technology equipment in the eight states bordering on the Great Lakes. At least 100 new companies specializing in biomedicine and computer software have located within fifty miles of the Mayo Clinic in Rochester, Minnesota. Based on historical experience, we can expect that recent investments in research and development will create some new product lines and perhaps even new industries with high growth potential. Domestic products that incorporate substantial amounts of research and development will become competitive while more mature items are increasingly replaced by imports.

Investments in research and development constitute an important way that American industry can hold its own in the face of virulent foreign competition. Improving process technology or offering new and superior products is a far more positive approach—and essentially more effective—than seeking government protection.

In many industries, designing and marketing new and better goods makes the future bright for an advanced economy such as the United States. This nation frequently maintains its comparative advantage in R&D-intensive industries. In most cases, the keys to overseas sales penetration by American firms are product development and technological skills. Thus, increased application of the fruits of science and technology to American industry is an important reason to expect that today's gloom and doom will turn into tomorrow's economic expansion.

The Outlook

To sum up the major points made here:

- The competitiveness of many U.S. companies is being enhanced by the often painful changes provoked by greater competition. These responses range from outsourcing to reducing labor costs to fundamental corporate restructuring.
- Simultaneously, many U.S. firms are discovering that product quality rests primarily with the workers on the front lines of production rather than in quality control departments.
- At the same time, the expansion of military spending has resulted in an upturn in federal research and development that has powerful spillover effects in the civilian economy.

None of these three factors yields quick or dramatic changes. Yet the cumulative effects that they generate are likely to endure and to reinforce each other. Virtually all of the changes work in the same direction—toward generating new and better products that will result in more orders, production, employment, income, and profits for American investors, managers, and workers. These changes surely will not prevent the possibility of another recession during the second half of the 1980s. But they make for a brighter outlook for the period beyond.

Thus, it is reasonable to expect substantial improvement in the ability of American firms to compete in world markets in the years ahead. Likewise, the relative attractiveness of domestically produced products to American consumers should increase significantly. In any event, the industrial sector of the American economy is far from being in the sad shape that many fear.

In a journalistic version of Gresham's Law, it sometimes seems that bad news drives out good. It is not widely known that industrial production in the United States hit a new high in 1984 when the Federal Reserve's Index reached 122. During 1985, the Index of Industrial Production reached a plateau averaging 124. In fact, manufacturing's share of the real gross domestic product has held steady at about 25 percent for the last thirty years. Economic naysayers do not have a factual basis for their unalloyed pessimism. Manufacturing in the United States is not going "down the tube," nor are we becoming a nation whose major employers are hamburger stands and clothing stores.

On the other hand, the positive developments are not foregone conclusions. For one thing, foreign competitors can improve on their current strategies while U.S. companies try to catch up. For example, Japanese car makers have been moving into the larger, luxury model market that America traditionally has dominated. In addition, the Japanese arc differentiating their cars according to function, price, and appearance, attacking the American Big Three from many directions at once.

Another factor that may hurt the chances of an improved economy in the 1990s is further public policy changes that may not all be benign. Pressures to reduce the budget deficit may result in raising the tax burden on saving and investment. Indeed, the tax reform bill that the House of Representatives passed in December 1985 eliminates the investment tax credit, reduces the R&D credit, and cuts back on depreciation allowances.

Should protectionist pressures lead to the erection of additional trade barriers, much of the resulting burden would be borne in the form of higher costs imposed on the industries using higher-priced protected inputs. U.S. export industries would be especially vulnerable to retaliation.

In addition, a new round of burdensome domestic government regulation would raise the cost of compliance and deter companies from investment and innovation. Moreover, another shift in federal budget priorities—from defense to transfer payments—could dampen the upward trend of R&D spending. Yet the three key forces for enhanced competitiveness identified here appear to have considerable momentum, and the prospects for their durability are bright.

18

A New Social Contract for the American Workplace

The basic changes in business operations described in the previous selection require comparably fundamental adjustments in employer-employee relations. This article lays out a framework for making those adjustments.

Repeated waves of corporate restructuring and downsizing have soured the attitudes of many American workers. Managements' attempts at explanation have often backfired, further eroding morale and productivity.

Confirming evidence is contained in a recent survey of management views. Only 12 percent of companies said that they embarked on downsizing and other changes to improve profitability or to increase shareholder value. Rather, a major purpose of corporate overhaul in a clear majority of cases (60 percent) was "to improve employee satisfaction." Sadly, this is a clear example of what researchers call "cognitive dissonance"—the psychological conflict that results from holding incongruous beliefs simultaneously. Of course, employees are going to mistrust any management that attempts to peddle this patently unbelievable line.

There are two possibilities for interpreting the survey results. If the top executives of American companies really believe that they are downsizing to make their employees happy, they are not too bright and should be replaced quickly. However, to those who serve on corporate boards, this nonsense is not believable. Perhaps the staff assistant who filled out the form was trying to show that the boss was high-minded and socially responsible. In either case, the serious response is clear. Business can try to restore employee trust by leveling with the worker. It is not a matter of improving employee communications, but of correcting the basic deficiency in the management response. The substantive suggestion presented here is in the form of a new social contract for the American workplace.

The Current Situation

Publicly announced company downsizings are at a record high and that phenomenon shows no sign of ebbing. For many American workers, this means that the American dream has been shattered. However, too much of the focus has been on the people who are laid off. They surely merit serious concern.

Source: Murray Weidenbaum, "A New Social Contract for the American Workplace," *Challenge*, January/February 1995.

But the primary attention should be paid to the far larger number of those who stay on the job.

That is hard to do. The stock market loves news of restructuring or downsizing or any other euphemism for a corporation going on a crash diet. From the time that IBM announced (on July 27, 1993) that it would cut 60,000 jobs by year's end, the company's stock price rose 30 percent. Boeing announced a 21,000-person layoff on February 18, 1993, and its stock price increased 31 percent by the end of the year. By contrast, the S&P stock market index rose only about 8 percent during 1993.

But, with all due respect to the high-powered talent that advises large investors, short-term movements in stock prices are too simpleminded a measure to guide long-term company planning. Like the academician who could simultaneously publish and perish, some firms have succeeded in both cutting back the size of their workforces and reducing the productivity of those who remain.

A study of 271 manufacturing firms undergoing corporate restructuring found that employee morale plummeted with little or no quality improvement and very modest enhancement of the bottom line. A Conference Board survey of human-resource executives also examined the consequences of corporate downsizing. More than three-fifths of the respondents said that their firms experienced declines in employee morale.

A word of caution is in order. The entire U.S. workforce is not disgruntled and insecure. Organizational change has not touched all working Americans in the same way. Since 1973, interviewers of Roper Starch Worldwide have been asking Americans: "How satisfied are you with your chosen field of work?" The "extremely satisfied" response reached an all-time low in April 1994—27 percent of all employed persons surveyed, compared with 40 percent in 1976. However, most of the shift has been to the response "fairly well-satisfied." The data do provide support for the perception of people working harder, or at least longer. The percentage of workers completely satisfied with the number of hours worked reached an all-time low of 30 percent in 1994, falling from 45 percent in 1976.

A comprehensive Census Bureau study goes into statistical detail on corporate restructuring. It provides balance, as well as surprises. Of those companies who downsize, the number who succeed in raising productivity is larger than the total who experience declines. However, the largest group consists of firms who increase their productivity while they are *expanding* the size of their employment rolls. Indeed, the micro data are confirmed by the rising overall level of employment in the United States.

Downsizing is just one strategy in an array of alternative ways in which businesses can respond to rising competition. For the typical American firm, competition has become more virulent than in the past. Three powerful forces account for that: (1) the rise of foreign competition due to the increasing globalization of markets; (2) the rise of domestic competition due to the deregulation of the transportation and communication industries; and (3) the growth of new products and production processes as a result of an accelerated pace of technological advance.

New technology does more than make organizational change possible. It causes it. When senior executives can receive up-to-the-minute information on operations on a computer screen on their desks, a cadre of middle managers and corporate staffers is no longer needed to collect and interpret that information.

What does deserve greater attention than it has received thus far is the widespread reports of declining job satisfaction on the part of the workers who continue to be employed after downsizing. Why does an economist focus on such a "soft" and subjective factor? Because this helps to explain why so many companies report that their attempts at restructuring have not yielded the expected results in terms of improved business performance.

The Old Social Contract

It is always difficult to generalize across the broad spectrum of the American economy. Nevertheless, for some time, many people in private industry—blue-collar as well as white-collar, management as well as the rank and file—believed that they were working under a widely understood social contract. There always were important variations. Nevertheless, two common sets of elements were widely followed:

- Employees understood that they would have to provide satisfactory attendance on the job. They also would have to demonstrate an acceptable level of effort as well as loyalty to the organization.
- Employers, in turn, were expected to provide fair pay and fringe benefits, and advancement based on seniority and merit. And, to a greater or lesser degree, they were expected to provide job security.

It is instructive to quote the executive vice president of a major regional telephone company in charge of downsizing: "My dad would have thought I'm breaking a social contract we have with our employees." Along the same lines, a director of human resources stated: "Lifetime employment is not something we can guarantee any more. Not that we ever guaranteed it. But it was implied."

Years of complacency under the old social contract created high-cost labor systems with insufficient incentives for producing quality goods or providing quality services. In too many American workplaces, the old social contract called for blue-collar and clerical workers to check their brains at the door and simply follow orders.

The traditional social contract was never followed universally. Those who grew up in the depression years of the 1930s know that it was hardly an eternal verity. But, in the period since World War II, the dual set of responsibilities just described did characterize a great many American workplaces.

Whatever form it took, the old social contract is a dead letter today. Wave after wave of corporate downsizing eliminated it.

Toward a New Social Contract

Traditionally, large staff reductions only occurred during periods of crisis that justified hardnosed re-examinations of company activities and the resulting tough actions. Today, in contrast, continual downsizing and organizational restructuring have become an accepted way of business life. One key factor (often conveniently overlooked by top management) makes it especially difficult for corporate personnel to accept this state of affairs. That sticking point is the unfortunate coincidence between the rising uncertainty and belt-tightening that is facing most corporate employees and the increasingly generous compensation packages and the security in the form of "golden parachutes" that are granted to the most senior executives.

This is very sensitive ground, so let us tread it carefully. As an outside director of several corporations, I am an enthusiastic supporter of generous compensation for outstanding performance of key executives. Boards of directors should resist reducing those incentives simply because people in other parts of the company hierarchy are unhappy about them. However, those gripes should be taken seriously. The challenge is to develop a constructive response that simultaneously meets the needs of the rank and file while promoting the objectives of the enterprise.

This leads to developing a new social contract for the American workplace. It takes much soul-searching for a hard-nosed economist to support the notion of a social contract. However, the situation requires such a response. Low morale contributes to slow growth in productivity. Attempts to define a new workplace "social contract" are currently being developed by a disparate array of sources—the White House, Congress, executive suites, union leaders, and management consultants. There is some overlap of ideas from unexpected places.

Richard Gephardt, minority leader of the House of Representatives, contends that, if workers have a real stake in the company—if they share the rewards as well as the risks—they would be more innovative and more productive. The Clinton administration suggests that job security has given way to employment security as the reward for satisfactory job performance. This new definition of worker security means that workers are equipped to handle the next job—even if it is with another employer.

The AFL-CIO has developed a new model for the workplace in which decision-making authority is fundamentally redistributed from management to teams of workers. Also, the rewards from transforming the work organization are to be distributed on equitable terms—agreed upon, of course, through negotiations between labor and management. Given the low and declining rate of unionization in the private sector, we may wonder how those negotiations will be carried out. Nevertheless, the union acknowledgment of the basic changes in business decision-making now occurring surely is noteworthy.

Developing a new social contract for the typical workplace in the United States requires reconciling a variety of paradoxes. Productivity must be enhanced while often the workforce is reduced. Competitiveness must be increased while the firm is meeting costly new social mandates imposed by government. Corporate decision-making needs to be decentralized while the enterprise is meeting the requirements of rising governmental regulation of the workplace. Greater attempts to motivate American workers are made while the management is expanding the reach of the firm on a global basis. The only way for business executives to negotiate this maze is to address these paradoxes head on, and with candor. They need to avoid setting unrealistic expectations for employees, or for themselves.

The key to developing a new workplace compact is the same key that unlocks the door to high-performance workplaces built on trust and mutual purpose. It is effective communication. This means setting up a process of dialogue. Such two-way communication is very different from persuasion or education. It requires utilizing one of the truly neglected parts of the human anatomy—the ear. Management has to listen as well as talk.

Along these lines, the AFL-CIO acknowledges that "distrust between labor and management . . . is endemic to the old system. . . . The new system, in contrast, can function effectively only if those deep suspicions are dispelled and replaced by mutual respect." They are right. Yet that type of trust is hardly evidenced by the AFL-CIO's insistence that workers interact with management only through union representatives. It is the responsibility of management in each company to initiate the development of a new social contract suitable to its special situation. The motivation for business action is basic: It reduces the likelihood that government will step in to fill the void.

Here is an outline of a new social contract (see the accompanying box). The set of employer expectations of employees and the set of employee expectations of employers are both tall orders. But the most ambitious parts of the new social contract are the three *joint* expectations. This does not mean a literal partnership in the legal sense of the word. Rather, the precedent is the figurative partnerships between suppliers and customers that are growing rapidly in popularity in private industry. "Partnering," in this context, is quite demanding. It requires an understanding of each other's needs, common goals, commitment, trust, communication, and a willingness to work through problems.

Today's business leaders need the wisdom of Solomon to respond to the paradoxical demands facing them. On the one hand, they must control costs and improve customer satisfaction in order to remain competitive. On the other, they are being pressured by societal and government demands to provide costly added consideration to special subgroups of their workers. Management wants to reduce employee turnover and increase commitment, but it is difficult to do so while attempting to "cut all the fat" and asking for more output from each employee. Government tells management to improve competitiveness and focus on "employability." But it passes laws that make American businesses less competitive and American workers less employable.

The move to a new social contract in the workplace implies an important feedback effect on government policymakers. They have to acknowledge the fact that the locus of business decision-making is shifting back to where it belongs—the factory floor, the company offices, and the boardroom.

Historically, one of the most important characteristics of an effective business manager has been the ability to live with ambiguity. In the years ahead, all employees will need to develop that special ability. Whether employees and managers realize it or not, they are forming new social contracts to govern their places of work.

Box 1
Outline of a New Social Contract

Employer Expectations of Employees

- Performance to the best of one's ability
- Commitment to the objectives of the firm
- Participation (and making suggestions)
- Willingness to take training to improve productivity
- Ethical and honest behavior

Employee Expectations of Employers

- "Fair" pay and benefits proportionate to contribution to company success
- Security tied to fortunes of the company and ability to perform
- Respect, recognition and participation
- Opportunities for growth
- Safe and health workplace
- Access to timely information and openness by candid leaders

Joint Expectations

- Partnering replaces paternalism
- Employees are value-adding resources, not mere costs to be cut
- Employees and employers must focus on customer needs and desires

---

19

The Economic Effects of Corporate Takeovers

This article challenges the widely held view, especially among economists, that corporate takeovers are generally beneficial. The analysis shows that there are many losers as well as winners. Moreover, the results are counter-intuitive: the shareholders of the firms being taken over usually benefit; the shareholders of the "winning" firm often lose.

This article challenges the prevailing view in the scholarly literature, which purports to show that the battles for control of major American corporations yield positive results because the shareholders usually benefit. In the light of my own experience on boards of companies that take over as well as those that are taken over, I have made a critical review of the available studies. That has led to a different conclusion about the value of takeovers.

Most economic studies of takeovers are disappointing. They do not directly answer—or even ask—whether the performance of the new company is superior to that of the previous separate parts. That is an extremely difficult task. Those few who have tried to do it have come away with negative conclusions about the economic effects of takeovers.

It is much easier to examine what happens to the stock of the target company. Such data are readily available. Wonder of wonders, the stock market value of the target company invariably rises during the takeover battle. On reflection, would we expect anything else? What raider would make a bid for a company below its current market value? Naturally, the bidding for a company's stock raises its price. As we teach in Economics 101, an increase in demand for an item, without a commensurate increase in supply, will result in a higher price.

But the prevailing view in the economic literature goes beyond a restatement of the obvious to make a very heroic assumption: the rise in shareholder value of the target company reflects the likelihood that the new management will manage more effectively than the old. After all, in an efficient market why else would the share price rise? That is, why else would the raiders invest in the target company? That does sound fairly logical even if we discount a bit the efficiency of today's stock market.

Source: Murray Weidenbaum, "The Economic Effects of Corporate Takeovers," *Executive Speeches*, May 1988.

Yet the presumption of enhanced corporate productivity resulting from takeovers soon becomes translated into irrefutable fact. Why is it irrefutable? Not because of empirical studies which demonstrate the point. There is little evidence that tenderers in general have managed the businesses they acquired any more profitably than their peers or their predecessors. Rather, the presumption of greater productivity is supposedly irrefutable because this conclusion is the only one consistent with the efficient market hypothesis. It is fascinating to note how the efficient market hypothesis has become an article of faith for economists doing supposedly scientific stock market event studies.

Let us look more closely at those stock-market studies that lead to the conclusion that shareholders benefit from the change in corporate control. That the stock of the target firm rises during the takeover battle has been demonstrated very convincingly. But it is premature to jump to the conclusion that stockholders generally benefit from takeovers. After all, for each seller there is a buyer. What happens to the stock of the firm that does the taking over?

The answer to this question is downplayed in the takeover literature. The stock of the acquiring firm usually declines in the period following the announcement of the merger—sometimes substantially (between 5 and 42 percent) and in other circumstances imperceptibly (1-3 percent). All sorts of apologies are provided for this inconvenient conclusion. Inevitably, some question the statistical methodology used—although it is the same as that utilized for the enthusiastically embraced findings on enhancement of shareholder value of target firms. In fact the two sets of findings come from the same studies. Thus, the widely held belief that shareholders generally benefit from takeovers does not hold up to serious analysis. There are both winners and losers. But the results are counter-intuitive: the owners of the "winning" firms lose; the owners of the "losing" firms win.

Furthermore, it is not clear that the takeover process generates positive gains to society. Of the studies that show the dollar amounts of the gains and losses to both groups of shareholders, several show net gains, several net losses, but few of these results are statistically different from zero. Thus, from the viewpoint of society, little net benefit seems to accrue from the entire takeover process. In any event, we must question the motives of the "raiders" whose investment decisions generate losses for their own shareholders large enough to offset the gains of the shareholders of the companies they are taking over.

What motivates the managements of the acquiring firms? We can dismiss out of hand the visionary notion that the raiders are, in truth, such idealists that they are willing to use the resources of their own companies, at the expense of their own shareholders, in order to liberate the downtrodden owners of some other company.

Corporate managers are no different than other individuals. Self-interest should be expected to dominate their decision-making. To the extent that managerial interests do not correspond to those of their stockholders, conflict of interests in decision-making will arise. The same factors which at times encourage managers to be generous to themselves in using corporate resources can also be the driving force behind corporate acquisitions—which after all do increase the amount of corporate resources in their span of control.

Let us not underestimate the benefits from controlling larger enterprises. Let us focus on objective measures of this phenomenon. A recent study by the Conference Board underscores the point that increasing the size (rather than merely the profitability) of the firm promotes management's own interests. Statistical analysis confirms common sense observation. One-half of the variation in pay of a large sample of corporate chief executives was statistically explained by variations in company size, as measured by sales (no other factor, including profits, came close in importance). Moreover, in many sectors, bonuses were a greater percentage of salary the larger the size of the company. In plain English, on average, the bigger the company, the larger the reward to top management.

Viewed in that light, it is logical for the raiders to be willing to offer above-market prices for the shares of target companies. The academic supporters of takeovers look down at the "entrenched" managements of target firms because of their supposed lack of concern for their shareholders. To be consistent, it is equally hard to deify the managements of the "sharks," who often show little more regard for their own shareholders.

Nevertheless, these findings do not necessarily support the advocates of more government intervention in corporate governance generally and takeovers specifically. If we have learned anything from the long history of government regulation of business, it is that government often does more harm than good when it intervenes in internal business decision-making.

A more activist approach is likely to generate serious and often unexpected side effects—the "government failure" that so frequently accompanies attempts to deal with "market failure." There is little need for new laws on takeovers. Of course, the proponents of more government intervention in the economy are encouraged by headline-producing situations. That is the history of so much of the excessively burdensome regulation already on the books. To turn an old legal phrase, dramatic cases make bad law.

The proper answer to corporate takeovers can be found in the private sector, in the corporation itself. In addition to "takeover artists" and "entrenched managers," there is a third private sector force in battles for corporate control—the firms' own boards of directors. Unfortunately, many boards still view their prime task as supporting the management. Surely outside directors and senior managers who serve as inside directors should develop good working relationships. But they need to understand that, at times, their interests diverge.

As we have seen, the shareholders of the acquiring firm often do not benefit from takeovers. Who will protect their interests? The law on this point is very clear. The corporation's board of directors is elected to represent the shareholders.

The most important, and rarely performed, duty of the board is to learn how to say no. It often falls on the outside directors to favor a dividend increase over a marginal project, which is the pet of a key manager. A super generous corporate donation to the ballet may do wonders for the social life of the CEO, but it hardly benefits the shareholders. It is up to the board to oppose a prospective merger that would, over the long run, dilute the earnings of existing shareholders—and, in the short run, reduce the market value of their shareholdings. Similarly, it is the responsibility of the board of the target firm to decide when an offer for the corporation's shares is sufficiently attractive to accept over the protestation of the existing management.

The irony is that some of the problems of the takeover "targets" have arisen from their desire to be more socially responsible. The modern business literature tells management to balance the desires of employees, customers, suppliers, public interest groups, and shareholders. For example, the Committee for Economic Development, in its influential report on the social responsibility of business, states that the professional manager regards himself as a "trustee" balancing the interests of many diverse participants and constituents in the enterprise. It is interesting to note that shareholders are only listed as one among those worthy groups—and they are listed last.

If the raiders are opportunists, it is managements and boards of directors who have given them the opportunity. The record is clear: if the board will not make the difficult choices that enhance the value of the corporation, the takeover advocates will. Takeover mania is not a cause but a symptom of the unmet challenge. The complaisant director has not totally vanished from the boardroom.

The traditional view of the key role of corporate boards is to deal with the succession problem. Surely, cultivating, and selecting the firm's chief executive is a fundamental task. But perhaps the key responsibility of board members, and frequently an unfulfilled one, is to know when to say no to the management—on takeovers, investments, and other strategic issues.

20

The Evolving Corporate Board

The previous selection concluded that the corporation's board of directors is the alternative to government intervention in improving the performance of American business. This article proposes ways of enhancing the role of the board, an issue that remains relevant in the post-Enron environment.

In a period of takeover battles and dramatic replacements of top managements, the role of the corporate board of directors is rapidly evolving into a major strategic force in American business. The new activism on the part of corporate directors includes replacing the chief executive officers for such industrial giants as American Express, Eastman Kodak, General Motors, and IBM.

The burst of public attention to the corporate board is matched by widespread ignorance—both of how that important institution functions and how it has been changing in recent years. Thus, it is appropriate to examine the evolving role of boards of directors, with special attention to strengthening the board.

Three major criticisms have been leveled at the institution of the corporate board of directors:

The most frequently made criticism of the board of directors is that it is ceremonial, rubberstamping the views of management. One retired board chairman of a successful company describes the board of directors as the "Achilles heel of the American corporation." A leading scholar refers to the corporate board as an "impotent legal fiction." In his classic study of large companies, R. A. Gordon concluded that directors are closer to top management than to the stockholders and that ratification of management proposals by the board is largely a formality. He also reported that, as a result of its control of the proxy machinery, management more often selects directors than vice versa.

Myles Mace, in an authoritative study of corporate boards, reported that the role of directors is largely advisory and not of a decision-making nature. He quotes one company president as saying, "The board of directors serves as a sounding board. . . . The decision is not made by the board."

Robert Malott, an experienced corporate director and retired corporate chief executive officer (CEO), identified the biggest barrier to effective outside directorship as the old boy network that dominates some boards. This

Source: Murray Weidenbaum, "The Evolving Corporate Board," *Society*, March/April 1995.

makes it personally unpleasant for directors to question the performance of their peers "and often their friends."

A second, closely related criticism is that the board's deliberations are dominated by the CEO, who typically also serves as chairman. When the same person controls the agenda and conduct of boardroom proceedings as well as the day-to-day performance of the company, the power of the individual director may indeed become attenuated. Despite the rising number of outside directors and special committees of corporate boards, in most cases the center of power remains with the management. CEOs serve as chairman of the board in 80 percent of the larger corporations.

And last, the board is plagued with conflicts of interest. Corporate directors often are criticized for showing greater concern for the welfare of other companies. Many outside directors of corporations do business with the companies on whose board they serve. An analysis of 286 banks that failed in 1990 and 1991 revealed that in seventy-four cases the main cause of the failure was fraud and other abuses by directors and officers, such as receiving loans at very low rates. In 101 other instances, insider abuses contributed to the bank's insolvency.

In the case of the bankrupt Penn Central, a staff report of the Committee on Banking and Currency of the U.S. House of Representatives censured the company's board members for their excessive involvement in other corporate boards. The committee staff noted the subservience of many of the outside directors to the interests of the financial institutions of which they were officers. As the makeup of corporate boards shifts to containing a larger percentage of outside directors, the likelihood of such corporate "interlocks" could increase.

In the case of the larger firms, a problem is emerging in the form of opportunity for back-scratching when setting management compensation. The board's compensation committee is typically a group dominated by outside directors. Frequently, those outside directors are senior officers of other firms and are very sympathetic to motions for generous treatment of their counterparts. Aside from the intrinsic merits of the matter, their self-interest dictates such a stand. The compensation committees of their own boards are often similarly composed of CEOs of peer firms. Moreover, the management consultants advising those committees take full account of such peer-group action by the other boards. An upward ratchet effect results.

Other nominally independent outside directors may in practice represent another set of special interests—those of the local community. Senior officers of local firms that primarily sell goods and services to the surrounding area may see great value in the company donating lavishly to local causes, even if its markets are national or international. Another serious concern is the relationship of the inside directors to the chairman/CEO. After all, he is their day-to-day supervisor, usually with the effective authority to radically change their role in the company and even to fire them. It is rare to see a subordinate officer serving on a board dissent from the position taken by the CEO.

Efforts to Reform

Criticisms of the board have led to a variety of proposals to reform corporate governance. Over the years, Ralph Nader and his colleagues have developed numerous ambitious and far-reaching proposals to restructure the corporation. To give "all stockholders in corporate decision-making a real voice in corporate governance," Nader has advocated a Corporate Democracy Act. Under this proposal, the federal government would assume the chartering power now residing in the individual states. Nader would install full-time outside directors to take an active role in the governance of the corporation. Under the Nader approach, individual directors would be assigned responsibility for specific areas of concern, such as the environment or employee relations. He also has urged a mandatory mail plebiscite of shareholders on all "fundamental" transactions.

Several former corporate CEOs have offered more modest, yet substantial, suggestions for change in the structure of the American corporation. Harold Williams, former chairman of the Securities and Exchange Commission (SEC) and former CEO of Norton Simon, contends that the ideal board of directors would include only one company officer, the chief executive. All other board members, including the chairman, would be chosen from outside the company. His concept of outside directors excludes bankers, lawyers, or anyone else having business dealings with the company. In his view, outside-dominated boards could do a better job of representing the stockholders' long-term interests than executives who are responsible for day- to-day management.

There is considerable precedent for an outside director chairing the board meetings. That is the standard procedure at nonprofit institutions such as hospitals, museums, and universities, many of which rival in size and complexity all but the largest for-profit corporations. Also, many Western European companies normally follow this practice, as do American companies with concentrated ownership on the part of venture capitalists and other outside investors.

Williams, unlike Nader, would not allocate individual directorships to representatives of employees, consumers, minorities, or other groups. "It would be disastrous. . . . Constituency [representation] . . . makes the board a political body," according to Williams. Does his proposal infringe on private property rights? The former SEC chairman states that corporations are more than economic institutions owned by shareholders: "Corporate America is too important, and perceived as too powerful, to fail to address the kinds of issues that are noneconomic."

Harold Geneen, retired CEO of ITT, would go further than Williams, barring all members of management from serving on the board of the corporation for which they work. The CEO and other members of management would continue to attend board meetings, but they would be there to report to the board and to explain their actions.

In a variation of Geneen's approach, Walter Salmon, of the Harvard Business School and a veteran board member, suggests that the boards of larger corporations be limited to three inside directors—the CEO, the chief operating officer (COO), and the chief financial officer (CFO). As the current leaders of the corporation, the CEO and COO are there to communicate, explain, and justify strategic direction to the outside directors. Because CFOs share fiduciary responsibility with the directors for the financial conduct of the corporation, they should also have a seat on the board.

It does not seem likely that any of these sets of detailed proposals for the reform of corporate governance will be made compulsory. Yet legislators continue to introduce proposals for legislating some of these changes. In 1993, Representative Ed Markey (D-Mass.) urged that the federal government require that all board chairmen be outside directors. He would also limit the number of boards that a director can serve on. In the United Kingdom, the Cadbury Committee on Financial Aspects of Corporate Governance has urged that nonmanagement (that is, outside) directors serve on only one board.

Voluntary Changes in the Boardroom

While the criticism of corporate governance continues unabated, important changes in the boardroom are being made on a voluntary basis. These adaptive adjustments have resulted from significant shifts in the environment in which corporations and their boards function. First is increased government regulation and the threat of further intervention. The second influence is active concern with corporate governance by some large institutional investors (especially state and local government employee pension funds). Other factors include greater foreign competition, rising levels of litigation by shareholders, and criticism from the press. In part, the changes deflect or reduce the pressures for new statutes or regulations requiring compulsory modifications in corporate governance. Also, the increased liability of corporate directors for their actions is reinforcing the trend toward their greater involvement in company decision-making.

We can identify eight basic voluntary changes in the boardroom.

Outside directors have become a majority on most boards of large companies in the United States, and the move toward more outside directors continues. In 1938, only one-half of industrial corporations had majorities of outsiders on their boards. By 1992, the average corporate board had nine outside directors and three inside directors. Also, board size has declined somewhat, reflecting in part the reduced role of inside directors. In 1992, the typical board had fourteen directors, down from sixteen in 1982.

Some movement is also being made voluntarily toward the Geneen-Williams view on board composition. Of the hundred large corporations analyzed in 1992 by the executive search firm Spencer Stuart, eleven had boards comprised entirely of outside directors except for the chairman/CEO. In 1987, this was true of only three of the hundred firms. Simultaneously, the prevalence of "dependent" outside directors (that is, those who also provide services to the company) has diminished. In the 1970s, the average board included a commercial banker, an attorney, or both. That is true in only a small minority of instances in the 1990s.

A broader diversity of backgrounds is evident in the type of persons serving on corporate boards. Increased numbers of directors have public service, academic, and scientific experience. Boards also include rising percentages of women and minorities. A survey of top company board placements in 1992 indicated that approximately 30 percent were women or blacks. During the same period, the percentage of boards with ethnic minority members rose from 11 percent to 26 percent, those with academics from 36 percent to 52 percent, and those with former government officials from 12 percent to 31 percent.

Another trend in the composition of U.S. boards of directors is the rising number of directors from other countries. In 1992, twenty-two of the hundred large corporations surveyed by Spencer Stuart had a total of twenty-seven international outside directors.

Auditing committees have become a nearly universal phenomenon. Typically these financial oversight bodies are composed entirely of independent outside directors (an absolute requirement for firms listed on the New York Stock Exchange). The audit committees have direct access to both outside and inside auditors and usually review the financial aspects of company operations in great detail. As recently as 1973, only one-half of large U.S. corporations had auditing committees. Currently, the proportion is 99 percent.

In many companies, nominating committees propose both candidates for the board and senior officers. These committees usually have a strong majority of outside directors (typically, four out of five). However, these statistics do little to illuminate the continuing powerful role of the CEO in initiating or approving committee selections. In practice, most outside directors are selected by the chairman/CEO and in virtually all cases, he or she must be agreeable to their appointment.

In most large companies, compensation committees evaluate the performance of top executives and determine the terms and conditions of their employment. These committees are composed largely or entirely of outside directors. In practice, many of these committees rely extensively on outside consultants whose compensation surveys often set the framework for committee deliberations.

On average, about one out of five of the larger companies have established public-policy committees on their boards. These committees give board-level attention to company policies and performance on subjects of special public concern. Public-policy committees often deal with topics such as affirmative action and equal employment opportunity, employee health and safety, company impact on the environment, corporate political activities, consumer affairs, and ethics.

Internal management and accounting control systems have been strengthened. In part, the impetus for this has come from the need to comply with the provisions of the Foreign Corrupt Practices Act. The activities of the audit committees are surely a reinforcing factor. As a result, the flow of information to board members has been upgraded and expanded.

And last, *recruiting directors has become more difficult.* Increasing the role and the remuneration of directors has helped make board service more attractive. However, these positive factors are on occasion offset by a change in directors' liability insurance. In recent years, courts have narrowed the scope of the business judgment rule, which provides broad discretion to board members in carrying out their functions. The resulting increase in lawsuits against corporate boards has increased the costs of the insurance companies that have previously covered the bulk of such expenses. In turn, this has led to a marked decline in the willingness of carriers to write directors' and officers' liability insurance policies. As a consequence, some directors have reduced the number of boards on which they serve in order to concentrate on their responsibilities on the remaining boards.

Boards have traditionally responded strongly when corporations have faced real crises. In the early 1990s, outside directors began taking a more active stance in reacting to poor performance on the part of the managements reporting to them, thus hoping to forestall the development of crisis situations. In 1992, the General Motors (GM) board, led by outside directors, replaced the CEO and designated an outside director (a recently retired CEO of another major enterprise) as nonexecutive chairman.

In 1993, IBM, after replacing its CEO, created a new committee of outside directors to focus on corporate governance. The function of the new committee is to nominate new directors, handle proposals from shareholders, and oversee the functioning of the board. In the same year, Eastman Kodak replaced its CEO and formed a corporate directors committee of outside directors to oversee its basic strategy.

An important and voluntary institutional change occurred in 1994 when the board of directors of General Motors issued twenty-eight "guidelines on significant corporate governance issues." The GM guidelines formalize the stronger control over management that the board had moved to. Specifics include designating a lead outside director to chair three meetings of independent directors a year, giving the board rather than the CEO real authority to select new members, and creating a new director-affairs committee, whose duties include assigning members to board committees and evaluating the board's performance each year.

Such actions, although few, provide a powerful signal to top management that inadequate performance can result in their replacement by a hitherto supportive board of directors. It is especially noteworthy that these changes in management did not require a formal takeover ("change of control"), with its ancillary legion of expensive investment bankers, attorneys, and accountants.

Strengthening the Board

Despite the progress that has been made in recent years, most writers on the role of the corporate board reach some variation of the same dual conclusion: The board of directors is a vital part of the business firm, but it often does an inadequate job of carrying out its responsibility to represent the shareholders.

The following suggestions are offered in the spirit of strengthening the corporate board without setting up a mechanism competitive with the company management.

Recognize the extent to which takeover battles have occurred because of the cumulative inaction of some boards of directors. It is easy enough to denounce financial entrepreneurs who have little interest in the production of goods and services but who profit merely from making unsolicited takeover bids. But if they are opportunists, we must ask whether existing board and management practices have created these opportunities. A clue is given, perhaps inadvertently, by the Business Roundtable's lament that a successful corporate defense may involve drastic restructuring to maximize share value in the short run. Without endorsing the desirability of such a change, we can wonder whether it does reflect the true desires of many shareholders who indeed want to maximize share value in the short run as well as in the long run.

Despite their attraction to defending managements, legislative proposals to make unfriendly takeovers more difficult do not deal with the fundamental need to respond to the desires of the shareholders. That is both the basic responsibility of the board and the key to its potential power. Corporate officials, both board members and officers, may forget that shareholders continually vote with their dollars. The less frequently key issues are presented to the shareholders, the more likely they are to resort to their ultimate weapon—selling their holdings in a company whose policies they disagree with.

Some of the problems of the takeover targets may have arisen from the desire to be more socially responsible. Examples include Cummins Engine and Control Data Corporation, both of which suffered under managements with an unusual interest in broad social problems. Control Data Corporation, after an annual loss of $680 million, replaced its CEO, who had stressed corporate social responsibility. The new CEO bluntly stated that the previous management had not always "thought in terms of building shareholder value" and had not built a culture of controlling costs.

The heart of a positive response to the dissatisfaction with corporate performance is for directors to act more fully as fiduciaries of the shareholders, as the law requires. The same authorities who are almost universally critical of the way in which corporate boards operate are unanimous in their belief that a well-functioning governing board is essential to the future of the modern corporation. Virtually no one has concluded that the board of directors has outlived its usefulness. Even such critics of business as Ralph Nader would lodge the responsibility for governing the corporation in a revitalized board of directors.

The most fundamental need in corporate governance is educational— senior corporate officers must come to understand their high stake in enhancing the role of the board of directors. There would be fewer challenges to the existing managements of their companies if more boards acted from a day-to-day concern with the interests of their shareholders. The benefits of a more active board will not be attained without costs. Achieving a stronger and more effective board means sharing the authority now lodged in the CEO—and at times reaching somewhat different decisions. But that does not require the establishment of a competitive power center. It does mean being more conscious of the desires of shareholders and of the need to keep them more fully informed. Only one person—the CEO—can guide the corporation's day-to-day activities. That function cannot be performed by a committee.

Successful directors learn to monitor and question while creating an atmosphere of confidence in the management. Simultaneously, a truly secure CEO will not attempt to stifle criticism by individual directors. The legendary Alfred P. Sloan reportedly made the following statement at a General Motors board meeting:

> Gentlemen, I take it we are all in complete agreement on the decision here. . . . Then I propose we postpone further discussion of this matter until our next meeting to give ourselves time to develop disagreement and perhaps gain some understanding of what the decision is all about.

Retired officers of a company do not belong on its board. It is enough to have independent outside directors looking over the shoulders of the management, without the previous generation of management also doing so. The outsiders have less stake in defending the status quo than do the retirees, who may have created the existing conditions. There are advantages in retired corporate officers serving as directors of other companies, so long as they are not competitors of or suppliers to the company from which they have retired.

Corporate boards should consist primarily of independent outsiders. Outside directors should not represent banks, law firms, customers, or the community in which the corporation happens to have its headquarters. Such actual or potential conflicts of interest should be avoided. Nominating committees would do well to bear in mind the advice of management scholar S. Prakash Sethi that a board of directors is not a debating society: "While it is normal to have different viewpoints and expertise represented on the board, it is illogical to represent special interests on the board."

The board chairman should usually be an outside director in order to assure the independence of the board. Much depends on the attitude of the CEO to the board and to the specific challenges facing the company. There is no compelling need to modify the traditional arrangement in the case of a well-functioning company whose CEO also maintains an open, healthy relation with the board. In such circumstances, it would be silly to change merely for the sake of change.

However, when the company is not performing well or when the CEO regards the board as merely a legal necessity, then a departure from the status quo is warranted. Under such circumstances, it would be helpful if the presiding officer had relevant experience—the recently retired CEO of another firm or of a large nonprofit institution, for instance.

A few senior members of the management can be useful board members. The CEO would be appropriate. His or her presence on the board does not give rise to the problems that occur when operating officials are made board members—when they participate in reviewing their own operations and those of their colleagues. Because of the crucial relationship of financial reporting to the monitoring function, the chief financial officer probably also should be a board member. None of these inside directors can be expected to differ frequently with the CEO, thus emphasizing the need for a substantial representation of outside, independent directors.

Where the board chairmanship is filled by an outside director, the position should be a private role; the CEO should represent the firm to the public. Only the CEO and his or her subordinates can truly represent the firm in public arenas since they bear the responsibility and possess the authority to conduct the business of the company. This approach requires a high degree of good will on the part of both outside directors and corporate officers. The indispensable factor in ensuring an effective board is that directors and management be committed to making the board work. A great deal of effort and discretion is required on the part of outside directors to carry on an active and constructive role that is simultaneously probing and supportive.

Some institutional protections of the independence of board committees are necessary and are now often in place. Specifically, the audit committee—even if the corporation is not listed on the New York Stock Exchange—should consist entirely of independent outside directors. The compensation committee, which passes on the pay and fringe benefits of top management, should be similarly constituted. Also, the nominating committee, with a key role in selecting directors and senior executives, should be comprised of independent outside members.

The subject of board turnover is often a painful matter. A directorship is not a type of civil-service appointment, but it is not easy to dislodge a long-term director. Long-term directors become so accustomed to the existing way of doing business that they viscerally oppose innovation on the oldest bureaucratic grounds: "We have never done it that way."

A Look to the Future

A growing array of external forces impinges on the contemporary corporation. Some of these factors are financial and economic, focusing on the traditional functions of business enterprise. Others are social and political, dealing with business responses to other issues. Together, these influences will likely produce significant further changes in the composition of corporate boards of directors to increase the active involvement of corporate directors in the decision-making of the business firm.

Looking ahead, researchers and practitioners alike in the twenty-first century will probably still be speculating about the needed changes in the roles and activities of corporate directors. Fundamentally, this will reflect the fact that the corporation is a continually evolving institution in the U.S. economy and, as external requirements change, key elements such as the board of directors continue to adapt and modify their actions. Outside directors need to bear in mind that, in a very special way, the future of the corporation is in their hands.

21

Restoring Public Confidence in American Business

Despite the adoption of some of the recommendations contained in the previous selections, fundamental shortcomings in business performance became evident in the opening years of the twenty-first century. The dramatic bankruptcy of Enron highlighted the situation. This article presents ways of responding to the resulting loss of confidence in American business.

The private enterprise system in the United States is under severe attack, not from people who advocate socialism or another philosophical alternative, but from many citizens appalled by widespread reports of unethical and illegal decisions made by high-level business executives. The initial response has been by government officials—through new legislation from Congress and enhanced enforcement of existing laws by the Securities and Exchange Commission (SEC) and the Department of Justice. Government action is a very good start, but it is not enough.

Many of the governmental reforms have been necessary to address problems in corporate finance, ranging from the accuracy of financial reports to the role of auditors and audit committees. The government actions are valuable to improve the information on corporate performance on which investors rely when making their decisions.

Legislation, however, cannot deal with the fundamental problem: poor judgment and bad decisions by individual business executives. Some of those decisions have had a tragic impact on employees and shareholders who have lost their jobs or their retirement funds as a consequence of business leaders' actions.

Restoring public confidence in the conduct of American business is most fundamentally a challenge for business leadership itself. Until recently, corporate governance, or the way in which company business is conducted, was primarily the province of lawyers and other technical specialists, each of which continue to play an important role. A number of voluntary, private-sector actions in the area of corporate governance could also help restore public confidence in capitalism in the United States. The problems of corporate governance, however, are fundamental, and their solution requires more than a technical response.

Source: Murray Weidenbaum, "Restoring Public Confidence in American Business," *The Washington Quarterly*, Winter 2002-03.

The actions of American business leaders—not just shortcomings on the part of technical specialists—have generated the loss of faith on the part of the American people. Only sustained changes in the way that business is conducted—not talk but action—will convince the public that the reforms are real and enduring. Voluntarily yielding some of the powers of what many now call the "imperial presidency," so common in the private sector, is clearly a matter of enlightened self-interest on the part of top business management. The alternative—sooner or later—will be a new round of pervasive government regulation of business, arbitrarily reducing the discretion of management.

Reforms by Business

Corporate governance in the United States is facing an unprecedented variety of pressures to change. Although some of the shortcomings have endured over recent decades, several dramatic bankruptcies, most notably Enron in December 2001, triggered the current wave of concern. More recent reports of companies such as Tyco paying for millions of dollars of personal expenses of CEOs demonstrate that changes in accounting procedures do not suffice. The key issues that have been raised in the national media, as well as in a flurry of congressional investigations, focused too much on auditing firms, financial reporting, audit committees of boards of directors, and similarly important but essentially technical matters. Fundamental reforms in corporate governance surely must deal with financial issues, but they must extend beyond that to the role of the top management.

A typical corporation starts with a board of directors elected by the shareholders. That board, in turn, selects the top management to conduct the day-to-day activities of the enterprise. The board also forms committees to deal with specific matters such as audits, executive compensation, and nomination of board members and officers. A board may consist of "inside" directors (the chief executive officer [CEO] and other members of management) and "outside" directors, who only serve part-time. The typical board is chaired by the CEO and is comprised primarily of outside directors. Combining the roles of chief executive and board chair generates the potential for, and often ends up with, a very powerful leader who at times can intimidate a dissident board member.

None of the governmental actions to date address fundamental shortcomings of corporate governance such as the excessive concentration of power in the CEO, nor should they. In an economy organized mainly on the basis of private enterprise, correcting those shortcomings is a task for the private sector itself.

Beyond Legislation

Many companies have been well managed and produce extremely positive economic as well as financial results. Their senior executives, boards, and outside legal and accounting firms do the effective and honest job expected of them. The history of corporate governance in the United States clearly demonstrates the substantial ability of business to reform itself. In 1869, the New York Stock Exchange (NYSE) cracked down on the practice of "watering" stocks (issuing shares in secret). More recently, the NYSE in 1977 required each listed company to establish an audit committee composed of outside directors. In the 1980s, most companies, responding to the critics of corporate governance, voluntarily shifted the composition of their boards to a predominance of outside directors.

These and many other voluntary improvements in corporate governance support the notion that not every problem requires a solution based in Washington. Currently, many companies are beginning to treat the issuance of stock options to their executives as a business expense, rather than burying the information in an obscure footnote to their financial statements. Yet, recent events confirm that serious shortcomings still exist and must be addressed.

Scandalous decisions in giant corporations operating beyond the effective control of their boards of directors have drained public confidence. All business, not just corruptly led ones, could benefit from the types of necessary internal change proposed here. These reforms focus on particular aspects of company management including the CEO's role, the selection processes for various boards and committees, and the specifics of the auditing process. More fundamentally, they aim to meet the challenges that any and every business driven by competition and individual self-interest—those characteristics of American capitalism that at the same time can be credited for its unparalleled success—can expect to face.

How can public interests be protected in an environment dominated by neither sinners nor saints, and how can that protection be provided without inhibiting the efficiency of the private enterprise system that currently generates abundant goods and services, employment, income, wealth, innovation, and progress? Achieving those multiple objectives is a tall order. It surely requires humility in recommending specific courses of action. Unlike the media and congressional coverage of these matters, however, it seems more appropriate to start at the top of the corporate hierarchy rather than in the middle or at the bottom.

Reconsidering and Revising the Role of the CEO

As noted earlier, the CEO, as the corporation's leader, is the focal point of its governing power. He or she sets the organization's tone and runs day-to-day operations. The CEO also controls the resources to support management's ideas. Ninety percent of the time, CEOs chair the board of directors, conducting meetings according to agendas they set.

This procedure makes opposing the recommendations of the chairman/ CEO, much less pursuing other approaches, difficult for individual directors.

The CEO also often recommends the candidates for the board and frequently contacts potential directors. Board nominating committees that will recommend a new director whom the CEO opposes are most rare. Equally unusual are shareholders who reject the nominations contained in the annual proxy statement submitted for their review and approval.

On the surface, this mode of operation may resemble the structure of an efficient operation. In fact, this model often works quite well. Many dedicated CEOs use this system in an honest attempt to build an effective, profitable organization that produces goods and services that meet the needs of the public and does so in an ethical manner. CEOs can be quick to point out that they may have spent a lifetime with a company while directors, at best, are part-timers and shareholders are often mere transients.

Centralization of power in the CEO, however, has led to a variety of abuses. Skyrocketing CEO compensation is a dramatic symptom of the shortcomings of the status quo in corporate governance. An effective response must go beyond dealing with technical questions such as the accounting treatment of stock options or the adequacy of financial controls on reimbursement of the CEO's personal expenses. The issue boils down to the personal motivations of the CEOs themselves. Expecting subordinates to limit the fiscal appetite of a determined, greedy, and/or ethically insensitive CEO is folly.

The answer to this basic problem in corporate governance must come from above the CEO—from the boardroom. Many U.S. companies may find it appropriate to adopt the British tradition of appointing an outside director to chair the board and to conduct board meetings. The chairmen are usually very experienced and often prestigious persons who are at the stage of life where they are not viewed as a management challenger. Although usually occupied with their own professional matters, the chairmen devote sufficient time and effort to the position so that they are not merely figureheads. For example, Lord Alexander Trotman, retired CEO of Ford Motor Company, now serves as board chairman of Imperial Chemical Industries.

Few U.S. CEOs can be expected to welcome with enthusiasm such a dilution of their customary authority. The outside chairman, however, is not an unknown phenomenon in the United States. Major investors at times serve as board chairs of new enterprises. During transitional stages, outside directors have been designated chairman, at least for a limited period of time.

The views of John G. Smale, retired CEO of Procter & Gamble and former outside chairman of General Motors, are quite instructive. Smale notes that as a CEO/chairman he would not have welcomed a diminution of his authority and that he saw his outside chairmanship at the time as merely a transitional appointment. Reflecting back, he now believes that the board should be chaired by an outside director:

> If the purpose of a board is to represent the shareholders in overseeing management's conduct of the business, such a structure [an outside director serving as chairman]

seems considerably more logical than having the board chaired by a manager who is also the subject of such oversight.

Although granting too much authority to the CEO can be dangerous, the constraints that should be placed on the ultimate leader of any business also have limits. An effective enterprise requires a strong CEO. No committee— and that is the organizational form of any board —should try to run a business. Every director should understand that the CEO is the day- to-day leader of the enterprise and provides its public face. That recognition does not, however, require a weak or passive board.

Strengthening the Board of Directors

As a longtime corporate director, I can attest from experience that boards of directors often seem asleep at the switch. In the midst of rising public criticism of business, the truly independent members of corporate boards can play a more vital role than ever to assure shareholders and society as a whole that business is being responsibly managed. Most directors take their role very seriously. The lapses from good practice, however, attract public attention and give business in general a bad reputation.

When we consider the disgrace that has been heaped upon some Enron directors, it seems clear that exercising independent judgment is not just the prerogative of an outside director. Acting independently of management's interests—overruling a poorly thought-through proposal for expansion, for example—is a basic way of protecting the individual director's integrity as well as that of the enterprise.

In this regard, several director-selection practices should be avoided because they limit the board's independence. Examples include celebrity directors who do not understand the basics of corporate governance; overly committed directors who serve on eight or ten or more boards while holding down a full-time job; personal friends of the CEO; and those directors who simultaneously serve as high-priced consultants or suppliers to the corporation.

Successful board members avoid the extremes of becoming either sycophants or rivals to the management. The board's basic task is oversight— advising and questioning management rather than blindly issuing approvals or independently trying to run the business. No legislation can mandate such wisdom on the part of directors but more public attention to the conduct of boards may encourage a greater dedication to the task.

To improve corporate governance, key board committees must be bolstered. Quite properly, attention has been focused on the audit committee; its watchdog functions are being enhanced. Yet, the role of the relatively recently emerging governance committee (which increasingly replaces the nominating committee) likewise should be developed. Governance committees now regularly review the CEO's and the board's performance. The results of those reviews should be a high-priority item on the full board's agenda.

Similarly, if CEO compensation has at times become excessive, that development is an indictment of the compensation committee, which also deserves more notice.

The compensation committee should consist entirely of truly independent directors, and oftentimes it does. But the selection and pay of outside compensation advisers, whose advice is usually given great weight by the committees, should be determined by the committee and not by the management whose compensation is being decided. This situation is an example of the inability of many corporate legal advisers to detect and blow the whistle on what, at least to a layman, appears a blatant conflict of interest: management selecting the individuals who draw up management's compensation plans and then advise the board on those same compensation matters.

Waking Up the Audit Committee

The NYSE has rules requiring each listed company to establish an audit committee consisting entirely of outside directors. Nevertheless, the effectiveness of audit committees is clearly, to say the least, uneven. Enron's audit committee met all of the formal NYSE and SEC requirements. Yet, it failed to blow the whistle on the outrageous financial practices that were perpetrated on unsuspecting shareholders.

A well-functioning audit committee is truly the conscience of the corporation. Its members review the work of the organization's own internal auditors as well as the activities of the outside accounting firm, which conducts an independent audit of the company's finances. Audit committees have a broad charter to question and investigate the various operations of the company to ensure their financial integrity. In a world of increasingly sophisticated financial techniques, Enron's audit committee as well as the entire Enron board seems to have violated one of the most elementary rules of management: if you do not understand something, do not approve it.

No new legislation is needed for audit committee members to show a greater spirit of inquiring independence. An arm's-length relationship between the audit committee and company management is essential to establish and maintain that independence. As the NYSE proposed, that means no former executives of the company, no consultants to the company, and no employees of companies that sell significant amounts of goods and services to the company should serve on the audit committee.

Refocusing the Role of Accountants and Lawyers

The practice of using a firm that conducts a company's outside audit to perform a variety of other services for that company has fallen out of fashion. A great many companies—perhaps the majority—are phasing out the nonaudit functions of their external auditors. In some cases, these ancillary functions were never substantial or are now much smaller than a few years ago. The new corporate reform law quite substantially reduces the array of additional services that an auditor can perform for its client.

Yet, there are other troubling aspects of the role of the accounting firms that remain. Too much of today's auditing seems to focus on the computer systems that generate the accounting data, downplaying the traditional review of individual transactions. Both tasks need to be performed.

Lawyers have been remarkably successful in ensuring that so much of the liability for current corporate governance problems falls on the accounting profession and so little falls on the members of the bar. To add the proverbial insult to injury, at the same time that attorneys are so actively urging accounting firms to rid themselves of their nonaudit functions, they are campaigning vigorously to expand and strengthen the multidisciplinary practices of their own firms.

Concern for maintaining high levels of legal ethics should extend to the poor advice that some lawyers provided to the corporate decision-makers who did such a great disservice to investors, employees, and the public generally in the cases of Enron, Worldcom, Tyco, Adelphia, and so forth. Many of the highly criticized financial-activities actions by management and auditors alike had been blessed in advance by their house counsel, outside law firm, or both. There is enough criticism to go around, and the onus for bad performance should be shared fairly and more widely, including with Wall Street stock analysts and bond-rating agencies.

Restoring Public Confidence

Corporate governance in the United States is being challenged for good reason. Top management—boards and the most senior corporate officers—must take the lead in cleaning house. The incentive for such action is basic: to maintain the confidence of the investing public and to minimize the likelihood of yet another round of burdensome regulation. Fortunately, the history of corporate governance in the United States is one of voluntary change by individual companies in response to developing circumstances. The shift in board-of-director composition from mainly management directors to outside directors is a cogent case in point, as is the rise of independent audit committees.

The hallmark of strong management is the ability to respond to serious problems promptly and proactively; any management can react to the crises that inaction permits to develop. The challenge to American business now is to respond constructively to the severe challenges to corporate governance that it faces. An effective and timely response, more than any government action, will help to maintain investor and public confidence in the private enterprise system.

22

Economic Freedom and Private Enterprise

This article takes a rather philosophical approach to the public policy environment facing private enterprise in the United States.

The air is full of sounds of budgets being cut and taxes being reformed. But, it is useful to step back and ponder the fundamentals that underlie the heated debates of the moment. When the frenetic events of the day are evaluated in the more leisurely light of history, we will find that we have been engaged in an effort far more fundamental than raising the growth rate of the GDP or slowing the pace of the Consumer Price Index, worthy as these actions are.

The United States is currently making an unprecedented shift in the focus of economic decision-making, away from the federal government and to the many diverse and smaller organizations and institutions that serve individuals. Thus, it is not a question of whether it is more desirable to cut taxes or to reduce the growth of government spending, or to curtail government credit programs or to provide relief from regulatory burdens. All of these are part of a larger endeavor: to strengthen the performance of the private sector by reducing the power, the burden, and the obtrusiveness of the public sector.

This shift in national priorities is based on the general proposition that private citizens do not need government officials to make their decisions for them or to direct their daily lives. Most people—workers, managers, investors, buyers, and sellers—know what they want and how to obtain it. Over time, the aggregation of these individual actions generally results in the most appropriate distribution of our economic resources and the highest levels of well-being.

The best government economic policy, therefore, is the one that provides a stable environment in which private citizens can confidently plan and make their own commitments and choices. Those who advocate departures from this approach bear the burden of proof that government intervention will do more good than harm. Advocates of intervention must show in any given situation that "market failure" is greater than the "government failure" that often accompanies political and bureaucratic responses to economic and social problems.

This, in my opinion, is a useful and succinct statement of the principles of limited government consistent with an economic order organized primarily on the basis of private enterprises competing in a market system. It is hardly

Source: Murray Weidenbaum, "Economic Freedom and Private Enterprise," *Journal of Private Enterprise*, Fall 1986.

new. Adam Smith came to this same conclusion over two centuries ago when he first conducted his inquiry into the nature and causes of the wealth of nations. The society he envisioned surely was not anarchic. Rather it was characterized by limited government, with the expectation that government would perform well the important tasks that only it could carry out, notably defense and those major public works we now call infrastructure.

Freedom and the Marketplace

Let us begin by looking at the basics of a free economy. It is a world where people sometimes win—and sometimes lose—in their economic pursuits. Given adherence to mutually accepted rules, a free enterprise system teaches individuals how to avoid failure and pursue success. In a healthy market-oriented economy, individual entrepreneurs and companies that are efficient in meeting consumer needs are profitable. Those that fail to meet those needs, or do so at high cost, sustain losses. Thus, it is erroneous to refer to a "profit" system; more accurately, ours is a profit-and-loss system. The opportunity to earn a profit is only as available as the possibility of bearing a loss.

Government institutions, on the other hand, are not subject to such discipline. No federal agency ever has been forced to declare bankruptcy. Rather, the typical response for a federal department living beyond its budget is to urge the Congress to increase its use of public resources. Government programs often continue beyond their original justification and develop a life of their own. There is no shortage of critics who comment about the shortcomings of the "invisible hand" in the market economy. But, as we have learned so painfully and so often in recent years, the "fickle finger"—or rather the hard fist—of government usually generates far greater problems when it intervenes in economic decision-making.

The last half century provides an almost endless array of experiences with well-intentioned governmental interventions in private decision-making that did not work out. These examples of government failure range from the scandal-ridden Reconstruction Finance Corporation of the 1930s and 1940s to the waste-laden Office of Economic Opportunity of the 1960s and 1970s to the counterproductive farm subsidies of the Commodity Credit Corporation that have extended throughout the period.

It is not a question of altruism, but of enlightened self-interest, that motivates the individual and the business firm. A private enterprise system takes advantage of that fact. As Adam Smith put it, "it is not from the benevolence of the butcher, the brewer or the baker that we expect our dinner, but from their regard of their own interest."

It is ironic to listen to thoughtless statements that free market institutions are heartless enough to let people starve. The fact of the matter is that the capitalist nations of the world are feeding the socialist nations not on a charitable basis, but in the spirit of Adam Smith's baker.

The role of government in this context must be carefully defined. Supporting free enterprise does not mean being single-mindedly pro-business. That approach normally translates into a cozy partnership between government and business—subsidies and protection for failing industries, government planning, and other interventionist techniques usually justified on an "exceptions" basis.

Indeed, many day-to-day practices on the part of business executives merit our critical attention. We can begin with the very way in which the business community describes economic events. For example, employers rarely refer to competition in their labor markets. The more widely used term for other companies bidding away their workers by offering them higher wages and salaries is "pirating" employees. Similarly in product markets, competition is only favored in the abstract or in the case of potential suppliers to the firm.

We rarely hear the word competition used in the markets in which the company sells its goods and services. There, the preferred term is price "chiseling." That specifically refers to the ungentlemanly practice of lowering prices.

The expansion of foreign trade has given rise to its own specialized vocabulary. "Imports" is too technical a term for general business usage. More common is the phrase "unfair competition." The volume of foreign goods entering the United States is usually described as a "flood." And what is the desired response? Protection against imports is too blatant. "Fair trade" sounds much better. After all, it is only fair that we buy American-made.

Protectionism is a politician's delight because it delivers visible benefits to the protected parties while imposing the costs as a hidden tax on the public. Some day the public will learn that too well kept secret—that the higher prices that invariably result from protectionism are paid by American consumers. Ironically, in all too many cases, such as textiles and apparel, this burden hits most heavily on the poorest people in our country.

It does little to bolster citizen confidence in a private enterprise system when captains of industry on one day urge people on welfare to stop depending on government for handouts and, on the very next day, appeal to that same government for some special benefit. Subsidy, of course, is a very selective term in business English. It usually is preceded by the work "farm."

Euphemisms are widely employed by corporate executives. Thus, in standard financial reporting, companies earn profits—a phrase that conjures up the notion of positive achievement of their own doing. In contrast, firms suffer losses. That sounds like an unexpected blow inflicted by some sinister force in the external environment beyond corporate influence.

By no means is the use of euphemisms limited to members of management. Take the example of the "corporate activists." Judging by their self-designated title, you would expect that corporate activists were engaged in the worthy enterprise of attempting to energize a sluggish company or were concerned with improving the economic performance of American business. The typical "corporate activists" are oblivious to the economic role of private enterprise. Producing and distributing the goods and services that meet consumers' needs is too humdrum a task to attract their interest.

Rather, they see the resources of the private enterprise system as a means for achieving their social ends. One term they love to use is corporate or economic democracy. But, on the contrary, they refuse to abide by the decisions of democratic political processes. They will buy a few shares of stock in a company—not as an investment—but to use the annual meeting as an opportunity to try to force the company to follow their pet social or political goals. These are goals that they are unable to convince Congress to adopt—such as imposing our internal social standards on other countries.

Some unions and other activist groups favor such high-sounding phrases as "pay equity" and "comparable worth" to describe the effort to set arbitrarily the salaries of some members of the workforce without regard to competitive market levels. As economists, we know the sad results, as in public education where there are chronic surpluses of gym teachers amidst continuing shortages of math and science instructors.

Descriptions of comparable-worth systems remind me of the Middle Ages, when the priesthood sat in judgment on economic matters, depending on theological concepts to determine what they called the "just price." Activists today attempt to play a similar role, forgetful of the costly impacts of imposing dogma on a modern market economy.

The private sector did not invent obfuscation, nor are business executives its exclusive practitioners. We can recall the tale—perhaps mythical—of the federal inspector who examined two very similar rooms of government officials, none of whom were working at the time. His report was simple: "duplication."

Actions and Appropriate Inactions

At times, adhering to the principles of economic freedom requires specific actions and on the other occasions it necessitates forbearance. For example, promoting the concept of free enterprise requires that no favored treatment be given to any specific interest group or industry. It means restraining the tendency to reallocate resources from those who are entitled to them by virtue of their own ability to those who receive them by political fiat.

I still recall meeting in Washington with the representatives of an industry seeking a federal bailout. After I pointed out that such action was the economic equivalent of welfare, the leader of the group responded with great indignation, "Why, Mr. Chairman, welfare is for poor people."

For example, although economists may argue for a laissez-faire approach to hostile takeovers on the basis of free market principles, many corporations see no problem in appealing to government to intervene in their behalf. As a practical matter, they want to use the power of government to make it more difficult for "outsiders" to take over their companies.

There is no need to argue that all or even most takeover attempts are constructive—or even benign. What should concern the business proponents of more government intervention in private business decision-making is the array of effects that usually follow. The long and intricate history of government involvement in the private economy does not provide an inspiring basis for expanding the role of the federal government in corporate governance. Whether that intervention is made by the judicial. legislative or executive branch, government regulation often does more harm than good. Study after study shows that much government regulation frequently fails to meet the most elementary benefit-cost test.

Moreover, economic history teaches us that government intervention usually begets more government intervention. In the present situation, for example, if government should limit the maneuvers by corporate raiders, that would tilt the balance of power. Invariably, it would lead to pleas to restrict the defensive actions of company managements (and vice versa). Surely it is legitimate for well-financed groups of investors to attempt hostile takeovers of private companies. So, too, resistance by the target company's board of directors may be perfectly proper. To ascribe the public interest to just one side of the controversy is to ignore the fundamental role of competition in the marketplace.

Surely, leaders of interest groups also can be properly criticized for their intellectual shortcomings in dealing with important issues of public policy. An example is the inconsistent attitude of many proponents of welfare programs. Especially in these days where virtually every federal agency's budget is being cut, we hear howls of outrage from the supporters of food stamps, medicaid, public housing, and other "payments in kind."

But how do these same advocates of higher federal spending reply when some of us raise the simple statistical notion that such "income in kind" should be included when the government attempts to measure the number of people in poverty? The proponents of these programs contend that such reporting would be unfair. They point out that a dollar of spending for these social programs does not generate a dollar of benefit to the recipients. One enthusiast for these social programs admits that food stamps ". . . certainly aren't worth their face value in cash." He suggests that these items, should they be included in any measure of poverty, be discounted by 20 percent or even 40 percent.

The cynic in me says that we have the makings of a deal here. Eliminate food stamps and all other "payments in kind" and split the difference. Give the current recipients cash equal to one-half of the government's current cost for these programs and reduce the budget deficit by the other half. I readily forecast that the major complaints would not arise from the "clients" of these programs.

Our concern for the principles of economic freedom needs to be broad gauged. It cannot stop at the water's edge. Free-flowing international trade and investment—a free enterprise system writ large—offers greater economic welfare to people of all countries. The same specialization of labor and individual creativity that we see in our society can also be encouraged beyond our borders.

Special interests would have us close the door to the accomplishments of Japanese management, or to the natural abundance of French vineyards. But, when all the benefits of a more open economy are added up, it becomes clear that losses for domestic producers do not, and cannot, cancel out the gains that consumers receive from imports. Free trade, of course, must be a two-way street. To oppose protectionism here at home is proper but insufficient. We must also speak out just as strongly against restrictions on commerce imposed by other governments.

On reflection, some policy innovation may be useful; one was suggested a while ago by my favorite economic analyst, Russell Baker, the columnist for *The New York Times*. You may recall, back in 1981, the controversy about limiting the imports of Japanese cars. Baker, in his customary scholarly manner, examined the comparative advantages of both the United States and Japan. He found that the Japanese auto industry had productive capacity far in excess of its domestic requirements. Similarly, he noted that the United States was producing far more lawyers than we need.

Unencumbered by econometric analysis or weighty theory, Baker recommended a simple swap. For every 1,000 Japanese cars that enter the United States, we would send Japan 100 lawyers. He was not concerned about an ensuing flood of foreign-produced motor vehicles. Rather, he saw this type of tied trade as possessing self-limiting features.

As American attorneys entered the Japanese economy, he reasoned, that nation's productivity would erode. In contrast, the exodus of lawyers from the United States would contribute to a rise in the efficiency of our economy. Eventually, the economic competitiveness of the two nations would equalize. Baker felt so strongly about his plan that he suggested that we start the process by sending the Japanese 100 lawyers on the cuff!

The Costs of Economic Freedom

There are real costs of achieving and maintaining important values such as economic freedom. Friedrich von Hayek has written eloquently on the neglected aspect of the relation between freedom and economics. In *The Road to Serfdom*, he cautioned with great foresight against the dangers of growing government. Even earlier, in a less often quoted work, he made a point that seems as appropriate now as it did then. In *Freedom and the Economic System*, he wrote: "Freedom and Democracy are not free gifts which will remain with us if only we wish it. The time seems to have come when it is once again necessary to become fully conscious of the conditions which make them possible, and to defend these conditions even if they should block the path to the achievement of competing ideals." Thus, we need to recognize the material costs that are involved in achieving and maintaining a free society.

Freedom and the free enterprise system have come under attack in recent years as public concern has shifted towards the achievement of a number of other goals, including a variety of social concerns such as ecology and income redistribution. But when these non-economic concerns sap the vitality of the economic system, and ultimately reduce or limit living standards, it becomes time to redress the balance.

In that spirit, let us also focus on the limits of political decision-making. In a political setting, it is appropriate that the majority should decide. Yet, that is hardly the way to meet the great variety of consumer desires. Following universally the approach embodied in voting and the political process can cause needless losses in economic welfare. Let me illustrate that point.

When the original Henry Ford declared that automobile buyers could choose any color so long as it was black, prospective purchasers with different preferences had recourse to the products of other companies. But if instead the same Henry Ford had been Secretary of a nationalized Department of Automotive Production, the minority desires would have remained unfulfilled.

In our daily lives, there is rarely a need for unanimity of choice. This is where the market system automatically meets individual wants far more effectively than the best-intentioned political process. Returning to the example of the automobile, if 1 percent of the population desire a car painted in blushing pink, the market can meet their demand—provided they are willing to pay the cost. There is no need to impose a single dominant viewpoint on all automobile purchasers.

In many cases where government does intervene in our daily lives, there may be no need for a standardized response by a federal agency having jurisdiction over the entire nation. Americans in different regions have different needs and priorities, and a decentralized public sector—which is a fundamental characteristic of our federal form of government—can respond to those citizen desires far more effectively.

It is heartening to see the heightened public awareness of the tremendous ability of a private enterprise economy to meet the needs and desires of its citizens. This improved understanding is evidenced by and indeed it has been embodied in several basic changes in the American economy in recent years. The pace of new regulation of business has slowed down measurably, as warnings about the high cost of regulation have been taken seriously. Federal civilian spending has been cut back, as concerns about containing the growth of public sector have been heeded. Labor-management relations are sounding a more constructive note; the number of strikes is at an all-time low; many collective bargaining agreements have become more realistic, as workers and management alike respond to new economic realities.

Yet it is too soon to say how complete or how durable these changes will turn out to be. This is no time to rest on our laurels. We need only look at the current federal budget and congressional action on tax reform to see that the key problems addressed a decade or two ago are yet unsolved. We still need to continue urging tax reformers to pay adequate attention to the effects of their plans on saving and investment. We still need to urge major cuts in government spending in order to get the deficit down and to expand the private portion of the national economy. And we must continue to call public attention to the fact that federal credit programs are no free lunch, and that the costs of regulation may be hidden by government but that they are ultimately borne by the consumer.

It is essential that we relate sound economic principles to the important issues of the day. This challenge to economic education goes beyond classrooms and scholarly journals. Truly, our "classrooms" must be forums that command the attention of large numbers of our fellow citizens. The key "journals" in which we publish the results of our research and analysis must include the national media.

Conclusion

The concern for the private enterprise system is part of a larger national debate over fundamental values, and especially over the balance between the power of government and the freedom of the individual. Simultaneously, we must relate economic concerns to the broader interests of the public.

Capitalism has its faults. We should be honest enough to admit them and eager to correct them where we can—that is, where the attempts at improvement will not do more harm than good. We also need to be mindful of the fact that economic institutions, such as the business firm, are not multipurpose organizations. In the productive specialization of labor characteristic of a market economy the profit-seeking corporation is best suited to the production and distribution of goods and services to meet consumer needs.

Attempting to impose on the economic process a variety of high-minded social obligations erodes the ability of business to perform its true social function. That basic social function of business cannot be underestimated. It is providing consumers a rising degree of economic welfare. To restate the obvious, it is the private enterprise system that makes available food, clothing, shelter, and other necessities as well as luxuries of life. That basic function of business also means creating the economic base upon which a society can meet its important non-economic needs, which range from ensuring the national security to caring for the sick and the disabled.

Finally, we should remind our fellow citizens of the importance of maintaining a society containing a great variety of diverse, independent, voluntary institutions—in both economic and non-economic spheres of activity. Seen in that light, the concern with the future of our economic system is a reflection of the more basic desire to maintain and strengthen the free and voluntary society of which the economy is a vital but only a constituent part. Political freedom requires economic freedom. We foster one as we pursue the other.

For corroboration of that last point, just take a globe of the planet and spin it. By and large, you will find that the nations with a large and strong private sector are the countries with relatively free political institutions. In striking contrast, those nations where the state dominates the economy tend to be the totalitarian societies. That is hardly coincidence.

23

Arms and the American Economy

This widely-cited article showed the close relationship between the military establishment and the major military contractors. It helped to generate pressure to reduce the bureaucratic approach to military procurement and thus to reduce the close relationship between government and the private contractors.

The close, continuing relationship between the military establishment and the major companies serving the military market is changing the nature of both the public sector of the American economy and a large branch of American industry. To a substantial degree, the government is taking on the traditional role of the private entrepreneur while the companies are becoming less like other corporations and acquiring much of the characteristics of a government agency or arsenal. In a sense, the close, continuing relationship between the Department of Defense and its major suppliers is resulting in a convergence between the two, which is blurring and reducing much of the distinction between public and private activities in an important branch of the American economy.

This domestic convergence hypothesis needs to be distinguished from other analyses of the interaction between government and private industry. The analysis presented here does not evoke the conspiratorial flavor of so much of the discussions of a "military-industrial complex." Also, it is narrower than the contention of Professor John Kenneth Galbraith that modern large corporations are becoming part of the governmental administrative complex. To the contrary, an attempt is made below to demonstrate that the convergence phenomenon here described is limited to one branch of American industry. It will also be shown that the government-oriented corporation is becoming measurably different from large American business firms that primarily cater to industrial and consumer markets.

Public Assumption of Private Decision Making

In its long-term dealings with its major suppliers, the Department of Defense gradually has taken over directly or indirectly many of the decision-making functions which are normally the prerogatives of business management. Three aspects of this public assumption of, or active participation in, private decision making can be identified: the choice of which prod-

Source: Murray L. Weidenbaum, "Arms and the American Economy," *American Economic Review,* May 1968.

ucts the firm is to produce, the source of capital funds, and the internal operation of the firm. This government involvement in private industry arises in the case of the unique and large-scale nature of military weapon system procurement. It hardly characterizes the purchases of standard items by government agencies through fixed-price contracts awarded via sealed-bid competition.

By awarding massive contracts for research and development (R& D), the Department of Defense has come to strongly influence or determine which new products its contractors will design and produce. In the commercial economy, in contrast, research and development costs normally are only recovered to the extent that they result in the sale of profitable products. Hence, the decisions to embark upon a product research and development program are made by the sellers, who bear the risk of not recovering their technological investment.

Defense contractors sponsor and fund some of their own R&D effort, but the bulk is performed under government contract. Much, if not most, of the remainder is charged as allowable overhead on their government contracts, having met the approval of military reviewing officials. In good measure, military product design and development is not an intermediate good but an end product that the contractor produces for sale to the government under contracts awarded before the R&D is undertaken.

The military establishment also uses its vast financial resources to supply the bulk of the plant and equipment used by its major contractors and also a major part of the working capital that they require. Billions of dollars of outstanding "progress" payments are held by defense contractors. Military procurement regulations provide specific disincentives for the use of private working capital. Progress payments equal to 70-80 percent of the costs incurred on government contracts generally are provided without interest charge to the contractor. In contrast, should these companies decide to rely on private sources for working capital, the interest payments may not be charged to the contract and, hence, must come out of profits. Presumably, this arrangement results in smaller total cost to the government because of the lower interest rates paid by the U.S. Treasury on the funds that it borrows. However, the result also is to increase the extent to which public rather than private capital finances the operations of defense contractors. Hence, the financial stake that the military establishment has in the performance of its contractors is increased further.

The most pervasive way in which the Department of Defense assumes the management decision-making functions of its contractors is through the procurement legislation and regulations governing the contracts it awards, The Armed Services Procurement Regulation requires military suppliers to accept on a "take it or leave it" basis many standard clauses in government contracts which give the military contracting and surveillance officers numerous powers over the internal operations of these companies. These unilaterally determined grants of authority vary from matters of substance to items so minor that they border on the ludicrous. These restrictions generally have been imposed to prevent specific abuses which may arise. However, the cumulative and long-term impacts on company initiative and entrepreneurship are rarely considered. These restrictions represent a form of government regulation via its monopsonistic power rather than through the traditional independent regulatory agency.

The authority given to the customer includes power to review and veto decisions as to which activities to perform in-house and which to subcontract, which firms to use as subcontractors, which products to buy domestically rather than to import, what internal financial reporting systems to establish, what type of industrial engineering and planning system to utilize, what minimum as well as average wage rates to pay, how much overtime work to authorize, and so forth. An example of the more minor matters covered in the detailed and voluminous military procurement regulations is the prescription that the safety rules followed in the offices and factories of the contractors must be consistent with the latest edition of the Corps of Engineers safety manual.

The whole philosophy of close government review of the internal operations of its contractors is so deeply imbedded that insertion of statements such as the following in the Armed Services Procurement Regulation evoke no public or industry reaction: "Although the Government does not expect to participate in every management decision, it may reserve the right to review the contractor's management efforts, including the proposed make-or-buy program."

Cost-plus contracting by the military establishment has shifted much of the risk bearing from the industrial seller to the governmental buyer. Although the use of fixed price contracts has increased in recent years, a major share of defense contracts still is on a cost reimbursement basis. So long as this remains the case, the government determines which items of cost are "allowable" as charges to the contract and hence, for most practical purposes, which activities and which items of expenditure the company can undertake (disallowed costs directly reduce company profits).

The industry-military relationship is a dynamic one. Numerous changes are made in military procurement regulations in the course of a year, many of them extending the role of the military in the internal operations of the contractors. The list of unallowable costs of defense contractors now includes technical displays, unapproved overtime, business conferences, bid and proposal expense, employee moving expense, foreign office expense, operation of executive airplanes, New York purchase tax, personal property tax, patents expense, and public relations.

The procurement rules are very specific. In contracts for aircraft tires, tubes, and recapping, the contractor must purchase an amount of rubber from the government's stockpile equal to at least 50 percent of the value of the contract. Military contractors must buy all of their jewel bearings from the government-owned Turtle Mountain Bearing Plant at Rolla, North Dakota (such tie-in contracts, if made between two private firms, would run afoul of the antitrust laws). Help-wanted advertising is no longer an allowable cost if it is in color. Advertising for employees, if it is to be an allowable cost, must be authorized in advance.

Long- Term Impacts on the Private Sector

The close, continuing relationship of the major, specialized military contractors to the governmental establishment is resulting in long-term structural impacts on this segment of private industry. Numerous specific indications are available of the limited entrepreneurial actions of the government-oriented corporations. The dependence of the shipbuilding companies on government contracts and subsidies is well known. It has resulted in that industry's failure to undertake new product development on its own or otherwise effectively to compete in the open world market.

Similarly, the aircraft industry generally has made only half-hearted efforts to utilize its much vaunted engineering and systems analysis capability to penetrate commercial markets. Most of these attempts have been on a very small scale or were abandoned when substantial private risk capital was required. During defense cutbacks, these companies reacted passively to the developments, mainly curtailing their operations and waiting for government proposals to bid on civilian agency work on a cost-plus basis.

Interestingly enough, the major exception to this lack of entrepreneurship and willingness to bear risks in commercial markets is the Boeing Company, which has not won a major military competition since 1958. During the past decade, that company has invested several hundred million dollars of its own funds in commercial aircraft development, with considerable success.

The long-term impact of the governmental relationship on the private contractors may be examined by comparing the major defense companies with large industrial corporations of approximately similar size. The comparison indicates that the government-oriented companies possess important, measurable characteristics that differ from those of commercially oriented industrial corporations. These differences have been increasing in recent years. This would seem to support the contention that it is the military contractors who are drawing closer to the government and not, as Professor Galbraith contends, large corporations as a whole.

The following six companies were selected because their contracts from the Department of Defense and the National Aeronautics and Space Administration were in excess of three-quarters of their total sales volume in 1965: North American Aviation, Lockheed Aircraft, General Dynamics, McDonnell, Grumman Aircraft, and Thiokol Chemical. Hence, these companies are representative of the government-oriented corporation. In many other cases, necessary data on large defense contractors are lacking because the organizations are divisions of corporate conglomerates that only release financial data on the total company (e.g., Martin-Marietta, Litton Industries, and Textron).

Each of six companies in a civilian-oriented industry was chose simply on the basis of similarity of sales volume in 1965 between it and one of the companies in the defense/space sample. (Generally, they were adjacent firms on the *Fortune* list of the 500 largest industrial corporations.) Each group reported an aggregate sales volume of $7.3 billion. The general industry sample contained the following business firms: National Dairy Products, Firestone Tire, General Foods, Alcoa, Colgate-Palmolive, and Purex.

The two samples were compared, for the years 1962-65, also for the period 1952-55, on the basis of financial characteristics, stockholder factors, and capital structure. A span of years was chosen in each case to reduce the effect of erratic movements in individual years.

The differences were clear. Defense companies operate on much smaller after-tax profit margins than do typical industrial corporations. As a result of the large amounts of government-supplied capital, which are not reflected on the books, the defense contractors report far higher rates of capital turnover (i.e., dollars of sales per dollar of net worth). The higher turnover rates for defense companies more than offset the lower profit margins. Hence, their return on net worth (net profits as a percent of stockholders' investment) is considerably higher.

The differences between the defense firms and nondefense firms widened over the past decade. The sales margins of the defense firms were closer to the general industrial sample during the earlier period than during the more recent years. The same changes are noticeable for capital turnover and return on investment.

Despite the greater relative profitability, the evaluation by the stock market of the government-oriented corporations has been less favorable than of large business firms as a whole. This results, at least in part, from the inherent instability of the government market and the historical volatility of the fortunes of individual contractors. The relatively low payout ratio (the proportion of net income disbursed to stockholders in the form of cash dividends) may also have an adverse effect. Reflecting these factors, earnings of defense companies are more fully discounted, as shown by lower price/earnings multiples—10.9 versus 20.6 for the period 1962-65. The results for 1952- 55 were not substantially different.

Similar investor reluctance towards government-oriented corporations is evident in the bond market. Of the six firms in the general industry sample, during the period 1962-65, four were able to issue bonds with a rating of either A or Aa, one chose not to issue bonds at all, while the last placed its bonds privately. Out of the six companies in the defense sample, only one issued bonds in the market and these had a low rating of Ba-Baa. One of the firms placed its bonds privately. The results for 1952-55 were similar. These comparisons suggest that it is much easier for civilian-oriented firms to enter the bond market on favorable terms. It would be expected that this reflects the greater degree of risk imputed to bonds issued by defense firms.

An attempt to sum up the growing differences between government-oriented and commercially oriented corporations yields a paradox, but perhaps not an unexpected one. The close dependence of the government contractors on the volatile military customer results simultaneously in higher profitability and lower investor interest. The higher profitability arises mainly because of the free provision of working and fixed capital. The lower stock and bond market evaluation comes about, in part at least, because of the great volatility of military requirements and, hence, of the fortunes of individual contractors.

Another factor influencing investor attitudes may be the inability of these companies to operate successfully in commercial markets because of their orientation to government requirements. Certainly other large defense contractors—such as General Electric, RCA, Honeywell, Litton Industries, and AT& T—which receive the bulk of their sales from consumer and industrial markets encounter more favorable investor attitudes. With reference to the possibility of the disappearance of that line between the mature corporation and the state, the market at least seems to distinguish increasingly clearly between government-oriented and market-oriented corporations.

Some Policy Implications

Recent periods of defense cutbacks gave rise to demands for utilizing the research and development and systems management capabilities of military contractors in civilian public sector activities. Given another reduction in military spending in the future, such action may be an effective short-term means of preventing unemployment in defense areas. However, as a matter of long-term public policy, would it be wise for the nation to expand the use of that branch of industry which increasingly develops the characteristics and mentality of a government arsenal? To a considerable degree, the major defense companies rarely risk large amounts of their own resources in new undertakings, but primarily respond to the initiatives of the governmental customer. This course of action may be a valid profit-maximizing solution for these companies, but it hardly promotes the risk-bearing and entrepreneurship characteristic of private enterprise.

In encouraging these companies to expand into civilian government markets, are we in the process of setting up a civilian counterpart of what has been labeled, or perhaps mislabeled, a "military-industrial complex"? Or should more emphasis be given to the possibilities of encouraging, or at least not discouraging, the eventual movement of defense industry personnel, facilities, funds, and other resources to those other industries that are more accustomed to operating in a commercial business rather than government environment? Perhaps an added and unexpected benefit of arms reduction would be the opportunity to reduce this "seminationalized" branch of the American economy.

Even in extended cold war periods, the "convergence" tendencies of military contractors need to be held in check in order to maintain their present high rate of technological innovation which forms such a basic part of the nation's national security base. An important justification of the government-oriented corporation is that it is in a position most readily to undertake innovation. Yet innovation is likely to come forth only if there remains some risk of not innovating due to competitive pressures. Such pressures may come from existing military suppliers as well as from companies now oriented to commercial markets.

The optimal in the government-supplier relationship may be substantially short of either arsenalization or the informal contact of a free market. The desired result may be enough stability to assure technical competence but enough uncertainty to prod some mutual participation in the innovation process. In any event, some second thoughts may need to be given before the nation agrees to the almost uncritical demands for extending the use of the government-oriented corporation to other parts of the public sector.

24

Reforming Military Purchasing

This article continues the theme of the previous selection. The emphasis is on specific ways of reforming the defense-industry relationship so as to achieve national security objectives in a more cost-effective manner.

The continuing military power of the United States depends on a secure industrial base that can meet three key requirements. It must have the capability to supply current forces. It must have the ability to meet the needs of the military force structure in the future, and it must be able to design and produce new weapon systems.

The juxtaposition of declining military budgets and the continuing requirements of national security makes more urgent than ever the need to get more military output per dollar of cost. This article presents the case for achieving that objective by means of a fundamental overhaul of the process by which the defense establishment acquires weapon systems and other specialized equipment.

It is ironic that, during the 1980s when many federal departments and agencies focused on deregulation, the procurement rules of the defense establishment became more Byzantine in their complexity and increasingly burdensome to the companies designing and producing weapon systems. Although most studies of government regulation of business ignore this important sector, defense contractors (and major subcontractors) are subject to more detailed government control than any other branch of the American economy. Two retired senior officers describe the nature of military procurement succinctly:

> Although defense is not called a regulated industry, it is controlled by the government as though it were. All effort is controlled through congressional legislation and regulations such as the Federal Acquisition Regulation. . . . The defense buyer is in fact a regulator.

Because the military market is so completely subject to the changing needs of its one primary customer, relationships between buyer and seller differ fundamentally from those in civilian sectors of the economy. By its selection of contractors, the government controls who enters into and who leaves this market. It also determines the potential growth of these firms, and it is in a position to impose its ways of doing business on them and it does so.

Source: Murray Weidenbaum, "Acquisition Policy for a New Era," in Ethan Kapstein, ed., *Downsizing Defense* (Washington, DC: Congressional Quarterly, 1993).

The officials of the Department of Defense (DOD) make many decisions that are normally the responsibility of business management. In the words of one knowledgeable analyst, "private firms in the American defense industry are subject to public controls of unequalled scope and complexity."

Unlike other government involvement in private business, there is no separate regulatory commission. The most pervasive way in which the military establishment shares the management decision-making functions of its contractors is through procurement legislation and rules governing the awarding of contracts. These regulations require private suppliers to "take it or leave it" when it comes to standard clauses in their contracts that give the government sweeping surveillance and often veto power over the internal operations of these companies.

The authority assumed by the government customer is extremely wide-ranging, including power to review and veto a host of company decisions. Thus, when a business firm enters into a contract to produce a weapon system for the military, it takes on a quasi-public character. This is implicitly recognized by requiring the firm to conduct itself in many ways as a government agency.

Contrast the paperwork required of a major aircraft manufacturer for the development of a new military plane with that for the development of a jet airliner. The latter included the needs of both the airlines and the Federal Aviation Administration. The 400 pages of specifications required for the commercial market contrast with the 16,000 pages for the military. Likewise, the 250 separate commercial data submissions are modest compared with the 30,000 that the military need.

A series of widely publicized shortcomings in specific military procurements arose during the rapid buildup of the 1980s. Items such as hammers, toilet seats, and coffee makers were alleged to have been purchased for prices far exceeding those charged in the commercial marketplace (in most cases, careful analysis shows that the taxpayer was not "overcharged"). Nevertheless, the adverse publicity resulted in numerous changes in federal procurement policy, virtually all in the direction of tightening controls over contractors. Some examples provide an indication of the overall trend:

- The Pentagon has imposed higher administrative costs on defense contractors by virtue of more stringent government record-keeping requirements.
- Recent changes in the *Federal Acquisition Regulation* shift the burden of proof on the reasonableness of contractor costs from the government to the contractor.
- Frequent delays occur in awarding new contracts because of new procedures that give losing firms more opportunities to protest the awards. Many federal procurement offices now regularly extend their acquisition schedule to allow for the virtually predictable delays that result from contract protests.

- Contractors must fund a greater share of initial research and development (R&D) costs. They now share a substantial portion of development costs with the Pentagon, which means that they often incur a loss on these development contracts (in the past, R&D contracts were at times a minor source of profit).
- Contractors must pay for about one-half of their expenses for tooling and test equipment. In the past, these expenses were reimbursable under procurement contracts.

This bureaucratization of the defense acquisition process and resultant increase in overhead costs of government and contractors alike are in stark contrast to the downsizing and streamlining that have been occurring simultaneously in the civilian sector of American industry. Spurred on by foreign competition, companies in commercially oriented industries have chopped out layers of overhead, reduced internal reporting requirements, and given more discretion to operating managers. By doing so, they have lowered their costs and raised their productivity. There is a cogent lesson there for defense decision-makers.

Attempts at Reform

The Department of Defense (DOD) has tried repeatedly to reform the military procurement process. All sorts of efforts have been made over the years, ranging from introducing new purchasing concepts (such as total package procurement) to altering contractor incentives (with a variety of contractual forms). Unfortunately, by and large the past attempts have increased the paperwork flow and raised, rather than lowered, the overhead costs of producing goods and services for the military establishment.

For example, several years ago the three major federal procurement agencies—the General Services Administration, NASA, and the DOD—replaced their individual procurement guides with a jointly issued *Federal Acquisition Regulation (FAR)*. This one "regulation," it turns out, is a massive two-volume handbook. Although *FAR* limits each of the procurement agencies to issuing only those additional procurement instructions necessary to implement *FAR* in their own agency, inevitably the Pentagon bureaucrats took full advantage of that loophole. The DoD's *FAR* supplement (known as *Defense Acquisition Regulation,* or *DAR*) is even larger than *FAR. DAR* contains seventy parts, twelve appendices, two manuals, and six supplements. Daunting in their own right, *FAR* and *DAR* are amplified by a massive body of directives on the part of each of the military services and operating commands. According to former Navy secretary John Lehman, Jr., existing legislation and case law governing Navy procurement alone occupy 1,152 linear feet of library shelf space.

Every serious examination of the military procurement system concludes that—even when it achieves its substantive objectives—it is excessively bureaucratic and needlessly costly. A panel of senior government and business officials convened by the Center for Strategic and International Studies concluded: "About 25 percent of the cost of research, development, and procurement of military products is wasted as a result of unnecessary oversight, auditing and regulation; program instability and poor estimates; excessive performance requirements; and overspecification of product and process in defense acquisition."

In its own way, the military acquisition establishment has tried to be responsive to criticisms about the complexity of its procurement system. For example, the *DAR* permits contracting officers to use simplified order forms, but it needs an eleven-line sentence to explain when the basic ordering agreement can be used:

> A basic ordering agreement may be used to expedite contracting if after a competitive solicitation of quotations or proposals from the maximum number of qualified sources, other than a solicitation accomplished by use of Standard Form 33, it is determined that the successful responsive offeror holds a basic ordering agreement, the terms of which are either identical to those of the solicitation or different in a way that could have no impact on price, quality or delivery, and if it is determined further that issuance of an order against the basic order agreement rather than preparation of a separate contract would not be prejudicial to the other offerors.

Not surprisingly, many contracting officers prefer to bypass the "simplified" alternative.

To sum up the lessons from previous acquisition reform efforts, new requirements and reviews are typically added to the existing bureaucratic routine. Little if any effort is made to scrape off the old paint and varnish before applying new layers. Thus, the size of the regulations, the number of officials with review power, the overhead cost imposed, and the length of time required by the entire process expand over time. Moreover, the ability of entrenched management to sandbag the reforms cannot be ignored. As we will see, reductions in their numbers and a basic change in their composition and outlook are vital.

Major Shortcomings of the Acquisition Process

The fundamental shortcomings of the military acquisition process are well known:
1. The congressional tendency to micromanage the specifics of defense decision-making
2. The excessive variety of socioeconomic (that is, nonmilitary) objectives superimposed on the process
3. The deficiencies of existing acquisition personnel
4. The shortcoming in the performance of defense contractors.

The Congressional Desire to Micromanage

Much of the procurement complexity and costs result from the tendency of congressional committees and individual members to get involved in operational details, often referred to as "micromanagement." Back in 1970, the Blue Ribbon Defense Panel reported the existence of forty separate statutes governing defense procurement in addition to the basic armed services procurement legislation. The statutes cover such detail as assignment and adjudication of claims, judicial review of agency contract decisions, performance bonds, labor standards, antikickback provisions, conflicts of interest, use of convict labor, and procurement of supplies made by prisoners and the blind.

Since 1970 the tendency for Congress to pass such legislation has accelerated. Each legislative enactment generates a wave of implementing regulations. Between 1983 and 1988 alone, Congress enacted sixteen "micromanagement" types of provisions that complicate the military procurement process. A sampling of these special provisions gives the flavor: Codifying and repeatedly revising the description of allowable costs under DOD contracts; establishing requirements for the use of prequalification procedures; setting rank and grade for competition advocates; establishing tours of duty for program managers; setting rules for allocating overhead to spare parts; directing the use of work measurement standards in various contracts; and establishing rules governing contract costs for special tooling.

Micromanagement is not the result of mere congressional whims. At times, the adoption of these special provisions reflects the loss of congressional confidence in the candor and cooperation of the Pentagon, especially in responding to legislative mandates with which it does not agree. With a higher level of mutual trust, much of the congressional second-guessing would not be necessary. But without that trust, all of the legislative mandates and restrictions are ultimately unsatisfying.

Much of the congressional interference results from the desire to please constituents who want some special favors. An example of a congressional "query" in behalf of special interests was the request for an examination of the reduction in defense procurement of fresh fruits and vegetables from New Jersey sources. It turns out that weather conditions were an important explanation as well as a shift in military preferences to fruits and vegetables that are grown in other states.

The Variety of Socioeconomic Provisions

A large number of extraneous socioeconomic provisions are included, usually by statute, in the procurement regulations. Many of the congressional "add-ons" are designed to shelter an industry from foreign competition (such as prohibiting imports of mooring and anchor chains). Some of the special provisions are advantageous to specific groups or interests (such as small businesses, the blind, labor surplus areas, Vietnam veterans, and residents of Alaska and Hawaii). Congress authorizes DOD to pay a 10 percent premium in order to achieve the goal of awarding 5 percent of procurement, R&D, and construction awards to minorities.

The socioeconomic provisions share one common characteristic: none are related to enhancing national security. On the contrary, they avoid the need to request a separate appropriation to help a favored group by burying the favor in the military procurement budget. In a report on the defense technology base, the Congressional Office of Technology Assessment (OTA) concluded that the defense acquisition system is "a major contributor" to the long delays in getting new technology into the field. There are formidable barriers to exploiting technology developed in the civilian sector. OTA noted that, "While Congress did not intend the system to be slow, cumbersome, and inefficient, laws passed to foster goals other than efficient procurement have made it so."

Although it is difficult to quantify the cost of meeting the numerous regulatory requirements imposed on military procurement, researchers at the RAND Corporation did identify influences that could be measured: the increase in the number of congressional staff who work on procurement issues; the increase in the restrictions that Congress adds to the annual defense authorization and appropriation bills; the increase in administrative obstacles that prevent acquisition personnel from accomplishing their program objectives in a timely and efficient manner. There was widespread frustration among project-level personnel who believe they could do their jobs more rapidly and at less cost with fewer controls.

However, the RAND researchers found almost no evidence that regulatory activity had affected the performance or quality of the final product, either favorably or adversely. Given the overall positive assessment of American weapon systems in the recent Gulf War, that assessment comes as no surprise. However, in view of the substantial time and resources devoted to meeting regulatory requirements, the case for a dose of deregulation or at least substantial regulatory reform seems compelling.

Deficiencies of Acquisition Personnel

Much of the verbosity and specificity of military procurement regulations is an attempt to deal with the lack of training, technical skills, and experience of procurement officers. The shortcomings of quality are thus overwhelmed by sheer quantity. Prior to recent cutbacks, over one-half million military and civilian personnel spent all or a substantial part of their workday on acquisition activities.

The turnover rate for key procurement managers is awesome. A General Accounting Office survey found that the average tenure of a military program manager (including experience as a deputy program manager) was slightly over two years. During the eight-to-twelve years of its development, a typical weapon system may have four or five different military officers in charge. Identifying these shortcomings is much easier than rectifying them. For example, it would take an act of Congress to permit the military establishment to do something that is standard for private business—to reimburse civilian personnel for courses taken to enhance their job skills.

To deal with the qualitative shortcomings of its procurement people, the Department of Defense has inserted into the *DAR* pages and pages of the most naive and elementary language. For example, one section instructs acquisition personnel that, "Profit, generally, is the basic motive of business enterprise." We must wonder how people who need to be reminded about such a fundamental matter are assigned to the procurement function. Then, another section informs the reader that "In certain instances, a sound decision may be possible after a simple review. . . . Under other circumstances, a more comprehensive review and analysis will be required." The inclusion of such basics in the regulation itself is very revealing as to the presumed intelligence of the people who are given purchasing responsibility.

Another shortcoming of the traditional method of staffing the military procurement function is that the bureaucratic routine attracts bureaucratically oriented people. The result is that many forward-looking reforms are lost in the paperwork maze. For example, the current bureaucratic interpretation of the Truth in Negotiations Act virtually guarantees a vast paper-shuffling exercise every time a contract is awarded. The law recognizes that competition is the best assurance that the government will pay fair and reasonable prices. When adequate price competition is found to exist, there is no statutory requirement for the submission of the elaborate cost and pricing data otherwise required.

However, unless the contract was awarded exclusively on the basis of the lowest evaluated price, the *FAR* says that adequate price competition does not exist and all the special paperwork must be filled out. Even when adequate price competition is found to exist, the contractor must perform "cost realism analysis," which is almost as involved as in the uncompetitive case. Theoretically, then, so long as price is a substantial factor in the evaluation of competing proposals, the spirit of the law can be fully achieved by waiving the special paperwork requirements. But the procurement officials who write the implementing rules seem determined to maintain the status quo with all its complexity and overhead burden.

The military's contracting personnel are badly outranked by their industry counterparts in terms of experience and training. As a response, Congress and the Defense Department have instituted procedural "safeguards" and intricate internal review processes. Authority (mainly to say no) is dispersed widely among program managers, contract officers, senior military executives, auditors, and inspectors. Accountability is greatly diluted in the process.

Approximately forty line and staff officials have veto power over some part of the efforts of the program managers. One can insist that they use certain designated military specifications in awarding the contracts. Another can impose specific reliability requirements. Yet another can impose small business and minority business requirements. None of these staff people has responsibility for the success of the program. Program managers typically spend 50-70 percent of their time "selling" or "defending" their programs at higher levels. Some report that they have to go to forty meetings to get any significant decisions made on a single program.

In those cases where good people are attracted to military procurement work, the bureaucratic approach embedded in *DAR* and other procurement regulations diminishes their effectiveness—and encourages them to leave for more challenging assignments. A RAND report on this subject concluded that the imposition of detailed requirements erodes the program manager's authority and reduces the ability to conduct the procurement program efficiently. That conclusion should come as no surprise to anyone familiar with the details of the military acquisition process.

Shortcomings of Defense Contractors

Perhaps the most worrisome aspect of the expansion of procurement detail is the impact on the contractors. The cumulative effect of imposing an almost endless array of bureaucratic requirements on private enterprises that provide goods and services to the military establishment is to force them to adopt the thought processes of government arsenals. In the process, we lose the benefits of risk taking, initiative, and innovation, the key reasons for using private business in the first case.

As a result, contractors insulate their defense work from their mainstream commercial activities. Such action minimizes criticism by government auditors of the allocation of overhead costs and so forth. It also ensures that the commercial divisions will not be "contaminated" by the bureaucratic environment of the military procurement process and thus forget what they know about cost control and fast market response. However, there is an adverse byproduct of this separation of military and commercial work: the insulation of the military activity makes it less likely that the government will benefit from the rapid rate of technological innovation occurring in the companies' commercial research laboratories.

Companies go to great lengths to avoid the burdens of the military procurement system: one electronics company has two divisions, one producing defense components and the other making microchips for civilian markets. When the defense division needs some microchips, the civilian division gives the chips to it without charge—in order to avoid the oversight and regulatory burdens associated with defense business. The chips are worth about $200 each.

Approaches to Reform

Both sides of the military procurement relationship—government and industry—need to make a series of difficult adjustments to accord with the basic changes taking place in the military market. These new fundamentals include:

- fewer new weapon systems,
- reduced likelihood of a given system moving from R&D to production,

- reduced volumes of production,
- fewer companies competing for defense business, and
- greater intensity of competition among those that remain in the military market.

Any effort to overhaul military procurement should take account of the difference between the governmental (or legal) approach and the business (or economic) approach. The prevailing government/legal attitude is to regulate the process so closely that no errors occur, no matter how expensive the regulatory procedure becomes. Business executives and economists, in contrast, look at costs as well as benefits of rule-making. As noted by defense executive Jacques Gansler, "Trying to prevent almost all mistakes would be more efficient." The practical problem that arises in the public arena is that, in writing 15 million new contracts each year, the Department of Defense would commit over 1500 errors even if its actions were 99.99 percent perfect.

The Office of Technology Assessment reports that, because making errors in accounting on government contracts can lead to criminal charges against business executives, defense managers devote inordinate amounts of effort to matters of no economic consequence. Under the circumstances, it will take at least three major types of changes to truly reform military procurement: streamlining the regulations; upgrading the caliber of who administers the regulations; and, improving government-industry relationships.

Streamlining the Regulations

A sweeping overhaul of the entire government procurement process is the most effective remedy for the continuing proliferation of bureaucratic detail and trivia. That means eliminating all the socioeconomic provisions and the restrictive "micromanagement" provisions as well. Simplifying the entire military procurement procedure is also the most direct way of responding to the perennial complaints of small firms that they are scared away from defense work because of the complexity of the procurement process. Radically streamlined acquisition would also be a constructive response to the substantial erosion of the defense subcontractor and supplier base.

Comprehensive reform requires dividing military procurement into two broad categories: items that can be purchased readily from the private sector, and the acquisition of weapon systems. The great majority of all procurement actions—as well as a substantial proportion of the dollar volume of military contracting—covers equipment readily available from civilian-oriented companies. These items should be purchased in the same manner that civilian agencies do their buying: via sealed bids, responding to standard commercial, rather than detailed military specifications.

Some experts urge that only performance characteristics should be specified, with the contractor having discretion on the details of the design. Gansler would go further. He advocates eliminating the wall that now segregates the military and civilian industrial sectors, to allow the emergence of a single, multi-purpose industrial base. To do so, he would relax Pentagon-unique accounting standards and contract requirements, as well as ease military specifications.

For the second category—weapons acquisition—selection should be made on the basis of prototypes produced by two or more competing firms. Mounds of paperwork are not an adequate substitute. The winner of the "fly-off" competition should receive all or at least the majority of the production business. Where it is economical to do so, the runner up would get a smaller contract, but large enough to keep its production line going. After the first production batch from each of the two contractors, the military service could alter the proportion awarded to each. Thus, competition would continue throughout the production process.

The only consistently reliable means of getting the information needed to evaluate a proposed military system is to build prototypes and to test them ("fly before you buy"). Given the repeated shortcomings that have resulted from rushing weapon systems to premature production, we can brush aside the counterargument that prototypes are costly and time-consuming to build.

Under the present approach to military budgeting, the reluctance to subject a new weapon system to rigorous operational testing prior to making the production decision is not entirely irrational. It reflects the distorted incentives provided by "stop-and-go" military cycles. Given the vagaries of military appropriation practices, the military service developing a new weapon system often is willing to rush it into production without adequate testing in order to avoid a possible new wave of budget austerity which would result in cutting back or eliminating the project. A system already in production is less likely to fall to the budget axe than one in the R&D stage. The basic change needed is to lower the peaks and raise the valleys in military spending.

Upgrading Acquisition Personnel

Virtually everyone who has examined the military procurement process has focused on the crucial role of the people who award and administer contracts. The caliber of procurement officials must be raised, and also the authority of the manager of each weapon system must be increased commensurate with the responsibility of the job. The Minuteman and Polaris strategic missile programs are often cited as examples of good acquisition practice. In both cases, small teams of highly competent people were given the responsibility and the authority to do the job and, to a considerable degree, they were left alone.

Managers of the development and production efforts of new weapon systems have limited authority and few tools to manage their programs. They often function as little more than briefing specialists and marketing representatives, spending much of their time seeking additional funds and continued support for their programs. At least some of the officers assigned to supervise weapon production should be persons experienced in industrial management. They should also possess the authority needed to accomplish their jobs, be well compensated, and be accountable for the results.

It is essential to improve the training of the officers responsible for making multimillion (often billion) dollar decisions. The notion of upgrading the personnel assigned to the staff function of acquisition, however, flies in the face of the traditional focus of the military establishment on line management and combat responsibilities. Nevertheless, the viewpoint of the modern military officer needs to be broadened substantially in order to carry out the multifaceted role of conducting national security programs in a rapidly changing, high-tech, global environment.

However, this is more than a matter of education and training, important as those factors are. The cumbersome staffing structure of the military procurement process must also be overhauled and streamlined. A substantial reduction should be made in the total number of acquisition personnel, bringing it closer to the levels of comparable commercial business. Military program managers are usually separated from the undersecretary of defense for acquisition by five or six administrative levels. Each layer demands a right to review all progress reports and major proposals for change. Some of these layers have an extensive horizontal structure, so that the views of several different officers must be accommodated in order to pass through a particular layer or "gate."

The federal government should take a leaf out of the book of private business experience. Many large companies have gone through a painful downsizing in the course of which they have changed entrenched institutional cultures, enhanced decision-making, and stimulated innovation. The payoffs in terms of cost and efficiency have been substantial.

Improving Government-Contractor Relationships

The truly serious problems arise in buying items that are so advanced that they do not exist at the time of purchase—new generations of aircraft, missiles, space vehicles, and communication equipment. Ideally, the award should go to the company that will provide the optimum combination of high quality, low cost, timely delivery, and ready maintainability. However, it is difficult to ascertain those qualities ahead of time. The answer is not to award the development and production work to contractors who want the business so badly that they will underestimate cost substantially. Nor is it a bargain to go with a low-cost producer who will sacrifice quality, time, and readiness in order to minimize price. There is a way out of this dilemma.

In making the initial award on a new weapon system, military contracting officers should be required to take more fully into account the bidder's past record on defense work. The company's track record may be the best indication of future performance. Focusing on actual accomplishment also provides a powerful incentive for improving performance.

Contract forms should be revised to provide larger profits for successful technical and cost performance and, conversely, more severe penalties for a poor showing. Total earnings on defense work would not necessarily rise, but individual company earnings might shift substantially. This proposal requires considerable forbearance on the part of Congress and of citizens generally. A contractor who has performed very well should not be criticized for receiving "unconscionable" profits. Nor should the company that does poorly be bailed out.

Under the "fly before you buy" policy of former deputy defense secretary David Packard, competing contractors were required to build and thoroughly test working prototypes before the major production contracts were awarded. This approach yielded the F-16 fighter and A-10 attack plane, two of the most successful procurement projects of the postwar era in terms of both performance and cost. Unfortunately, Packard's approach was largely abandoned when he left.

Simultaneously, some of the "reforms" of the military procurement process instituted in the 1980s should be reversed. Military R&D contracts should not be viewed as "loss leaders" on the part of defense contractors hungry for future business. The DOD should pay for what it gets. Trying to shift the impact of the defense budget cuts to the contractors by financially squeezing them is not an effective substitute for just buying less.

Substantial excess capacity coupled with weak finances characterize the major defense contractors. Downsizing will enhance efficiency and make the survival of the key firms in the industry more likely. Mergers and consolidations will reduce the current number of players. Some of the financially weaker firms may be acquired by civilian-oriented companies. A smaller group of stronger firms will improve the long-term position of the defense industry in a post-cold-war environment.

Conclusion

More efficient and less burdensome acquisition of weapon systems can help the nation reach national security objectives with smaller military budgets. Maintaining a stable and predictable level of military acquisition is the most powerful incentive to greater efficiency in defense development and procurement activities. It obviates the necessity for individual services to move rapidly from development to production in an effort to protect a given weapon system from the budgetary knife.

Greater efficiency in defense spending will also generate several indirect but powerful benefits. Streamlining military procurement will remove many of the current roadblocks that inhibit the interchange of scientific and technological advances between military and civilian producers. Moreover, reducing the bureaucratic burdens imposed on government contractors will bring down their overhead cost structures and also enable them to compete more effectively in commercial markets.

25

Conversion and the Future
of Defense Contractors

A perennial question facing the defense industry following a reduction in military budgets is whether to attempt to diversify into civilian markets. This article, based on historical experience, concludes that such attempts at "conversion" are often doomed to failure.

Following the end of the Gulf War, the major defense companies are at a fork in the road. Do they take the path urged by many to convert to civilian production the excess capacity made available because of lower military budgets and thus obtain a civilian pay-off on the massive national investment in defense technology? Or do they take the tough-minded business approach of streamlining and slimming down from their current peaks?

The conversion approach has a great deal of appeal. It claims the benefit of keeping in place the jobs of defense workers who otherwise face extended unemployment. The cutback alternative, in contrast, smacks of austerity. It is designed to maintain the financial health of the firms as they reduce excess capacity of labor and capital and adjust to a very different set of market opportunities. There is no need to debate the conversion and cutback alternatives in the abstract. There is a substantial history of defense contractors trying to weather defense cutbacks via converting—or to use the more business-like term, "diversifying"—into civilian markets.

Conversion Experiences

Ever since the end of the Second World War, defense contractors have been trying to use their special talents in other areas of the economy. They have been extremely successful in diversifying into several large but very narrowly defined markets. For example, the expansion from aircraft to missiles and space vehicles was a natural but noteworthy progression. Because it happened without a great degree of economic disruption, few appreciate the tremendous transformation of the airframe manufacturers into aerospace designers and producers. Several large aerospace companies have also devel-

Source: Murray Weidenbaum, "Conversion and the Future Direction of Defense Contractors," in Jurgen Brauer and Manas Chatterji, eds., *Economic Issues of Disarmament* (New York: Macmillan, 1993).

oped and manufactured substantial numbers of civilian passenger aircraft although, except for Boeing, profitability has been illusive.

The numerous attempts on the part of the larger, specialized defense contractors to penetrate civilian non-aerospace markets have not met with similar success. Their failed attempts literally range from canoes to computers to coffins. A comprehensive study sponsored by the U.S. Arms Control and Disarmament Agency (ACDA) concluded, "There is a discouraging history of failure in commercial diversification efforts by defense firms." According to ACDA, the profitability of non-defense, non-aerospace diversification efforts is usually below that experienced in defense.

The reasons for these conclusions are numerous. The Battelle Memorial Institute reports that, in order to be cost-effective, defense plants have been designed with a single product or production process in mind: "Therefore, by their very nature, these production facilities do not easily lend themselves to reuse."

Most of the diversification ventures outside the defense/aerospace markets have been abandoned or sold off. The remainder generally operate at marginal levels. These negative experiences have been so frequent—and many of them have so drained the companies—that they now constitute a major obstacle to further diversification efforts. A survey of defense firms by the Center for Strategic and International Studies (CSIS) reported that a majority believe a reorientation to civilian production is "neither feasible nor desirable."

Nevertheless efforts by some defense contractors to enter civilian, non-aerospace markets continue. In 1983, Grumman introduced the Kubvan, hoping to open a new market for aluminum truck bodies. It abandoned the effort two years later. It sold its solar energy division in 1985 and Pearson Yacht in 1986. Another major military supplier, McDonnell Douglas, also experienced hard knocks on the road to commercial diversification. In 1983, the company purchased Computer Sharing Services with the objective of making its information service group a major segment of the corporation. After losing $333 million in 1989, the company reduced the commercial part of the information systems operation and in 1990 it sold its computer maintenance and hardware distribution operation.

Likewise Boeing reported a cumulative deficit in its non-aerospace, non-government sales over the 1980s. It had entered the mass transit business to offset the decline in its helicopter business. After encountering much grief in dealing with the Department of Transportation, several large cities and union restrictions, it left the business. At its peak, Boeing's transit production employed only 550 workers, compared to 9,000 employees laid off by its helicopter division.

Curtiss-Wright provides the most extreme example of the shortcomings of naive conversion efforts. This pioneering aviation firm—which built more aircraft during World War II than any other U.S. company—assumed that the military market would never recover from its post-World War II lows. The company diversified into a host of miscellaneous industrial product areas. Curtiss-Wright never achieved its previous heights. While its former competitors now enjoy annual sales of aircraft, missiles, and space vehicles measured in the billions of billions, the company's annual revenues from its assortment of parts and components are in the millions.

In 1989, General Dynamics announced that it had "decided to stick to the defense business" and pursue only those new programs for which the government need is "strong and valid." That statement can be appreciated by examining the accompanying financial report, which showed a substantial cumulative loss in the company's non-governmental programs over the previous eight years.

Why Did Diversification Go Sour?

A pertinent anecdote is told by Seymour Melman, a staunch advocate of "conversion" planning. He described the case of a defense firm attempting to produce a class of civilian vehicles. The chief engineer said that, since their people had previously been building vehicles with the speed of sound, designing and producing something that would move at 50 miles an hour would be like falling off a log. Melman reported, "They fell off."

A common set of themes arises from studying the diversification experiences of military contractors. The major defense companies are very special business organizations. They are very good at what they are set up to do—to design and produce state-of-the-art weapons—but to do so they differ from typical commercial companies in terms of technology, organizational structure, marketing and financing.

Compared with commercially oriented companies, U.S. defense firms have relatively low capitalization, little if any commercial marketing capabilities and limited experience in producing at high volume and low unit cost. Moreover, their administrative structure is geared to the unique reporting and control requirements of the governmental customer. Those defense firms that do operate in civilian markets maintain operationally separated, insulated divisions that have little contact with each other, merely reporting to the same top management.

In the CSIS survey cited earlier, 71 percent of the defense firms stated that the Pentagon's procurement policies make it difficult for defense firms to enter or flourish in civilian markets. Bolstered by in-depth interviews, CSIS concluded that the Department of Defense acquisition system is a major obstacle to civilian diversification, and that military production has evolved into a business culture quite distinct and closed off from normal commercial culture. CSIS quoted one industry representative as typical: "With this high overhead, together with the facilities, manpower, and systems oriented toward that type of work, it is extremely difficult to find civilian markets where we can be cost-competitive."

The lack of commercial marketing experience is another familiar refrain in defense industry circles. Grumman developed and tried to sell a minivan years before Chrysler popularized the vehicle. The project failed because of the lack of a distribution system. It is not hard to understand why company managements have become so reluctant to move from fields they have mastered into lines of business quite alien to them. Their lack of knowledge of non-defense markets is pervasive. It includes ignorance of products, production methods, advertising and distribution, financial arrangements, funding of research and development, contracting forms and the very nature of the private customer's demands.

Clearly, the type of company that can successfully design and build a new multibillion dollar ICBM network or space exploration system has a very different capability from that of the soap, steel, toy or other typical cost-conscious but low-technology company operating in the commercial economy. The point made here was underscored recently when the chief executive of Martin Marietta, a large and relatively successful defense contractor, was asked by the Russians how to convert a tank-producing facility into a refrigerator factory. His response: tear down the tank plant and build a new refrigerator factory.

The Future of Defense Contractors

The most likely outcome is a substantial decline in the overall volume of defense business for the 1990s, but with defense spending remaining high by historical standards. Such fluctuations in business opportunities are not unique to defense companies. Other sectors of the economy regularly adjust to market shifts as part of the normal workings of a private enterprise system.

The Major Prime Contractors

There is great variety among the major contractors and in their dependence on the military market. Many of the large aerospace companies—such as General Dynamics, Grumman, Lockheed, Martin Marietta, McDonnell Douglas, and Northrop—rely on the Department of Defense for most of their income. Some, notably General Dynamics, are widely diversified within the military market, producing aircraft, missiles, tanks and submarines. Others, such as Martin Marietta, have gained fairly secure niches within that market. Still others, such as McDonnell Douglas, have diversified to a significant degree into commercial aircraft work (but without attaining profitability). Most of these companies should be able to weather the storm, albeit not at their current volumes of sales and employment.

Companies like Grumman and Northrop, who are dependent on just a few weapon system contracts, are likely to be in for a difficult time, depending on the future of those specific military products. They are surely more vulnerable than the more diversified defense contractors and are responding accordingly. Northrop reduced its research and development effort by 46 percent in real terms between 1985 and 1989. Grumman's company-initiated R&D slipped by 78 percent during that period.

Because of the military's great dependence on the major defense prime contractors for designing and building key weapon systems, their survival as a group seems assured. Nevertheless, substantial excess capacity, coupled with weak finances, characterize this key segment of the defense industrial base.

Divisions of Civilian-Oriented Companies

In contrast, other major defense contractors look primarily to commercial markets for the bulk of their sales. Examples of large companies with important defense segments include Boeing, General Motors, Honeywell, Rockwell, Tenneco, Texas Instruments, Textron, and TRW.

These firms will benefit from the expansion of civilian markets, especially if macroeconomic policy succeeds in maintaining high aggregate levels of economic activity. Because their contracts with the Pentagon are generally less profitable than their commercial sales, some of these companies will respond to shrinking military markets by phasing out defense business or trying to sell their defense segments.

Smaller Contractors and Subcontractors

Less attention is usually given to the very large array of small business, some of which are prime contractors, and the far greater number that are subcontractors to the large firms. Some of them will be hurt in the defense transition, especially as large prime contractors pull business back into the parent company. Many of the smaller firms tend to be more capable of dual military-commercial work than the larger and often more muscle-bound prime contractors. In quite a few cases they abandoned the military market during the 1980s in favor of less regulated and more profitable commercial work.

Facing Common Problems

How should defense contractors react to the current and impending reductions in the military market? The politically popular alternative is to tell them to convert their operations to other pursuits. But that flies in the face of experience, especially for the larger firms. Seasoned industry executives show a more chastened and informed view. Stanley Pace, retired chief executive of General Dynamics, says, "We've all come from smaller companies. We can all go back to being smaller companies." Similar sentiments are voiced by Malcolm Currie, chairman of Hughes Aircraft: "The defense industry does not have to be at its present peak size to be a very healthy, profitable, vital industry."

Many contractors are laboring under heavy indebtedness. The ten companies making up Standard & Poor's aerospace index more than doubled the ratio of their long-term debt to shareholder equity in recent years. There is considerable diversity among major defense contractors. At the beginning of 1990, Grumman's total debt equalled a painfully high 100 percent of its net worth and the ratio for Lockheed was 91 percent. In contrast, the debt-to-equity ratio for Boeing was a modest 5 percent.

A substantial reduction in size is the most sensible response to the greatly reduced market for military equipment that seems likely in the 1990s. The sooner the major contractors reduce their excess capacity—through restructuring, mergers, sales of assets, or simply closing down unneeded facilities—the greater will be their ability to withstand the competitive rigors of the new military marketplace. This prescription is not so radical as it may seem at first sight. Many mergers have occurred in the defense industry over the years: McDonnell Aircraft acquired Douglas Aircraft, Electric Boat merged with Consolidated Aviation to form General Dynamics. Rockwell International is the result of consolidating North American Aviation and Rockwell Standard. Boeing acquired Vertol Aircraft. United Technologies combined United Aircraft and a variety of civilian companies such as Carrier and Otis Elevator. In the 1980s, several aerospace prime contractors acquired smaller electronics firms and other key subcontractors.

The shape of things to come may be seen by looking across the Atlantic. The consolidation of defense firms is a clear trend in Western Europe. In recent years, Germany's Daimler-Benz acquired Messerschmitt-Bolkow-Blohm. Britain's Plessey was taken over by a combination of Germany's Siemens and the United Kingdom's General Electric Company.

Responding to Changes in the Military Market

Despite a temporary but modest resurgence of orders to support operation Desert Storm, the current outlook for defense companies is not very bright. In fact, many of them continued to lay off workers during that war. The great bulk of the direct costs of the Persian Gulf conflict were for military pay, personnel equipment for desert operations, fuel, ammunition and transport. The weapons used generally came out of existing inventories. Not all of these items will be replaced.

The defense business always has been subject to sharp swings in a special cyclical pattern unique to national security trends. A combination of continued budgetary pressures to cut defense expenditures and the greatly reduced tensions between the two military superpowers is resulting in a downward path for the military budget, especially the procurement of major weapon systems.

Barring an unforeseen expansion in the military budget, the major defense firms will look significantly different by the mid-1990s from what they do today. They will be down substantially from the peak size they attained in the 1980s and there may be fewer of them. But to the extent that they avoid wasteful and fruitless "conversion" attempts and simply streamline their operations, they can achieve that new condition with few bankruptcies or hostile takeovers and with reasonable levels of profits and jobs.

To the extent that unmet commercial needs exist, they are being adequately met by those commercially oriented companies which are highly experienced in those markets. An indication of the future of the defense industry was Lockheed's painful decision in early 1990 to close down its aircraft production at Burbank, the city where it was founded. Honeywell spun off its torpedo and munitions business to its shareholders after trying unsuccessfully to sell it to other companies. Emerson Electric also spun off its defense divisions. Varian Associates dropped most of its defense operations to focus on more profitable lines of electronic equipment.

On the positive side, defense contractors can be expected to continue to search for new applications of their existing product lines, especially in markets close to the ones they now dominate. Grumman is working on a $1 billion contract with the U.S. Postal Service to build over 99,000 delivery trucks. The Sikorsky Division of United Technologies produced $206 million of helicopters for the Coast Guard for intercepting drug smugglers. Lockheed sold two radar planes to the Customs Service for $58 million. Boeing has sold some of its Vertol helicopters to oil companies to service offshore drilling platforms.

Also Martin Marietta won a $900 million contract from the Federal Aviation Administration to help overhaul the nation's air traffic control system. In the aggregate, however, these close civilian applications of military products are a minor fraction of the government market. The $1 billion being spent annually for drug interdiction equipment is dwarfed by the $120 billion allocation each year to the development and acquisition of weapon systems. Moreover, it is too soon to say whether these new diversification efforts will be any more successful financially than the poor record of earlier attempts.

Two Different Approaches

Defense companies can choose between two different models of corporate behavior in responding to large cutbacks in the military budget. To simplify, let us call these the Boeing and Grumman approaches. When faced with a very large decline in the orders for its basic aerospace product line back in 1971, Boeing took the painful actions required to reduce the size of the company substantially. Little effort was made to diversify into new markets. Over one-half of the entire workforce was laid off. One wag rented a billboard for a memorable message, "The last one out of Seattle, please turn off the lights." Boeing's cutbacks were painful, extending to experienced engineers and skilled workers with considerable seniority, but the reduction in size left the company in a strong enough financial position to lead the next upturn in commercial aircraft sales and production. The result is a world-class corporation with a record high workforce.

Grumman, in contrast, followed the advice of those advocating "conversion" of the defense industry. It invested much of its resources in non-aerospace diversification efforts. The result has been unsuccessful, in the process weakening Grumman's basic financial condition. To add the proverbial insult to injury, it did so without achieving the job creation objective that motivates the conversion approach. Subsequently, Grumman was acquired by another defense contractor, Northrop.

It is ironic that the strongest support for the conversion of defense companies comes from those who had most strongly attacked the wasteful cost-plus operating environment of the "military-industrial complex." It should be expected that they would welcome the opportunity to move resources out of those companies to more efficiency-minded civilian-oriented enterprises.

As the Persian Gulf experience demonstrated, the United States still needs a powerful military establishment and a strong base of defense contractors— just not at their present size. Change is an essential aspect of a modern competitive economy. In the 1980s, the tremendous expansion of the aerospace and other defense companies required the attraction of people and capital from other parts of the economy, often to the discomfort and displeasure of those other companies and their managements, stockholders, and suppliers. We should not expect that type of movement always to be in one direction. Nor should we anticipate that the current ranking of defense contractors will prevail over the coming decade.

Some perspective will benefit both the defense companies and their employees, including those who fear that they will soon lose their jobs. They could do worse than cite the compelling words of a long-term critic of high levels of military spending: "Even if Fidel Castro shaved off his beard and became a fellow of the Heritage Foundation, we would still need the military-industrial complex for quite a while longer."

26

The U.S. Defense Industry After the Cold War

This article was written after the Cold War but before the terrorist attack of September 11, 2001. It provides some insight into national security planning during that period.

The U.S. defense industry is adjusting to the end of the Cold War more rapidly and effectively than expected. Many of the changes have been painful, but while today's national security decision-makers can count on the presence of a strong defense industrial base, that positive situation cannot be taken for granted in the years ahead. This article offers one economist's evaluation of the challenges facing the U.S. military establishment and the private sector companies on which it so strongly relies.

To judge the adequacy of the future defense industrial base in an uncertain post-Cold War environment is indeed a challenge. It requires dealing simultaneously with a set of paradoxical needs: to develop an international orientation at a time when the nation is focused on domestic concerns, to consider expanding military outlays in a period of budgetary austerity, and to worry about the adequacy of competition for the production of weapon systems when the economy is in the midst of a wave of mergers, consolidations, and downsizing.

This is a tall order, so let us begin with fundamentals. As an ex-defense industry planner, I instinctively start by examining the major threats to the national security. To state the obvious—although it may not be so clear to all Americans—the United States continues to exist in a dangerous world.

The Changing Threats to National Security

The danger to U.S. security is no longer an array of Soviet strategic systems aimed at this nation. Those missiles and bombers may not now be aimed at the United States, but—and this is a crucial "but"—the uncertain control over the technological and military resources developed by the Soviets is far from comforting. Developing countries in Asia have been acquiring a wide variety of high-performance aircraft, tanks, and missiles from the spin-off nations of the former Soviet Union. China is emerging—once again—as a great power, both economically and militarily. Credible sources report that China is buying Russian-made destroyers armed with supersonic missiles.

Simultaneously, large and indeterminate assortments of terrorists and other troublemakers are developing the capability to do considerable harm to the people of this country and its allies. Biological weapons, which are far easier to manufacture, transport, and disseminate than any other type weapon of

Source: Murray Weidenbaum, "The U.S. Defense Industry After the Cold War," *Orbis*, Fall 1997.

mass destruction, are of growing importance in the post-Soviet environment. Anthrax, for example, can be made by a biology student in a lab the size of a microbrewery. A small suitcase can contain enough to kill hundreds of thousands of people. As for the delivery platform, anthrax can be readily sprayed from a crop duster.

Between 1991 and 1996, about 5,000 employees left the Ukrainian Southern Machine Building Plant. That facility specializes in developing and producing SS-18 missiles. During the same period, the All Russian Scientific Research Institute of Experimental Physics, which specializes in nuclear warhead R&D, also lost about 5,000 people. All in all, the numbers of unemployed scientists and engineers in Russia and other parts of the former Soviet Union are at a record high. Reports like these are juxtaposed with news that Libyan and Iranian "university representatives" are stepping up efforts to recruit various categories of scientists.

Today's situation requires a response different than the Cold War norm— in terms of intelligence and communication, force structure, planning and strategy, and research, development, and production capability. But that does not necessarily mean a drastically lesser response. The United States needs to be able to deal with a new spectrum of conflicts, ranging from low-intensity warfare, to serious situations of global crime and lawlessness, to conventional confrontations between major national powers.

Viewed in this fight, the current practice of cutting back the military equipment and personnel required during the Cold War is not the end of the process of adjusting to a changed external environment. Rather, it is the beginning. At a time of tight budgeting, it is foolish to devote the limited funding to activities supported more by sentiment for the past than by the needs of the future. While military pork was never fully justified, the "opportunity cost" of such indulgences is higher than ever.

Maintaining an Adequate Industrial Base

The key task is to maintain the capacity to design and produce the military systems and forces needed to deal with future threats. The concern with the defense industrial base is far more than dealing with contract forms, cost controls, and business procedures. It is a matter of maintaining an appropriate and adequate military arsenal in a dangerous world. To restate the challenge facing defense planners: how, at a time of profound downsizing, do they keep the defense industry's innovative, managerial, and technological strength so vital to the national security? Downsizing in this regard is no euphemism for marginal reductions. The nation faces levels of funding for military research and development and procurement that, in real terms, are less than one-half of the 1985 numbers.

Compounding the loss of much of its traditional military market, the defense industry has had to fend off substantial political pressures to "convert" its resources to civilian markets. The conversion proposals that were successfully resisted, would have involved large government subsidies and an array of new controls. All this would have been aimed at forcing management to shift attention to civilian non-aircraft markets, which most of these companies have flubbed time and again. Such dissipation of their limited resources would have left these enterprises in weakened financial condition. It also would have threatened the technological strength of the defense industrial base.

Fortunately, the major defense companies followed a different and more sensible set of approaches, each of which reflected tough-minded and realistic management decisions. The result has been a financially stable set of primes. This has been true for most traditional defense contractors. Faced with the likelihood of being awarded fewer major contracts in the years ahead, many of the historic primes merged with or acquired some of their traditional rivals. Marriage partners included Lockheed and Martin, Northrop and Grumman, and Boeing and McDonnell Douglas.

These and other important defense contractors eliminated large divisions that were viable but not industry leaders. General Dynamics sold its space systems to Martin and its tactical aircraft business to Lockheed, while acquiring Bath Iron Works. General Motors's Hughes subsidiary is selling its defense electronics activity to Raytheon, which has acquired Texas Instruments's defense unit. Ford's Aerospace, IBM's Federal Systems Division, and Unisys's defense systems operations all went to Loral (on its way to Lockheed Martin). Northrop Grumman acquired Vought Aircraft and Westinghouse's defense work. Boeing bought the military segment of Rockwell (formerly North American Aviation).

Not surprisingly, some serious critics bemoan the prospect of declining competition for military contracts, predicting that a reduced number of competitors will bring about higher prices and poorer products. As a general proposition, competition is good, so more is better than less. However, that traditional approach to military procurement as well as to the antitrust laws is now passé. In the past two decades, the antitrust authorities allowed a host of mergers between active competitors in major civilian markets. In the 1960s and 1970s, comparable corporate marriages probably would have been challenged if not stopped.

Since 1980, many successful mergers have occurred among large banks (Chase Manhattan and Chemical), retail chains (May Department Stores and Associated Dry Goods), communications companies (Bell Atlantic and NYNEX), and manufacturers (Kimberly-Clark and Scott Paper). The civilian economy is much healthier for that consolidation. We have not witnessed the bursts of price increases that might have been expected to accompany the declines of measured competition. Rather, American consumers are enjoying the most benign inflation situation in many years—and with high and rising levels of employment.

The new approach to antitrust enforcement is not one of laxity. Instead it reflects the changing nature of the marketplace, especially the globalization of business and the rise of cross-border competition. The case of the military marketplace is similar but not identical. The emerging military market cannot be accurately described as a monopoly. Perhaps the most strikingly unique characteristic of defense procurement is that, even after the current merger wave, production capability will probably far exceed the procurement of defense products.

It is frightening to think of the consequences if the conventional antitrust approach had been applied to the recent wave of defense industry mergers and acquisitions. The result would have been a larger number of financially weak firms—a much greater concern to the national security than speculation about the creation of an American "Krupps." Most of these companies would have lacked the critical mass required to maintain high levels of research and development. Shareholders would not have been the only losers. The national security would have suffered an erosion in the quantity and likely the quality of defense technology.

The reality is that in the foreseeable future the Department of Defense will be ordering fewer weapon systems from a smaller group of companies than was usual during the Cold War era. There may well be a shift in formal emphasis from price competition back to design competition. But, below the surface, technological superiority has continued to be the key factor in the selection of prime contractors on major projects.

One helpful change in defense contracting procedures would be a substantial raise in the rates of return on research and development. Military R&D no longer can be viewed as a loss leader. Contractors must be given a greater incentive to devote their resources to R&D even in the absence of large production orders.

Overall, the defense industry is in far better shape than might have been expected from the loss of so much of its basic market. It is not surprising that, despite the massive cutbacks in U.S. defense spending, no plea was heard for taxpayer bailouts of faltering defense contractors. No Chrysler-style corporate loan guarantee program was even requested.

On the positive side, progress has been made in streamlining the Byzantine procurement process, resulting in reduced overhead costs for both buyers and sellers. The Federal Acquisition Streamlining Act of 1994, though far from a panacea, has been a constructive force, as have efforts to eliminate some military standards and to utilize more commercial practices.

Guidelines for the Future

The interaction between the requirements estimated by defense planners and the economizing efforts of budget officials is inherently a bargaining process. But the need for sound budgeting of defense is hardly a transient phenomenon. It was noted over a century ago by C. F. Bastable in his classic work on public finance:

> To maintain a due balance between the excessive demands of . . . military officials, and the undue reductions . . . sought by the advocates of economy, is one of the difficult tasks of the statesman.

27

How Much Defense Spending Can We Afford?

This article was written in early 2003, as the United States was preparing for war with Iraq. However, the conclusions are geared to a longer-run view of the role of defense in the American economy.

At a time when international tensions and budget deficits are both increasing rapidly, many Americans are raising a perennial question: How much military spending can the United States afford? The truth is that the country can afford to devote a substantially larger share of its resources to military purposes than it now does. That simple conclusion, however, is only the beginning of serious analysis of the subject.

A host of related questions quickly come to mind: What is the real cost of maintaining a large military establishment? Are there limits to the size of the military budget? How much military expenditure is enough? Does military spending stimulate or retard economic growth? What is the exact relation between spending on guns and on butter? Economic analysis can cast considerable light on these important issues and help us to formulate budget priorities. In the end, though, it is mainly political criteria that must determine how much of our resources we allocate to national defense, and a political question as to how much we are willing to spend.

The Real Costs

The costs of military spending are usually described in billions of dollars or as a percentage of the gross domestic product (GDP). These substantial costs, however, can more meaningfully be expressed in the number of men and women pulled away from civilian pursuits, the technology diverted to military ends, the many barrels of oil pumped from the earth, and the vast amount of space taken up by military equipment and debris. In short, the real costs of military activities are measured in human and natural resources and in the stocks of productive capital absorbed in producing, transporting, and using weapons and other military equipment. It is in this broader sense of opportunities lost that military spending should be considered.

Not only do we lose the opportunity for civilian use of goods and services, but we also lose the potential economic growth that these resources might have

Source: Murray Weidenbaum, "How Much Defense Can We Afford?" *The Public Interest*, Spring 2003.

brought about. For example, the production of a military capital asset such as a missile may entail the same amount of economic activity as the production of a civilian capital asset such as machinery for a truck factory. But while the former will eventually be exploded or buried, the latter would continue to enhance the nation's productive capacity over an extended period of time.

Thus, the real cost to society of allocating productive resources to military programs is not the money spent but the fact that these resources are not available for other purposes. In general, more missiles and tanks mean fewer new cars, homes, and schools.

This trade-off occurs no matter how the military budget is financed. If the economy is near full employment and the military outlays are financed through taxation or through borrowing from the private sector, part of these expenditures will be undertaken at the expense of private investment and part from reduced current consumption. A portion of the individual incomes and corporate profits given up in the form of higher taxes would otherwise have been saved and invested in new capital facilities. If, instead, the deficit is financed through increases in the money supply, the same shift in resources is achieved by inflation as the Department of Defense bids resources away from other uses. Thus, at least part of the burden of defense expenditures will be borne by future generations, since they are deprived of the returns on the curtailed private investment.

Yet in practice, not all resources used in military programs have been diverted from other uses. Some of these resources might not have been employed at all if it were not for the expansion of defense activities. Additionally, certain categories of defense activity, while absorbing resources that the civilian economy would use, replace similar goods and services that the civilian economy would otherwise have had to provide. The food, clothing, and shelter provided to members of the armed forces is a case in point. Even if we had no military establishment at all, a portion of the nation's output would still be devoted to feeding, clothing, and sheltering these people. Likewise, some of the military's research and development is part of the economy's investment in future growth and would probably be undertaken, at least in some form, in peacetime.

Guns or Butter?

Economists disagree as to whether increases in military spending come primarily out of resources that otherwise would be devoted to investment or to consumption. Because investment contributes far more directly to economic growth, the cost in terms of lost opportunities is higher when military spending is pulled from investment resources than when taken from money that would otherwise go toward current consumption—that is, for items that generate little or no future benefit.

The argument that military demands substantially crowd out private investment rests on the notion that a large and growing federal deficit forces the Treasury to expand its presence in capital markets. This puts upward pressure on interest rates. In turn, rising interest rates inhibit private capital formation. Intuitively, it would seem that the expanding deficits that so often accompany a military buildup contribute to rising interest rates. However, the empirical evidence on the causal relationship between budget deficits and interest rates is not very impressive. From 2001 to 2003, for example, military outlays and the budget deficit were both rising at a time when interest rates were declining or stable at a very low level. Clearly, other factors were the main determinants of interest rates at the time.

During World War II, when the U.S. economy was pushing very hard against the limits of productive capacity, the rapid expansion of military demand had a strong negative effect on civilian investment. Studies of more recent time periods show that, on the whole, defense spending has not drained investment funds from the civilian economy. The share of GDP devoted to nonmilitary investment has not suffered on account of a larger defense share; rather, it is primarily consumption that is affected. Bruce Russett of Yale University expressed these findings succinctly: "Private consumption has indeed been the largest alternative use of defense money. Guns do come partly at the expense of butter."

Evidence for that proposition is obtained by comparing the structure of the American economy of 1929 (as far back as comparable statistics are available) with that of the late 1990s. Two major changes took place during that seventy-year period: a rise in military outlays from 1 percent to about 4 percent of the GDP (down from a peak of over 10 percent in 1960-62) and a decline in the size of personal consumption expenditures from 73 percent to 67 percent of GDP. To some extent, this pattern reflects the unwillingness of the public to pay for wars by curtailing civilian spending by government. Financing the resultant budget deficit requires pulling resources out of the private sector, the largest part of which is personal consumption.

This pattern does not always hold. Although consumers bore the economic brunt of the Vietnam War, consumption was hardly affected by the Korean conflict. And while state and local government purchases declined relatively during World War II and the Korean War, they gained some ground during the Vietnam War. At times, the military effort may actually generate additional private investment to support the war production effort.

Such aggregate comparisons, however, obscure important qualitative differences. Many resources devoted to military programs are very specialized and not quickly transferable to or from civilian uses. Compared to the modest ratio of military spending to GDP, the military establishment accounts for far larger shares of the nation's capital formation, research and development, and high-tech production. A large reduction in, say, procurement of supersonic aircraft will not necessarily be offset—even after a reasonable adjustment period—by a comparable expansion in production of civilian high-tech goods and services.

The sectors of the economy producing equipment for the armed services are important but also narrow. The fundamental civilian orientation of this nation's economic activity can best be judged by examining the reactions that occur in that basic barometer of capitalism, the stock market. Marxist economists—who believe that military spending is necessary for the viability of the capitalistic system—might find the way in which the financial community reacted to recent wars very puzzling. As the *Financial Times* put it during the Vietnam War, "There is no greater nest of doves, outside the campuses, than Wall Street." Contrary to supposed precedent, stock prices rose on the mere rumor of peace: "Peace Reports Ignite Brisk Market Spurt," stated the headline of an article in the *Christian Science Monitor.* The article went on to report that hopes of peace in Vietnam had triggered a two-day buying spree in which the Dow Jones average rose in heavy trading.

More recent experience confirms this tendency. The poor performance of the stock market in the fall of 2002 was blamed, at least in part, on investor worries about a possible war with Iraq. On balance, military buildups may generate some positive response in financial markets, but the prospect of war itself does not.

Politics not Economics

There is no simple or generally agreed upon method of measuring the "burden" of military programs on the economy, nor is there any convenient indication of what, if any, economic ceiling exists for such programs. With certain qualifications related to the costs of lost opportunity in civilian production, available economic research tends to support the view that the United States can "afford" whatever level of military outlays it believes is necessary.

This conclusion is the result of studies begun in the 1950s and 1960s on the economics of disarmament, when military spending was a much larger share of the GDP than it is today. In 1958, the Committee for Economic Development concluded that the risk that military outlays of 15 percent or more of the GDP "will ruin the American way of life is slight indeed." Later analyses have also found that if necessary the American economy can sustain a higher level of such spending than was experienced during the Cold War. And a comprehensive review of a variety of econometric studies of the relationship between military spending and economic growth led Todd Sandler and Keith Hartley, authors of a comprehensive compendium on the economics of defense, to conclude that the net impact on growth is negligible.

Political factors are also important in weighing the economic effects of military spending. According to Harvard political scientist Samuel Huntington, "Arguments that significant increases or decreases in defense spending were economically feasible rested on the assumption that there would be widespread public support for such changes." During the Vietnam War, it appeared at times that this nation was testing the outer limits of public support—at least for that type of military venture. The late Edward Mason, an economist at Harvard University, has also argued that the effective limit on defense spending is political, concluding that there is not much doubt that in the face of deepening emergency even higher expenditures would be accepted." As a practical matter, it seems that Mason is right.

Thus, the pertinent question in current debates on military spending is not the ability of the U.S. economy to produce the goods and services required by the armed forces but the willingness of the public to devote a substantial share of its resources to that purpose.

A Military-Industrial Complex?

The same studies that show that the American economy can sustain higher levels of military spending also indicate that economic growth and prosperity do not require the current level of national security expenditure. The President's Committee on the Economic Impact of Defense and Disarmament, chaired by economist Gardner Ackley, reported in 1965 that "experience testifies to the ability of the American economy to adjust successfully to major reductions in defense expenditures." The Ackley Committee drew on the adjustment experiences following World War II and the Korean War. The post-Vietnam adjustment furnished another case in point. In its report in 1969, the Cabinet Coordinating Committee on Economic Planning for the End of Vietnam Hostilities concluded that "prosperity has not depended on the defense buildup and will not need high military spending to support it in peacetime."

In a variety of econometric simulations performed since then, scholars have estimated that a short transition would occur after a large cutback in spending for national security programs. Temporarily, unemployment would rise as the economy's growth rate slowed down. Subsequently, however, the peacetime economy would follow a more rapid long-run growth path.

Indeed, that has been the experience in the recent past. Following an initial adjustment period—with its attendant pain and uncertainty—many localities end up with a stronger economy after a substantial defense cut. A study of 100 former military bases reported that, during the period from 1981 to 1986, 128,000 new civilian jobs replaced the 93,000 military jobs that were lost. The 7 percent average annual increase in employment at these sites compares favorably to the 2 percent average annual increase in employment nationally during the same period. Three-fourths of the closed bases became industrial or office parks; colleges and vocational-technical schools occupy most of the remaining sites.

Other examples of successful transitions have been reported in more re- cent periods (the conversion is far from instantaneous, taking three to five years on average). These positive results are not surprising considering the valuable assets that the military often leaves behind—land, buildings, air- strips, deepwater harbors, and rail lines, as well as water, sewer, gas, and elec- tricity lines.

On balance, the belief generally held among economists—an idea not as universally accepted by policymakers—is that, given a reasonable period of adjustment, the American economy can attain prosperity with a greatly re- duced military establishment. The people, occupations, and industries ben- efiting from the changes in sectoral demands will likely be different from those that participated most actively in the military buildup. This is a fact with more powerful political and social implications than economic data reveal. The costs of change may justify government-provided transitional assistance (such as special unemployment compensation and retraining al- lowances) for those who suffer initially from the shift in national priorities.

A Political Decision

Economic analysis does not suggest that a certain share of GDP be allo- cated to defense. But it does provide a few facts that deserve a prominent place in the ongoing debate over the right level of military outlays. However measured, the defense program is a minor player in the American economy today—it accounts for one-twenty-fifth of the GDP and an even smaller pro- portion of the nation's work force. Moreover, the economic importance of this sector of the economy has been declining for many years. Economic activity in the United States marches to the beat of civilian drummers, both domestic and international. Our massive economy is neither propelled nor redirected by modest shifts in the relatively small share of national resources devoted to military purposes. Furthermore, the powers of adjustment in the American economy are substantial.

The adjustments required by defense cutbacks are not different from the responses that occur regularly from shifts in consumer demand, from new products or technological changes that eliminate markets for older products, or from changes in the pattern of international trade. Major readjustments in the use of resources continually occur in the U.S. economy and, on the whole, do so fairly successfully.

This is not an argument for adopting any particular level of military out- lays. Rather, the amount of resources that the United States devotes to defense should be determined fundamentally through the political process, and on national security grounds—with due regard for the other demands on the public purse and the dictates of efficiency in the use of public resources.

The Economics of War and Peace

With a war in Iraq looming and the war on terror expanding in scope, it is a propitious time to review what we know about the impact of military activity on the American economy. We must discard notions based on World War II experience—that was a different age and few "lessons" from that time apply to the current situation.

At the start of World War II, the United States had a small and inadequate military establishment, and its defense industrial base was of similarly modest size. We were forced to create a new military-oriented production industry and to manufacture a wide array of armaments for the rapidly expanding armed forces. That burst of military demand—which was sustained until the end of World War II—was a key factor in ending the Great Depression.

The experiences of the period following the end of the Cold War provide a vivid contrast. The substantial reduction in military spending—the procurement of weapon systems was reduced more than one-half from the peak achieved in the mid 1980s—did not interfere with a prolonged economic boom. In fact, the shift from military to civilian priorities contributed to the strength and duration of the economic upturn of the 1990s.

Meanwhile, the economic impact of the Gulf War and the war in Afghanistan was fundamentally different from our experience in World War II or even the Korean and Vietnam Wars. During the Gulf War and the war in Afghanistan, the United States experienced limited recessions, rather than war-induced prosperity. In both cases, but especially in the case of the war in Afghanistan, it was the successful conclusion of the military effort that gave the nation's economy a shot in the arm. In contrast, short and mild recessions followed the end of the Korean and Vietnam Wars.

Wars and defense spending in general can neither be justified nor rejected out of hand on economic grounds alone. The United States can afford to engage in military conflicts if it decides that this is in its best interests but the health of the American economy does not require any specific level of military outlays. Yet Adam Smith's forecast comes to mind: "The first duty of the sovereign, therefore, that of defending the society from the violence and injustice of other independent societies, grows gradually more and more expensive, as the society advances in civilization."

28

The Costs of Government Regulation of Business

This selection was prepared at the request of the Congressional Joint Economic Committee and published as a special Committee Print. The resultant distribution of this report helped to elevate the subject of government regulation to a significant and continuing issue of public policy.

The process of regulation of business activity via governmental rules and regulation generates a variety of impacts, direct and indirect, intended and unintended, desirable and undesirable. Proponents of governmental intervention stress the benefits that are expected to flow or the social problems to be solved. The costs that are involved tend to be discounted or even ignored ("If we can put a man on the moon, why can't we clean up the Mississippi?").

The purpose of this report is to examine the various costs that are incurred in the process of government regulation. By raising the public information level, it is hoped that governmental decision-making in this important area can become a more balanced process, giving equal weight to the costs and other disadvantages as well as the benefits and other advantages of proposed actions. The result, hopefully, will be the attainment of important national objectives with greater effectiveness than characterizes the present situation.

The impacts of government regulation of business are felt in every part of the economy:

1. *The taxpayer feels the effect.* Government regulation literally has become a major growth industry, an industry supported by the taxpayer. The cost of operating federal regulatory agencies is rising more rapidly than the budget as a whole, the population, or the gross domestic product.
2. *The motorist feels the effect.* Federally mandated safety and environmental features increased the price of the average passenger car by $666 in 1978. Compliance with those regulations thus costs American consumers $7 billion a year in the form of higher priced cars. In addition, the added weight of the cars is increasing fuel consumption perhaps by as much as $3 billion annually.

Source: Murray Weidenbaum, *The Costs of Government Regulation of Business*, Joint Economic Committee Print (Washington, DC: U.S. Government Printing Office, 1978).

3. *Business feels the effect.* There are over 4,400 different federal forms that the private sector must fill out each year. That takes over 143 million man-hours, the economic equivalent of a small army. The Federal Paperwork Commission estimates that the total cost of federal paperwork imposed on private industry ranges from $25 billion to $32 billion a year.

4. *The homeowner feels the effect.* Regulatory requirements imposed by federal, state, and local governments are adding between $1,500 and $2,500 to the cost of a typical new home. Applying the midpoint of that range ($2,000) to the 2 million new homes built in 1977 results in an added cost to homeowners of $4 billion last year.

5. *The consumer feels the effect.* The costs of complying with government regulations are inevitably passed on by business to the consumer in the form of higher prices. The aggregate cost of complying with federal regulation came to $62.9 billion in 1976, or over $300 for each man, woman, and child in the United States. The estimated $62.9 billion of costs imposed on the private sector is 20 times the $3.1 billion spent to operate the regulatory agencies in the same year. If we apply the same multiplier of 20 to the amounts budgeted for regulatory activities for more recent years, we can come up with approximations of the private sector's cost of compliance and thus with the total dollar impact of government regulation. On that basis, it can be estimated that the costs arising from government regulation of business (both the expenses of the regulatory agencies themselves as well as the costs they induce in the private sector) totaled $79.1 billion in the fiscal year 1977 and may reach $96.7 billion in the current fiscal year. On the basis of the budget estimate for the fiscal year 1979 the aggregate cost of government regulation may come to $102.7 billion, consisting of $4.8 billion of direct expenses by the federal regulatory agencies and $97.9 billion of costs of compliance on the part of the private sector. Although there is no assurance that larger budgets for federal regulatory agencies generate a constant multiplier effect on the private sector, the analysis in this report tends to show that the data used here for private sector regulatory costs are substantially underestimated.

6. *The worker feels the effect.* Government regulation, albeit unintentionally, can have strongly adverse effects on employment. The minimum wage law has priced hundreds of thousands of people out of labor markets. One increase alone reduced teenage employment by 225,000, with a disproportionately large impact on nonwhite youngsters. Many industry facilities and entire factories have been closed down—with substantial but unmeasurable effects on employment—because of the high costs of meeting environmental, safety and other regulatory requirements.

7. *The investor feels the effect.* Approximately $10 billion of new private capital spending is devoted each year to meeting governmentally mandated environmental, safety, and similar regulations rather than being invested in profitmaking projects. Edward Denison of the Brookings Institution has estimated that in recent years these deflections of private investment from productive uses have resulted in a loss of approximately one-fourth of the potential annual increase in productivity.

8. *The nation as a whole feels the effect of government regulation in many ways.* The adverse consequences range from a slowdown in the availability of new pharmaceutical products to the cancellation of numerous small pension plans. The aggregate response to the proliferation of government regulation is a bureaucratization of American business. These undramatic but fundamental effects occur because of the diversion of management attention from traditional product development, production, and marketing efforts designed to provide new and better products and services, to meeting governmentally imposed social requirements.

The New Wave of Government Regulation

It is hard to overestimate the current rapid expansion of government involvement in business in the United States. Certainly the majority of public policy changes affecting business-government relations in recent years has been in the direction of greater governmental intervention—environmental controls, job safety inspections, equal employment opportunity enforcement, consumer product safety regulations, energy restrictions, and recording and reporting of items ranging from illnesses to foreign currency transactions. Indeed, when we attempt to look at the emerging business-government relationship from the business executive's viewpoint, a very considerable public presence is evident in what ostensibly, or at least historically, have been private affairs.

No one who operates a business today, neither the head of a large company nor the corner grocer, can do so without considering a multitude of governmental restrictions and regulations. Costs and profits can be affected as much by a bill passed in Washington as by a management decision in the front office or a customer's decision at the checkout counter. Management decisions fundamental to the business enterprise are increasingly becoming subject to governmental influence, review, or control, decisions such as: What lines of business to go into? What products can be produced? Which investments can be financed? Under what conditions can products be produced? Where can they be made? How can they be marketed? What prices can be charged? What profit can be made?

Virtually every major department of the typical industrial corporation in the United States has one or more counterparts in a federal agency that controls or strongly influences its internal decision-making. The scientists in corporate research laboratories now receive much of their guidance from lawyers in federal, state, and local regulatory agencies. The engineers in manufacturing departments must abide by standards promulgated by Labor Department authorities. Marketing divisions must follow procedures established by government administrators in product safety agencies. The location of facilities must be in conformance with a variety of environmental statutes. The activities of personnel staffs are increasingly restricted by the various executive agencies concerned with employment conditions. Finance departments often bear the brunt of the rising paperwork burden being imposed on business by government agencies who seem to assume that information is a free good—or in any event that more is always better than less.

The new types of governmental regulation of business are not limited to the traditional regulatory agencies, such as the Interstate Commerce Commission, the Civil Aeronautics Board, and the Federal Communications Commission. Rather, the line operating departments and bureaus of government—the Departments of Agriculture, Commerce, Health, Education, and Welfare, Interior, Justice, Labor, Transportation, and Treasury—are now involved in actions that affect virtually every firm.

Impetus for this expanded government participation in economic activity is being provided by a variety of consumer groups, environmental organizations, civil rights advocates, labor unions, and other citizen's institutions. In many cases, the increasing regulation reflects public and congressional concern that traditional federal and state-local programs have not been effective. The new wave of regulation is also reinforced by the belief that the private sector itself is responsible for many of the problems facing society—pollution, discrimination in employment, unsafe products, unhealthy working environments, misleading financial reporting, and so forth. The present trends in federal government regulation in the United States do not represent an abrupt departure from an idealized free market economy, but rather the rapid intensification of the long-term expansion of government influence over the private sector.

Government regulation at times can be justified as a logical response to imperfections in the private economy or what economists call "failures" in the normal market system. Examples of such situations are pollution of the environment, inadequate industrial safety practices, and long-term health hazards. Voluntary action to deal with such problems may place a firm under a competitive disadvantage. The specific company attempting to correct the situation would tend to bear the full costs, while the benefits of the improvement would be widely dispersed in the society. "Free riders" who do not make the expensive changes may nevertheless share in the benefits (those "externalities" that economists write about).

An example of this situation is provided by the regulation of pollution standards in the motor vehicle area. The basic justification for government setting standards for automobiles—particularly in the pollution area where so much of the benefit goes to society as a whole—was clearly stated by a president of Chrysler:

> . . . a large part of the public will not voluntarily spend extra money to install emission control systems which will help clean the air. Any manufacturer who installs and charges for such equipment while his competition doesn't soon finds he is losing sales and customers. In cases like this, a government standard requiring everyone to have such equipment is the only way to protect both the public and the manufacturer.

The current wave of government regulation is not merely an intensification of traditional activities. In good measure, it is a new departure and requires a new way of thinking. The standard theory of government regulation of business, which is still in general use and has dominated professional and public thinking on the subject, is based on the model of the Interstate Commerce Commission. Under this approach, a federal commission is established to regulate a specific industry, with the related concern of promoting the well-being of that industry. Often the public or consumer interest is viewed as subordinate, or even ignored, as the agency focuses on the needs and concerns of the industry that it is regulating.

In some cases—because of the unique expertise possessed by the members of the industry or its job enticements for regulators who leave government employment—the regulatory commission may become a captive of the industry that it is supposed to regulate. At least, this is a popularly held view of the development of the regulatory process. Actual practice of course varies by agency and jurisdiction and over time. In addition to the ICC, other examples of this development, which have been cited from time to time, include the Civil Aeronautics Board, the Federal Communications Commission, the Federal Energy Regulatory Commission, and the Federal Maritime Commission.

Although the traditional type of Federal regulation of business surely continues, the new regulatory efforts established by Congress in recent years follow a fundamentally different pattern. Evaluating the activities of these newer regulatory efforts with the ICC type of model is inappropriate and can lead to undesirable public policy. The new federal regulatory agencies are simultaneously broader in the scope of their jurisdiction than the ICC-CAB-FCC model, yet in important aspects are far more restricted. This anomaly lies at the heart of the problem of relating their efforts to national interests.

In the cases of the Environmental Protection Agency, the Equal Employment Opportunity Commission, the Consumer Product Safety Commission, and the Occupational Safety and Health Administration, the regulatory agency is not limited to a single industry. For each of these relative newcomers to the federal bureaucracy, its jurisdiction extends to the bulk of the private sector and at times to the public sector itself. It is this far-ranging characteristic that makes it impractical for any single industry to dominate these regulatory activities in the manner of the traditional model. What specific industry is going to capture the EEOC or OSHA? Or would have the incentive to do so?

Yet in comparison to the older agencies oriented to specific industries, in many important ways the newer federal regulators operate in a far narrower sphere. That is, they are not concerned with the totality of a company or industry, but only with the limited segment of operations that falls under their jurisdiction. The ICC, for example, must pay attention to the basic mission of the trucking industry, to provide transportation services to the public, as part of its supervision of rates and entry into the trucking business. The EPA's interest in the trucking industry, on the other hand, is exclusively in the effect of trucking operations on the environment. This restriction prevents the agency from developing too close a concern with the overall well-being of any company or industry. Rather, it can result in a total lack of concern over the effects of its specific actions on a company or industry.

If there is any special interest that may come to dominate such a functionally oriented agency, it is the one that is preoccupied with its specific task—ecologists, unions, civil rights groups, and consumerists. Thus, little if any attention may be given to the basic mission of the industry to provide goods and services to the public. Also ignored are crosscutting concerns or matters broader than the specific charter of the regulating agency, such as productivity, economic growth, employment, cost to the consumer, and effects on overall living standards. While the traditional regulatory agencies may be overly concerned at times with economic growth and productive efficiency, the newer programs move to a different beat. Their impetus comes from such social considerations as improving the quality of life, both on and off the job, and changing the distribution of income.

Important cases combine a blend of the old and new forms of regulation. The Securities and Exchange Commission is a good example. In one aspect of its activities, it regulates a specific branch of the economy, the securities industry. Yet, many of its rules also influence the way in which a great many companies prepare their financial statements and reports to shareholders. Economy-wide regulatory agencies are not a recent creation. The Federal Trade Commission has existed for six decades. Moreover, a few one-industry agencies continue to be created, notably the Commodity Futures Trading Commission, which regulates the financial markets dealing with products of agriculture and other extractive industries.

Varying alliances arise in promoting a given type of regulatory activity—or in pushing for reform. The business firms and labor unions in a given regulated industry often become strong supporters of the traditional industry-oriented commission which they have learned to live with, if not to dominate. They may join ranks to oppose efforts by consumer groups and economists to cut back on the extent of the protective regulation. This has been most apparent in the railroad and trucking industries.

In contrast, consumer groups advocate expanding the newer types of crosscutting or functional regulation. In this effort, they often are joined by labor unions, particularly in the occupational health area. Here, reform efforts may be led by coalitions of business groups and economists, who are concerned with the excessive costs and other consequences of the specialized regulatory activities. These alliances may shift from time to time. Specific safety regulations for automobiles may be opposed by unions and companies in the motor vehicle industry—although the two groups may differ strongly on job safety standards. Labor, management, and local governments may present a united opposition against specific environmental efforts which are viewed as hurting the economies of their community, although some of these groups may advocate general ecological advances. The older consumer organizations may become more concerned with the ultimate cost to the consumer of expanding governmental activities than the newer and more militant groups that emphasize public control over private sector activities.

Although the precise changes that will occur in the years ahead are basically a matter for conjecture, the overall trend seems to be fairly clear: On balance there is likely to be more and not less government intervention in internal business decision-making. No balanced evaluation of the overall practice of government regulation comfortably fits the notion of benign and wise officials always making sensible decisions in the society's greater interests. Numerous adverse side-effects are evident, as well as substantial benefits to society.

The Impacts of Government Regulation

The initial and direct effects of government regulation can be measured by the budgets of the regulatory agencies themselves. These governmental outlays indicate the costs of regulation which are borne by the taxpayers. The cost of operating federal regulatory agencies is rising more rapidly than the federal budget as a whole, the population of the country, the gross domestic product, or any other applicable basis for comparison.

The bulk of the regulatory budget is devoted to the newer areas of social regulation, such as job safety, energy and the environment, and consumer safety and health. The costs to the taxpayer are obviously not trivial, but the key effects of government regulation are in terms of the compliance by the private sector.

At first blush, government imposition of socially desirable requirements on business through the regulatory process appears to be an inexpensive way of achieving national objectives. This practice apparently costs the government little and represents no significant direct burden on the taxpayer. But the public does not escape paying the cost. Every time, for example, the Environmental Protection Agency imposes a more costly (albeit less polluting) method of production on any firm the cost of the firm's product to the consumer will tend to rise. Similar effects flow from the other regulatory efforts, including those involving product safety, job health, and hiring and promotion policies.

These higher prices represent the "hidden tax" of regulation that is shifted from the taxpayer to the consumer. The regulatory "tax" would not be shifted in this manner if the mandated effort—for example, environmental cleanup—were conducted or at least financed by the government itself. Moreover, to the extent that government-mandated requirements impose similar costs on all price categories of a given product (such. as passenger automobiles), this hidden tax tends to be more regressive than the formal tax system. That is, the costs may be a relatively higher burden on lower income groups than on higher income groups.

The indirect costs of regulation can be substantial. The paperwork and ancillary requirements of federal agencies inevitably produce a "regulatory lag," a delay that can run into years and can be a costly drain on the time and budgets of private managers as well as public officials. The Federal Trade Commission averages nearly five years to complete a restraint-of-trade case. It took the Federal Power Commission eleven years to determine how to regulate the price of natural gas all the way back to the wellhead. The regulatory lag is lengthening. Ten years ago, the director of planning of the Irvine Co. obtained in ninety days what was then called zoning for a typical residential development. A decade later, the company received what is now called entitlement to build for one of its developments, following two years of intensive work by a specialized group within the company's planning department aided by the public affairs staff. The preparation of environmental impact statements has become a major source of paperwork. The report for one offshore oil field in the Santa Barbara Channel, for example, required nearly 1,300 pages and took two years to prepare.

A study covering twenty-one residential development projects in the New Jersey Coastal Zone estimated the direct regulatory expenses for a single-family house at $1,600 during the period 1972-75. The costs covered some thirty-eight separately required permits, including preliminary plan, performance improvement bond, sewer plan, tree removal permit, final plans review, road drainage permit, and coastal area facilities permit.

Government inspectors are increasingly frequent, albeit unwelcomed, visitors to business premises. Milk processing experiences an extraordinary variety of inspections. More than 20,000 state, county, local, and municipal milk jurisdictions exist in the United States. Milk plants are inspected about twenty-four times annually, even though the Public Health Service recommends only twice a year. One milk plant, licensed by 250 local governments, three states, and twenty other agencies reported that it was inspected forty-seven times in one month.

In the more traditional areas, many regulations deal with natural monopolies, such as in the case of utilities. In some of these one-industry regulatory efforts, however, the government actions may be anticompetitive and thus ultimately costly to the consumer. Interstate trucking furnishes a cogent example, where federal regulation is in large degree a barrier to entry protecting existing firms against possible new entrants.

A recent report prepared at the Center for the Study of American Business at Washington University estimates that the aggregate cost of complying with federal regulation came to $62.3 billion in 1976 or 20 times the direct cost to the taxpayer of supporting the major regulatory agencies.

The basic approach followed in the study was to cull from the available literature the more reliable estimates of the costs of specific regulatory programs, to put those estimates on a consistent and reliable basis, and to aggregate the results for 1976. Where a range of costs was available for a given regulatory program, the lower end of the range was generally used. In many other cases no cost estimates were available. Thus, the numbers in the study are low and underestimate the actual costs of federal regulation in the United States.

Regulation and Innovation

As William Carey of the American Association for the Advancement of Science has stated, "Government may imagine that it is neutral toward the rate and quality of technological risk-taking, but it is not . . . regulatory policies aimed at the public interest rarely consider impacts on innovation." The adverse effect of regulation on innovation is likely to be felt more strongly by smaller firms and thus have an anticompetitive impact.

One hidden cost of government regulation is a reduced rate of introduction of new products. The longer it takes for a new product to be approved by a government agency—or the more costly the approval process—the less likely that the new product will be created. In any event, innovation will be delayed.

Professor Sam Peltzman of the University of Chicago has estimated, for example, that the 1962 amendments to the Food and Drug Act are delaying the introduction of effective drugs by about four years, as well as leading to higher prices for pharmaceutical products. As a result in large part of the more stringent drug regulations, the United States was the 30th country to approve the antiasthma drug metaproterenol, the 32nd country to approve the anticancer drug adriamycin, the 51st to approve the antituberculosis drug rifampin, the 64th to approve the antiallergenic drug cromolyn, and the 106th to approve the antibacterial drug co-trimaxazole.

According to Thomas Moore of the Hoover Institution at Stanford University, regulation by the Interstate Commerce Commission delayed the introduction of unit trains by at least five years and delayed full use by the Southern Railroad of the "Big John" cars used to carry grain. Ann Friedlander has estimated the loss in the railroad industry due to retarded innovation at between $12 million and $41 million a year.

Regulation and Capital Formation

Federal regulation also affects the prospects for economic growth and productivity by levying a claim on a rising share of new capital formation. This effect of regulation is most evident in the environmental and safety areas. According to the U.S. Council on Environmental Quality, private capital outlays for pollution control in 1975 were $3.8 billion higher than would have been the case in the absence of federal environmental requirements.

Similarly, the McGraw-Hill Department of Economics estimates the cost to American industry of meeting the occupational health and safety regulations at about $3 billion a year. Thus, these two programs alone account for 6 percent of total capital spending in the private sector of the American economy.

Regulation and Small Business

Government regulation, often unwittingly, tends to hit small business disproportionately hard. Most of this impact is unintentional, in that the regulations typically do not distinguish among companies of different sizes. But in practice, forcing a very small firm to fill out the same forms as a large company with highly trained technical staffs at its disposal places a significantly greater burden on that smaller enterprise. This general point is supported by data and examples for such different governmental regulatory activities as the Environmental Protection Agency, the Employee Retirement Income Security Act, National Labor Relations Board, Occupational Safety and Health Administration, and the Securities and Exchange Commission.

A current example of government regulation affecting small business disproportionately is the proposed standards for air-lead exposure levels promulgated by the Occupational Safety and Health Administration. The impact of these standards has been examined in a study by Charles River Associates. In the battery industry, which is made up of 143 firms, OSHA lead regulations are estimated to result in much larger per unit production costs for smaller plants than for larger plants. Because of large differential costs and the fact that battery prices would only rise to cover the unit costs of the larger firms, smaller plant operators would be forced to absorb the differential in costs. In many cases the amount absorbed would eliminate entirely the plant's profitability. According to the study, about 113 single plant battery firms would be forced to close, eliminating half of the productive capacity not operated by the five major battery companies.

It is much more difficult to assess the impact of regulations that are merely burdensome to small business, such as filling out government forms and responding to information requests by regulatory agencies. The Commission on Federal Paperwork reports that 5 million small businesses spend $15-$20 billion, or an average of over $3,000 each on federal paperwork. Not all examples of the heavier burden of regulation on small business have to do with the newer regulatory agencies. A National Labor Relations Board election is a good example. The cost per employee of an NLRB election is smaller for the large firm ($102 for companies with over 1,000 employees) and larger for the small firm ($135 for firms with fewer than 100 workers).

Regulation and Business Functions

One of the immeasurable effects of government regulation is what it does to the basic nature of the private enterprise system. To the extent that management's attention is diverted from traditional product development, production, and marketing concerns to meeting governmentally imposed social requirements, a significant bureaucratization of corporate activity results.

In the occupational safety and health area, professional safety staffs are often diverted from their basic function of training workers in safer operating procedures to filling out forms, posting notices, and meeting other essentially bureaucratic requirements. OSHA directives, for example, contain very specific requirements for virtually every piece of equipment used in the production of steel. These requirements range from such major items as coke ovens all the way down to such minutiae as the ladders used in plants and the mandatory 42-inch height from the floor for portable fire extinguishers.

The results measured by any improvements in safety are almost invariably disappointing. Two major studies of the occupational safety and health (OSHA) program to date have yielded negative findings. Nicholas Ashford concluded that "The OSHA Act has failed thus far to live up to its potential for reducing job injury and disease . . . OSHA has had little measurable impact in reducing injuries and deaths."

Robert Smith reported similar findings, ". . . the estimated effects [of OSHA] on injuries are so small that they cannot be distinguished from zero." Apparently, the original concern of the public and the Congress to reduce accidents has been converted to obeying rules and regulations. The disappointing results lead to a predictable reaction: Redouble the existing effort—more rules, more forms, more inspection, and thus higher costs to the taxpayer and higher prices to the consumer. Statistics on occupational injuries and illnesses are hardly reassuring. The number of workdays lost to injuries and illnesses per 100 workers actually rose, to 54.4 in 1975 from 53.1 in 1974.

Approaches to Regulatory Reform

A new way of looking at the microeconomic effects of regulatory programs may be helpful to public policymaking. A parallel can be drawn to macroeconomic matters, where important and at times conflicting objectives are recognized and attempts at reconciliation or trade-off are made (for example, as among economic growth, income distribution, and price stability). At the microeconomic level, it may likewise be appropriate to reconcile the goals of specific government programs with national objectives.

Healthy working conditions, for example, are an important national objective, but not the only important national objective. Society supposedly should avoid selecting the most costly and disruptive methods of achieving a higher degree of job safety. Similarly, environmental protection, product safety, and other regulatory efforts should be related to costs to the consumer, availability of new products, and the employment of the work force. In part, this reconciliation can be made at the initial stages of the governmental process, when the president proposes and the Congress enacts a new regulatory program.

Benefit-Cost Analysis

One device for broadening the horizons of government policymakers and administrators is the economic impact statement. Policymakers could be required to consider the costs (and other adverse effects) of their actions as well as the benefits.

This is not a novel idea. In November 1974, President Gerald Ford instructed the federal agencies under his jurisdiction to examine the effects of the major regulatory actions on costs, productivity, employment, and other economic factors. This first step was subject to several shortcomings. Many of the regulatory agencies—ranging from the Consumer Product Safety Commission to the Federal Trade Commission—are so-called independent agencies that are beyond the president's jurisdiction in these matters.

Second, even in the case of the regulatory activities that come within presidential jurisdiction, the existing policy is limited to the regulations that, in the issuing agency's own estimation, are "major." Third, the agencies covered by the executive order are only required to examine the economic aspects of their actions. The weight they give to economic factors remains in their discretion—to the extent that congressional statutes permit them to give any consideration to economic influences at all.

A broader approach may be warranted, one with a strong legislative mandate. In the fashion of the environmental impact statements Congress could require each regulatory agency to assess the impact of its proposed actions on the society as a whole, and particularly on the economy. Much would depend on the "teeth" put into any required economic impact statement. Merely legislating the performance of some economic analysis by an unsympathetic regulator would serve little purpose beyond delaying the regulatory process and making it more costly. But limiting government regulation to those instances where the total benefits to society exceed the costs would be a major departure from current practice.

To an eclectic economist, government regulation should be carried to the point where the incremental costs equal the incremental benefits, and no further. Indeed, this is the basic criterion that is generally used to screen government investments in physical resources. Overregulation—regulation for which the costs exceed the benefits—would be avoided.

Changing Attitudes Toward Regulation

Basically, however, it is attitudes that need to be changed. Experience with the job safety program provides a cogent example. Although the government's safety rules have resulted in billions of dollars of public and private outlays, the basic goal of a safer work environment has not been achieved.

A more satisfying answer to improving the effectiveness of government regulation of private activities requires a basic change in the approach to regulation, and one not limited to the job safety program. Indeed, that program is used here merely as an illustration. If the public policy is to reduce accidents, then public policy should focus directly on the reduction of accidents. Excessively detailed regulations are often merely a substitute—the normal bureaucratic substitute—for hard policy decisions.

Rather than emphasis being placed on issuing citations to employers who fail to fill forms out correctly or who do not post the required notices, it should be placed on the regulation of those employers with high and rising accident rates. Perhaps fines should be levied on those establishments with the worst safety records. As the accident rates decline toward some sensible average standard, the fines could be reduced or eliminated.

But the government should not be much concerned with the way a specific organization achieves a safer working environment. Some companies may find it more efficient to change work rules, others to buy new equipment, and still others to retrain workers. The making of this choice is precisely the kind of operational business decision-making that government should avoid, but that now dominates many regulatory programs. Without diminishing the responsibility of the employers, the sanctions under the federal occupational safety and health law should be extended to employees, especially those whose negligence endangers other employees. The purpose here is not to be harsh, but to set up effective incentives to achieve society's objectives. This can be a preferred alternative to government specifying the details of what it considers to be "acceptable" private action.

With reference to consumer protection regulation, an information strategy may often provide a sensible alternative. For the many visible hazards that consumers voluntarily subject themselves to, perhaps the most important consideration of public policy is to improve the individual's knowledge of the risks involved rather than to limit personal discretion. In their daily lives, citizens rarely opt for zero risk.

Alternatives to Regulation

The promulgation by government of rules and regulations restricting or prescribing private activity of course is not the only means of accomplishing public objectives. Codes of behavior adhered to on a voluntary basis may often be effective. Trade associations on occasion have served such a useful function in upgrading the level of business performance.

Government itself has available to it various powers other than the regulatory mechanism. Through its taxing authority, the government can provide strong signals to the market. Rather than promulgating detailed regulations governing allowable discharges into the nation's waterways, the government could levy substantial taxes on those discharges. Such sumptuary taxation could be "progressive," to the extent that the tax rates would rise faster than the amount of pollution emitted by an individual polluter. Thus, there would be an incentive for firms to concentrate on removing or at least reducing the more serious instances of pollution.

The use of taxation would neither be meant to punish polluters nor to give them a "license" to pollute. Rather it would be using the price system to encourage producers and consumers to shift to less polluting ways of producing and consuming goods and services. The cost of removal of pollution for each organization, compared to the size of the tax, would determine the level of environmental cleanup that it pursues. Those that can control pollution more cheaply will clean up more (and thus pay less tax). Those with higher control costs will clean up less (and pay more pollution taxes). This approach attempts to achieve a given level of environmental quality with minimum resource use by equalizing the marginal cost of pollution control.

In the case of the traditional one-industry type of government regulation (as of airlines, trucking, and railroads) a greater role should be given to the competitive process and to market forces. Unlike the newer forms of regulation, the older forms are often mainly barriers to entry into a given industry, protecting existing firms from competition by potential new entrants. It is in this sense that deregulation is a viable option.

Any realistic appraisal of government regulation must acknowledge that important and positive benefits have resulted from many of these activities— less pollution, fewer product hazards, reducing job discrimination, and other socially desirable goals of our society. But the "externalities" generated by economic activity cannot justify government attempting to regulate every facet of private behavior. A reasonable approach to this problem requires great discrimination in sorting out the hazards that it is important to regulate from the kinds of lesser hazards that can best be dealt with by the normal prudence of consumers, workers, and business firms.

29

The Case for Economizing on Government Controls

This, my first journal article on the subject of government regulation, spelled out the case for reviewing and modifying the proliferation of regulation that was underway. Together with a host of follow-on and derivative writings, it helped to move the subject of regulation from the exclusive domain of the scholarly journals to the public arena.

It is always tempting to compare the ugly reality of what we oppose with the enchanting ideal of what we propose. This surely seems to be the case with the current wave of expanding government controls over the private sector.

Are some consumer products unsafe? Are some working conditions unhealthy? Are some physical environments deteriorating? Are some employers discriminating in their personnel practices? The standard answer seems to be clear: Establish another corps of federal officialdom with power to right these wrongs.

Of course, one must possess the personality of a Scrooge to quarrel with the desirability of safer working conditions, better products for the consumer, combating discrimination in employment, or reducing environmental pollution. And, to be sure, the programs established to deal with these issues have at times yielded substantial benefits to the public.

But, unfortunately, any realistic evaluation of the actual practice of government regulation does not comfortably fit the notion of benign, beneficent, and wise men and women making altogether sensible decisions in the society's greater interests. In my study of the subject, I find instead waste, bias, stupidity, arrogance, concentration on trivia, conflicts among the regulators, and, worst of all, arbitrary and often uncontrolled power. Let me cite chapter and verse.

The Costs of Regulation

Mandatory auto buzzers and harnesses (the widely detested "interlock" system) will rapidly fade into history as an example of the highhandedness and wastefulness of government regulation. Over 40 percent of the owners of those expensive contraptions disconnected them or otherwise found ways of avoiding their use prior to their elimination by Congress. Nevertheless, the

Source: Murray Weidenbaum, "The Case for Economizing on Government Controls," *Journal of Economic Issues*, June 1975.

phenomenon of government adding to the costs of private production of goods and services as a convenient way of achieving public objectives without spending much, if any, government money seems likely to continue.

Less dramatic but often equally expensive types of federal regulation remain with us. The agencies carrying them out are surely proliferating. In the past decade alone, we have seen the formation of the Consumer Product Safety Commission, the Occupational Safety and Health Commission, the Environmental Protection Agency, the Federal Energy Administration, the Cost Accounting Standards Board, the National Bureau of Fire Prevention, the Mining Enforcement and Safety Administration, the National Highway Traffic Safety Administration, the National Transportation Safety Board, the Federal Metal and Nonmetallic Mine Safety Board of Review, and the Occupational Safety and Health Administration.

A direct private cost resulting from the expansion of government controls is the growing paperwork burden imposed on business firms: the expensive and time-consuming process of submitting reports, making applications, filling out questionnaires, replying to orders and directives, and appealing in the courts from other rulings and regulatory opinions. As of June 30, 1974 there were 5,146 different types of approved public use forms, in addition to tax and banking forms. Individuals and business firms spend over 130 million man-hours a year filling out all the necessary federal reports.

The lack of understanding between regulators and those they regulate is vividly conveyed in the interchange reported by a small manufacturer who attended a federal meeting on the paperwork burden. When he was advised not to worry about the matter personally but have his staff complete the forms, he replied: "When I attend this meeting the staff is right here with me. It's me."

A small, 5,000-watt radio station in New Hampshire reported that it spent $26 just to mail to the Federal Communications Commission its application for renewing its license. An Oregon company, operating three small television stations, reported that its license renewal application weighed forty-five pounds. At the other end of the spectrum, one large corporation, with about 40,000 employees, uses 125 file drawers of back-up material just to meet the federal reporting requirements in the personnel area. The departmental manager contends that one-third of his staff could be eliminated if there were no federal, state, or local reporting requirements.

There are many other hidden costs that arise as a result of federal regulatory legislation. The Jones Act, requiring cargo shipments from one U.S. port to another to be made by U.S. vessels, adds 8 to 10 cents per million cubic feet to the cost of transporting liquified natural gas between Alaska and the West Coast. Attempts to avoid this "tax" result in the roundabout and more expensive process whereby Alaska exports the gas to other countries, and the mainland United States imports it from the South Pacific and Russia.

Another hidden cost is the reduced rate of innovation that may occur as the result of government controls. The longer it takes for some change to be approved by a federal regulatory agency—a new or improved product, a more efficient production process, and so forth—the less likely the change will be made. Professor William Wardell of the University of Rochester School of Medicine and Dentistry has concluded that as a result of more liberal policy in the United Kingdom toward the introduction of new drugs, Britain experienced clearly discernible gains by introducing useful new drugs, either sooner than the United States or exclusively.

The private costs of government regulation arise in good measure from the attitudes of the regulators. To quote a member of the Consumer Product Safety Commission: "When it involves a product that is unsafe, I don't care how much it costs the company to correct the problem." In one recent case where an offending company had not posted a label on its product bearing the correct officialese ("cannot be made non poisonous"), it was forced to destroy the contents. If you do not care about costs, apparently you do not think about such economical solutions as pasting a new label on the can.

In contrast to the attention given to the benefits that are expected to flow from each and every regulation, the costs usually are ignored. Let "them" pay for it; "they" can afford it; that seems to be the public attitude. The economic model underlying this approach is quite unusual. Government mandated costs of private production are assumed neither to be shifted forward to consumers nor backward to the factors of production. The costs presumably simply come out of profits, but without interfering with the needed flows of saving and investment—the proverbial "free lunch."

Trivia and Nonsense

An expected result of the lack of attention to the costs of regulation is the opportunity for bureaucrats to engage in exercises in trivia and, on occasion, sheer nonsense. What size to establish for toilet partitions? How big is a hole? (It depends upon where it is.) When is a roof a floor? What colors should various parts of a building be painted? How frequently are spittoons to be cleaned? There actually are people willing to take tax dollars to establish and administer regulations dealing with these burning issues.

Picture the plight of the small businessman who tries to deal with the Occupational Safety and Health Administration (OSHA) rules without paying for expensive outside assistance. I have tried to by requesting copies of the introductory materials provided by the agency. Some examples stagger the mind. Let us begin with a supposedly simple matter, the definition of an *exit*. The dictionary says that *exit* is "a passage or way out." To OSHA, an *exit* is "that portion of a means of egress which is separated from all other spaces of the building or structure by construction or equipment as required in this subpart to provide a protected way of travel, to the exit discharge." Obviously, I had to define "a means of egress" as well as an "exit discharge." Leaving seems to be easier than entering, at least the Kingdom of OSHA.

Exit discharge is defined merely as "that portion of a means of egress between the termination of an exit and a public way." OSHA defines "means of egress" as "a continuous and unobstructed way of exit travel from any point in a building or structure to a public way and consists of three separate and distinct parts: the way of exit access, the exit, and the way of exit discharge. A means of egress comprises the vertical and horizontal ways of travel and shall include intervening room spaces, doorways, hallways, corridors, passageways, balconies, ramps, stairs, enclosures, exits, escalators, horizontal exits, courts, and yards." Exit is a comparatively easy one. Try ladder, where the reader literally has to cope with three renditions of the same tedious set of definitions plus one trigonometric function.

The operation of the Occupational Safety and Health Act provides a pertinent example of how government regulation can lose sight of the basic objective. If a company without its own specialized safety personnel invites OSHA to come to the plant to tell the management which practices need to be revised to meet the agency's standards, it instantly lays itself open to citations for infractions of OSHA rules. In order to circumvent the problem, one regional office of OSHA suggested that companies take photographs of their premises and send them to OSHA for off-site review. If the inspectors do not actually "see" the violations, they cannot issue citations for them.

Which Good is Better?

The proliferation of government controls has led to conflicts among controls and controllers. The task of washing children's pajamas in New York State exemplifies how two sets of laws can pit one worthy objective against another.

In an effort to halt water pollution, New York State banned the sale of detergents containing phosphates. Less than two months later, a federal regulation took effect requiring all children's sleepwear to be flame-retardant. New York housewives faced a dilemma, because phosphates are the strongest protector of fire-retardancy. Phosphates hold soil and minerals in solution, preventing the formation of a mask on the fabric that would inactivate flame-resistancy. Soap and, to a lesser degree, many nonphosphate detergents redeposit those harmful items during the wash cycle. What does a conscientious mother do in a phosphate-banned area to avoid dressing her child in nightclothes that could burn up? Smuggle in the forbidden detergent? Commit an illegal act of laundry?

The controversy over restrooms furnishes another example of the conflict among different regulations. The Labor Department, under the Occupational Safety and Health Act, has provided private industry with detailed instructions concerning the size, shape, and number of toilet seats. On the basis of a long accepted biological argument, some type of lounge area is required to be adjacent to women's restrooms. However, the Equal Employment Opportunity Commission requires that male toilet and lounge facilities, although separate, must be equal to those provided for women. Hence, either equivalent lounges must be built adjacent to the men's toilets, or the women's lounges must be dismantled, OSHA and state laws to the contrary notwithstanding.

Arbitrary Power

The instances of waste and foolishness on the part of government regulators pale into insignificance when compared to the arbitrary power that can be exerted by federal regulators. To cite a member of the Consumer Product Safety Commission: "Any time that consumer safety is threatened, we're going to go for the company's throat."

That this statement is not merely an overblown metaphor can be seen by examining the case of Marlin Toy Products, Inc. of Horicon, Wisconsin. The firm's two main products, Flutter Ball and Birdie Ball, were plastic toys for children, identical except that one contained a butterfly and the other a bird. The toys originally held plastic pellets that rattled. If the toys cracked, the pellets could be swallowed by a child. This led the Food and Drug Administration to place the products on its ban list. The company recalled the toys and redesigned its product line to eliminate the pellets and thus be removed from the ban list.

Now enter the newly formed Consumer Product Safety Commission (CPSC), which had assumed responsibility in this area. Because of an "editorial error," it puts Marlin products on its new ban list, although there is no longer any reason to ban them (the commission incorporated an out-of-date FDA list). The error was called to the commission's attention, but it replied that it was not about to recall 250,000 lists "just to take one or two toys off." Marlin Toy Products reports that it was forced out of the toy business due to the federal error. It is ironic to note that the commission, which specializes in ordering companies to recall their products if some defective ones have been produced, refused to recall its own defective product.

As for the constitutional protection against unreasonable search and seizure, OSHA inspectors have so-called no-knock power. They can to enter the premises of virtually any business in the United States without a warrant or even prior announcement. Jail terms are provided in the law for anyone tipping off an OSHA "raid."

The Possible Shape of Things to Come

A society, acting through government, can and should act to protect consumers against rapacious sellers, individual workers against unscrupulous employers, and future generations against those who would waste the nation's resources. But, as in most areas of life, the sensible questions are not matters of either/or, but rather of more or less. Thus, we can advocate stringent controls to avoid infant crib deaths without simultaneously supporting a plethora of detailed federal rules and regulations dealing with the color of exit lights and the maintenance of cuspidors.

We need a fundamental rethinking of the attitude that government increasingly should involve itself in what traditionally has been internal business decision making. The nation needs to recognize the costs as well as the benefits of government regulation of private activity—and to seek more cost-effective approaches.

30

A New Approach to Regulatory Reform

In response to critical analyses such as the previous two selections, ambitious efforts have been made to reform the government's regulatory process. Progress to date, however, has been very limited. Further improvements must take account of the successes and failures of these prior experiences.

Over the years, many attempts have been made to reform government regulation, but success has been limited. These efforts have been hampered by distrust on both sides of the regulatory debate. Individuals committed to protecting public health, safety, and the environment are suspicious of any effort that is seen as obstructing or delaying their objectives. In contrast, people advocating the reduction of "big government" decry those who would proceed rapidly to address various problems with costly remedies.

To reconcile these two polar extremes, or at least to narrow the gap between them, it is necessary to raise the level of understanding of the galaxy of issues involved. That requires a far better flow of information, one based on sound science and professional analysis. Moreover, a broader approach is in order in the regulatory process than has been customary.

The most carefully constructed and well-grounded analysis, however, can antagonize citizen groups, which may jump to the conclusion that wetlands are about to be paved over or national forests sold to the highest bidder. Any successful and comprehensive reform must have a perspective that is not threatening to the widespread concerns of citizens—and that positive approach to achieving the nation's social priorities must be translated into reality.

In that spirit, the various parties to the regulatory debate should recognize that the American people believe there is a legitimate need for government regulation to achieve economic and social goals of high priority to the nation. There are many areas in which regulation is accepted without question. Airline safety is an obvious example; the public is reassured by the licensing of pilots. Similarly, restrictions on child labor in the United States are no longer controversial. Agencies such as the Environmental Protection Agency (EPA), the Equal Employment Opportunity Commission (EEOC), the Food and Drug Administration (FDA), the Federal Trade Commission (FTC), and the Occupational Safety and Health Administration (OSHA) may be viewed

Source: Murray Weidenbaum, *A New Approach to Regulatory Reform*, Center for the Study of American Business, Policy Study 147, August 1998.

as bureaucratic and burdensome "alphabet soup" by those subject to their rulings, but the public at large strongly supports continuing government involvement in their areas of responsibility.

However, the process of regulation—the way in which a national concern is translated into a specific rule—is not widely understood. It does not begin when a government agency issues a ruling. Rather, it starts much earlier, when Congress passes a law establishing a regulatory agency and gives it a mandate to issue rules governing some activity. The writing of the specific statute, which has been largely ignored by most efforts at regulatory reform, is usually the most important action in what is an extended rule-making process. Basic defects in the enabling legislation cannot be cured by the regulatory agency or anywhere else in the executive branch.

Regulatory proceedings are not, for the most part, mere matters of procedure and conformance. Rather, they spring from the desire for clean air, safe drinking water, safe workplaces, reliable financial markets, improved medicines, and competitive industries.

Yet, achieving these desirable results is far more complicated than commonly understood. It is not simply a matter of Congress proclaiming worthy goals or an executive branch agency promulgating rules to that effect. The regulatory process is fundamentally bureaucratic, with all the powers and shortcomings associated with government. Even at its best, regulation is a blunt and imperfect tool. Far too often, it imposes costs that greatly outweigh the benefits achieved, often unnecessarily.

Setting the Stage for Reform

In seriously considering the subject of regulation, an important distinction needs to be made between two types: *economic regulation,* historically used by such agencies as the Federal Communications Commission (FCC), the Maritime Commission, and two agencies which Congress has terminated, the Civil Aeronautics Board (CAB) and the Interstate Commerce Commission (ICC), and *social regulation,* performed by EPA, OSHA, and similar government agencies of fairly recent origin. The characteristics of the two types of regulation are different and so are the ways of improving them.

Economic regulation relates primarily to such aspects of business as prices, profits, entry, and exit. Typically, an agency or commission regulates a specific sector of the economy, such as transportation, communications, utilities, or banking. Social regulation, in contrast, is characterized by the use of agencies organized along functional or issue lines (ecology, discrimination, product safety) rather than industry categories. Many of these agencies have power to regulate across all industries, although their jurisdiction is limited to one aspect of business activity.

Since the 1970s there has been a strong and consistent effort to reform or eliminate economic regulations where competition adequately serves the public interest. Thus, the CAB and the ICC have been terminated; the Securities and Exchange Commission (SEC) no longer regulates brokers' commission rates; and the FCC is beginning, somewhat fitfully, to let competition replace rate regulation in the rapidly changing telecommunications industry.

The staffing of federal economic regulatory agencies (nearly 30,000 persons in 1997) is dwarfed by the much larger array of inspectors, reviewers, and other officials of federal agencies engaged in social regulation (almost 94,000 in number). However, there has been no sustained effort to reduce social regulations. On the contrary, the recent tendency has been to expand the scope of this activity.

In some cases, citizens become so used to regulation that they forget the value of marketplace competition in protecting consumers. For decades, regulation by the ICC was accepted by the trucking industry as a fact of life. But since the effective dismantling of these controls in the early 1980s, thousands of additional firms have entered this market, and the cost of transporting goods in the United States has been reduced by billions of dollars a year. The demise of the ICC goes unmourned.

Thus, substantial progress has been made in deregulating some key sectors of the economy—notably transportation, communication, and financial services—in which competition does an effective job of protecting consumer interests. The United States has enjoyed large productivity gains in these sectors relative to other industrial economies because it has successfully challenged the traditional approach of selecting regulation or public ownership and opted instead for the relatively "radical" solution of competition.

It is helpful to recall the limits as well as the advantages of the market mechanism. Marketplace competition is not an effective way of directing people to follow very specific courses of action. Control of automobile traffic provides an example. Traffic lights, stop signs, and similar command-and-control devices are an accepted part of everyday life. However, for producing changes in behavior that are less specific or that differ among individuals or organizations, economic incentives can be useful. For example, lower fees for toll bridges during off-peak hours can reduce the congestion facing the command-and-control traffic system at peak hours of usage. Likewise, a statutory or administrative command-and-control apparatus can set a specific level of air or water purity for society to strive to achieve, but emission fees or tradable permits can achieve this same level at lower cost than conventional regulatory control mechanisms.

The marketplace does not function perfectly. But the relevant question in any given instance is whether it works better than regulation. The response is less a matter of philosophy than of practicality. The answer can be "yes" or "no," depending on such factors as the type of regulation and the state of technology.

The costs imposed by regulation also are often broader than many people realize. In addition to specific equipment that may have to be added to an automobile or to a production line to meet a federal requirement, the government directive may also have powerful indirect influences. A case in point is the value of time that people must spend waiting in line for permits and inspections or filling out forms.

The impact on consumers can be even less transparent, especially since regulations often have unintended consequences. Take the case of a federal requirement that the household ladder be made safer. Such an action not only increases the cost of the product, but may make it more difficult to use. As a result, many families may forgo purchasing this more expensive and less convenient item and stand on chairs or tabletops instead. The unintended adverse result, the reduction of safety in the home, would not be apparent from merely reading the proposed rule.

In another ironic example, the current narrow tolerance standards on pesticide residues on fresh fruits and vegetables do more than merely increase the costs of nutritious foods. A diet rich in fruits and vegetables may reduce cancer rates far more than would eliminating trace pesticides on those foods. Because the standards are so tight, many low-income persons, in particular, do not eat sufficient fruits and vegetables; these foods have become too costly. On balance, cancer rates may actually be higher because pesticide restrictions are too rigid. That unintended result only becomes apparent when we trace through the effects of the government's rule making. Clearly, the rhetorical claim that onerous regulation is always justified because "lives are more important than dollars" is far too simplistic.

On the other hand, critics of regulation must keep in mind the many instances in which regulations, sometimes with very large costs, have served the public interest. Thus, EPA's two-decade-old regulation requiring refiners to stop adding lead to gasoline was an effective way to eliminate hazardous lead particles from exhaust fumes. The costs were substantial; the rule required refiners to adopt more expensive refining techniques, since lead had been a low-cost octane booster. But these costs were exceeded by the important public health gains that resulted from lower levels of lead in the environment.

It is heartening to realize that changes in the regulatory process do not have to start at square one. The appropriate question no longer is, "Are you for or against environmental or workplace regulation?" That question has long been answered. The relevant questions relate to how those regulatory mandates are carried out—to the degree of rule making and the specific approaches directed by a statute or a government agency. Most studies of government regulation conclude that adopting sensible reforms could result in greater social benefits being achieved with the same resources now committed to complying with regulations—or equivalent benefits at much lower economic cost. In this regard, regulatory failure in the public sector can be as costly as market failure in the private sector.

The Need for Change

In the aggregate, the costs of government regulations exceed the budgetary cost of all federal domestic discretionary programs. The widely used estimate prepared by Thomas Hopkins shows that complying with federal regulation cost $677 billion (or over $3,000 per capita) in 1996 and will cost $721 billion in the year 2000. Moreover, those regulatory costs fall disproportionately on small businesses; the burden of compliance for firms with fewer than twenty workers in 1992 was about 90 percent higher per employee than for companies with 500 or more workers.

From a more aggregate viewpoint, regulation impairs economic growth. It is estimated that, when the Clean Air Act of 1990 is fully implemented in 2005, it (in combination with preexisting environmental regulation) will have reduced the nation's capital stock by 4 percent, increased the cost of capital by 5 percent, and reduced the real gross domestic product by more than 3 percent.

Regulatory costs, of course, are only half the equation. Were it evident that the benefits of most of the vast array of current regulations justified their economic costs, we should consider these costs well spent. But there is no sound basis for jumping to this conclusion.

It is widely acknowledged that the positive results of many regulatory activities are subject to sharply diminishing returns. Benefits may greatly exceed costs for early interventions, but subsequent actions tend to produce smaller benefits at sharply rising costs. Reports on major environmental regulations reinforce these concerns. A study using the government's own regulatory impact analyses reveals that only 38 of the 83 major regulations analyzed by five major federal agencies from 1990 to 1995 met a benefit-cost standard. In the case of EPA, 40 of its 61 regulations failed a benefit-cost test.

In addition to generating direct costs, regulation often retards the innovation process. An example is in the treatment of new medical software that models the reaction of cancerous tumors when treated with a specific dose of radiation. The FDA has ruled that this software must be approved as a "medical device." As a result, even a slight change in computer code can require time-consuming and expensive reapproval. Yet, the FDA regulations on medical devices surely did not contemplate the inclusion of medical computer software.

The extensive regulatory reviews to which many new products are subjected in the United States inevitably raise the cost of product innovation and increase the uncertainty of financial success. However, many companies bypass these barriers to innovation by establishing research laboratories and production facilities abroad. Pharmaceutical and medical equipment firms provide striking illustrations. Companies moving to the Netherlands, for example, are not encountering a weak or ineffective regulatory environment, but one that is more flexible and efficient.

In many instances, contemporary regulatory activity is a vestige of responses to problems that have long since passed. A clear example is the Davis-Bacon Act, which prescribes "prevailing" wages on government construction contracts that are generally above the market wages received by other workers in construction jobs. The statute, which was enacted in the depths of the Depression of the 1930s, was designed to prevent sweatshop conditions in the building trades. Sixty years later, the original justification has long since disappeared, but the statute and its regulations survive in full force.

Another example of the persistence of obsolete rules is found in the administration of the Resource Conservation and Recovery Act (RCRA). EPA's Office of Solid Waste (which administers RCRA) originally placed silver on its toxic characteristic list because silver was so listed by EPA's Office of Drinking Water. However, in 1991, the Office of Drinking Water eliminated the standard for silver because it determined that silver in drinking water had no adverse effects on humans. Yet, silver remains on RCRA's list of toxic substances.

It is easy to identify regulatory programs that have serious deficiencies and elicit widespread objections. But no one sets out deliberately to create burdensome and ineffective rules. Many of the underlying statutes have created huge and unnecessary costs because Congress responded to the concerns of some citizen groups without sufficiently analyzing the proposed solutions. A powerful example is asbestos removal.

Congress passed a sweeping law that led cities and states to spend nearly $20 billion removing asbestos from public buildings, although EPA concluded that ripping out asbestos was an expensive and dangerous mistake: the removal effort *increased* the asbestos fibers circulating in the air. Compounding the problem, many regulatory statutes, especially in the areas of environment and job safety, prohibit or severely restrict any use of economic analysis in the executive branch's rule making process.

One universal shortcoming of standard regulation is apparent. Each statute or rule is promulgated in isolation, as if no others existed. If there is any lesson that we have learned in recent decades, it is that regulation is a powerful remedy that should be used only in situations where markets do not work adequately. Given the huge amount of regulation in force today, a compelling case can be made for economizing on the government's regulatory power. Like any strong medicine, regulation should be used carefully and with full attention to its adverse side effects.

The United States substantially underinvests in information on regulatory programs and should significantly increase the resources devoted to that purpose. Government regulatory activities involve hundreds of billions of dollars annually in benefits and costs. Yet, those who issue and enforce these regulations usually have little knowledge of the magnitude of their impact—

especially who bears the costs and who receives the benefits. Government agencies now spend $50 million or less each year to deal with these issues. Expenditures of several times this amount on such informational and analytical activities would be fully justified.

Benefit-cost analysis can also serve broader purposes such as thinking systematically about social issues and more fully understanding the implications of selecting one plan of action over another. Alternative approaches may not involve regulatory powers at all. However used, a careful calculation of advantages and disadvantages provides an essential discipline to improve the current arbitrary procedure.

To avoid problems inherent in placing monetary values on human lives, benefit-cost analysis sometimes can be structured in terms of lives themselves. For example, sodium nitrite, which is used to preserve food, is a mild carcinogen. Its use creates the possibility that a limited number of people will develop cancer. On the other hand, a far larger number of people would die of botulism if nitrites were not used as a preservative in meat. A comparison of the costs and benefits of restricting the use of nitrites in meats indicates that more lives are saved by its continued use. This type of comparison was the basis for the FDA's sensible decision not to ban nitrites in meat and, instead, merely to urge a reduction in their use.

Previous Attempts to Reform Regulation

A brief examination of previous attempts at reform provides a useful background for preparing recommendations to reform the regulatory system.

Since 1974 every president of the United States has attempted to improve the regulatory process. President Gerald Ford launched an effort to modernize economic regulation, particularly with respect to rate regulation of the transportation and financial industries. President Jimmy Carter maintained the momentum with the elimination of the CAB, the reduction of restrictions imposed by the ICC, and the creation of intense price competition in the financial industry. Both presidents also established formal systems to review new government regulations before they were issued. Every subsequent president has carried forward this general approach. Important lessons can be learned from their successes as well as their failures.

President Ford's concerns about the inflationary impact of federal activities, especially regulation, marked the beginning of an organized, comprehensive effort at regulatory reform. He established procedures for preparing "inflation impact statements" to illuminate the economic impact of regulatory proposals. The statements were prepared by the various executive agencies and reviewed in the White House. Because the so-called independent agencies are not subject to the jurisdiction of presidential executive orders, Ford and his staff could only try to coax them into following the spirit, if not the letter, of his directive. With some exceptions, the agencies paid merely lip service to this initiative. Nevertheless, this basic way of performing regulatory reviews has continued under successive administrations, with revisions in the details reflecting experience gained over the years.

To formalize regulatory review, President Carter replaced Ford's "inflation impact statement" with a new "regulatory analysis." For all new regulations with an estimated economic impact of $100 million or more, preparation of a regulatory analysis was required prior to the publication of the regulation in the *Federal Register*. Each analysis included a description of the proposed rule, an identification of alternative ways of achieving the policy goal, and an examination of the economic impact of the regulation. A rudimentary cost-effectiveness test was also required to enforce the requirement that "the least burdensome of acceptable alternatives has been chosen."

On balance, however, the 1970s will be remembered for an outpouring of new federal rules and an expansion of the number and size of regulatory agencies. The agencies subject to presidentially ordered regulatory review generally considered benefit-cost analysis merely to be the final hurdle to clear *after* they had completed the regulation design.

The Paperwork Reduction Act of 1980 created the Office of Information and Regulatory Affairs (OIRA) in the Office of Management and Budget to supervise enforcement of the law's objective of reducing federal reporting requirements. In 1981, President Ronald Reagan expanded OIRA's mission to encompass review of regulations promulgated by executive branch agencies.

A presidential order issued in 1981 stated, "Regulatory action shall not be undertaken unless the potential benefits to society from the regulation outweigh the potential costs to society." The presidential directive also required agencies to prepare a "regulatory impact analysis" subject to review by OIRA for each "major rule" pending. A federal agency could not publish a notice of proposed rule making until an OIRA review was complete and its concerns had been addressed. President George Bush continued President Reagan's reforms.

President Bill Clinton reaffirmed OMB (via OIRA) as the central agency to review proposed regulations. However, under his order, regulatory agencies have to find only that the benefits of the intended regulation "justify" its costs. Like its predecessors, the Clinton administration issued formal guidelines on performing economic analysis, but they were honored more in the breach than in the observance. In the case of EPA, only six of forty-five "significant" rules issued from April to September 1994 contained the required determination that the benefits justified the costs.

On balance, the formal systems of review put in place by presidents from Ford through Clinton helped convince often reluctant officials of government agencies to analyze the implications of their rules before issuing them. That approach has been somewhat successful in getting regulators and their supporting interest groups to develop data on the costs and the benefits they impose on society. However, the impact of such analyses on the actual decision-making of the regulatory agencies has been very limited.

Proposals for Reforming Regulation

Specific proposals for reforming regulation need to be developed within a broader framework. The following four basic standards for justifying and evaluating regulation are an attempt to provide such a useful framework:

1. *Regulation is warranted only when private markets do not work as well as regulation to protect citizens and consumers.*

   A worthy objective does not necessarily create a need for regulation. Government regulation is already a very large presence in the American economy, and clearly the American people believe that it is needed to achieve many important economic and social goals. But the ability of competitive markets to protect the public is very powerful. Therefore, the burden should be on those who would replace the market with additional regulation to demonstrate with solid information and careful analysis that the public would benefit from a further extension of government into the private sector.

2. *Regulatory authority should not be exercised capriciously, and the delegation of such authority by Congress to regulatory bodies should be limited to ensure this.*

   Often officials lack the authority to correct an error quickly, even when they would like to do so. For example, the EPA admitted it erred in listing the household antibiotic Bacitracin as an "extremely hazardous" substance. However, the agency was precluded from deleting that erroneous listing without going through the same burdensome process that it does in listing a very hazardous product.

3. *Congress and the regulatory agencies should objectively evaluate the expected benefits and costs of proposed major regulatory efforts, using professional scientific advice. Such an evaluation also should be applied periodically to major existing regulations.*

   Government decision-makers involved in the regulatory process necessarily perform a rudimentary form of cost-benefit analysis when they make judgments about programs, whether they know it or not. It is vital that they think hard and analytically about these important decisions, using the best available information. The regulatory process would be improved if decision-makers relied more heavily on sound science, including peer review of the technical basis for new regulations. Too often, regulators are influenced more by emotional and widely publicized fears and claims of interest groups than by professional analysis. As a result, priorities of federal agencies frequently do not reflect the relative seriousness of the numerous hazards and risks to which the public is subjected.

4. *Where feasible and effective, regulations should be applied with a "soft touch" that allows flexibility of response, including the use of market incentives instead of command-and-control directives.*

A regulatory system based on incentives to "do the right thing" can be both more effective and less costly. In pollution control, this means changing people's incentives so that not polluting becomes cheaper and easier than polluting. This approach also is far less onerous when government is dealing with the average citizen than the more traditional approach, which imposes highly specific and often extremely complex directives and then emphasizes seeking out wrongdoers for punishment. On occasion, simply setting performance standards may suffice, with the private sector having the flexibility to use the most cost-effective approach in achieving those standards.

The Task of Congress

The basic thrust of regulatory reform should be shifted. Virtually all reforms to date have focused on improving the way in which government agencies write regulations to carry out laws already enacted. Although this activity is useful, it ignores the compelling fact that the key decisions occur earlier in the process—when Congress writes an Occupational Safety and Health Act or an amendment to the Food, Drug, and Cosmetics Act or other important regulatory law, usually with hundreds of pages of detailed specifications.

Each congressional committee should be required, when drafting a regulatory statute, to present estimates of the expected benefits and costs of the regulatory program in the report accompanying the legislation. The committee should affirm that these benefits justify the program in light of its estimated costs. Such a statement, and the benefit-cost analysis supporting it, should be required before a legislative proposal can be reported to the full House or Senate.

The way regulatory statutes are now written frequently precludes the agencies from even considering the most cost-effective approaches. Key provisions of the Occupational Safety and Health Act, the Federal Food, Drug, and Cosmetics Act, the Clean Air Act, the Safe Drinking Water Act, and the Superfund Act implicitly, or explicitly, prohibit the regulators from taking account of economic impacts when setting standards. Despite well-intended presidential directives, it is impossible for regulators to strike any sensible balance between the costs they impose and the benefits they generate when the basic regulatory laws prohibit costs from being considered at all.

Congress should eliminate provisions in existing regulatory statutes that prevent or limit regulatory agencies from considering costs or comparing expected benefits with costs when designing and promulgating regulations. Regulations that seek to reduce health or safety risks should be based on scientific risk-assessment and should address risks that are real and significant rather than hypothetical or remote.

The Task of Regulatory Agencies

The current efforts of government agencies to examine the impact of proposed regulations before issuing them need to be strengthened. By statute, these requirements should be extended to the so-called independent commissions, such as the Federal Energy Regulatory Commission, the Federal Trade Commission, the International Trade Commission, and the Nuclear Regulatory Commission.

Congress should legislate provisions for regulatory review by OIRA similar to those contained in the executive orders promulgated by presidents Reagan and Clinton. A firm statutory basis would help to provide continuity in this important activity. In addition, Congress should codify in a single statute a requirement that regulatory agencies analyze the impact of significant regulatory initiatives *before* they are undertaken. Such an analysis of expected benefits and costs should be made a routine part of the drafting of new regulations by the various federal agencies.

Difficulties in estimating costs and benefits should not deter efforts to analyze the impact of regulations before they are issued. For example, uncertainty about the dollar benefits of air pollution control is not primarily a problem of statistical measurement. Rather, it may mainly reflect the unpleasant fact that we are unsure how many asthma attacks will be prevented or how much agricultural crop damage will be avoided by a specific emissions reduction. Such uncertainty should be recognized in the analysis, but should not be used as an excuse to proceed without analysis.

Furthermore, in making decisions and setting priorities based on risk, agencies should use best estimates rather than worst-case projections of risk. OSHA has based occupational cancer risks on the unrealistic assumption that a hypothetical worker is exposed to the risk eight hours every day, five days a week, for 50 weeks a year for 45 years. Similarly, the EPA sometimes assumes that an individual is exposed to emissions at a distance of 200 meters from the factory, 24 hours a day, every day for 70 years.

Concluding Thoughts

None of the procedural changes proposed here will succeed in truly improving the regulatory process unless they have the support of the public. It is the public that receives the benefits and pays the costs generated by the very substantial involvement of government in business decision-making. Thus, the emphasis in considering these proposals should not be on the effects on either business or government—but on the American people.

A final barrier to careful analysis is the common and erroneous perception that the costs of government regulation are of little concern to citizens because they are simply "paid by business." By and large, those costs are ultimately borne by the individual workers and consumers who make and purchase the products and services produced under regulation. Moreover, much of the rule making extends to all employers, be they profit or nonprofit, in the public sector or in the private sector.

The criticism in this report of the government's response to public concerns about worker safety, the environment, and similar issues does not imply that those public concerns are not legitimate or should be ignored. The analysis here, rather, leads to the compelling conclusion that the American people deserve better results from the very substantial amounts of resources, time, and effort devoted to government regulation than is now the case. Air ought to be cleaner, water purer and workplaces safer, at the same time that consumer living standards are higher.

31

Making the Marketplace Work
for the Environment

This article goes beyond criticizing the shortcomings of government regulation. It focuses on alternative ways of meeting society's social objectives, notably improving the quality of the environment.

There is a high common ground on which economists and environmentalists can meet and thus mutually help to generate more sensible public policy. Several basic ideas, readily supported by both groups can help to attain that common ground. A strong economy requires a healthy environment. Even the most theoretical economist breathes the same air and drinks the same water as members of the Sierra Club. In fact, he or she may be a dues-paying member.

Also, a strong economy provides the resources for human activity, including dealing with ecological problems. It generates the rising living standard that enables citizens to deal with serious concerns beyond the immediate one of paying for everyday necessities. Balancing economic and ecological concerns is hardly an either/or matter.

Any doubt on that score can be resolved by examining the plight of many Eastern European nations. Their weak economies have been unable to support the environmental cleanup taking place in Western societies. The result has been an "ecological Twilight Zone," where even the snow is black. Fines levied on polluters are ineffective in socialized economies because the government, as owner of almost all property, ends up paying the penalties.

Public Support and Individual Reluctance

Every poll of citizen sentiment shows overwhelming support for doing more to clean up the environment. An April 4, 1990 public opinion survey by *The New York Times* and CBS News reported that 74 percent of the sample agreed that the environment should be protected "regardless of cost."

Despite a plethora of new laws and directives by the Environmental Protection Agency (EPA) plus hundreds of billions of dollars of compliance costs expended by private industry, the public remains unhappy with the results. An August 1990 survey, released by Environment Opinion Study, Inc., asked respondents, "In general, do you think there is too much, too little or about

---

Source: Murray Weidenbaum, "Making the Marketplace Work for the Environment," in Kenneth Chilton and Melinda Warren, eds., *Environmental Protection* (Boulder, CO: Westview Press, 1991).

the right amount of government regulation and involvement in the area of environmental protection?" Two-thirds answered that there was "too little" involvement, while only one in ten persons believed there was too much.

Unfortunately, the same citizens who want environmental improvements "regardless of cost" vociferously oppose the location of any hazardous waste facility in their own neighborhood. Nor are they keen on paying for the cleanup. Of course, they strongly favor cleaning up the environment, but each prefers to have the dump site located in someone else's backyard and to have the other fellow pay for it.

An example of this situation is the reaction of the citizens of Minnesota to a $3.7 million grant from the EPA to build and operate a state-of-the-art chemical landfill that could handle hazardous wastes with a high assurance of safety. In each of the sixteen locations that the state proposed, the local residents raised such a fuss that the state government backed off. Ultimately, the unspent grant was returned to EPA. The Minnesota experience is not exceptional. The EPA was also forced to stop a project to test whether the sludge from a municipal waste treatment plant could be used as a low-cost fertilizer. The public opposition was fierce, even though the EPA was going to use federally owned land and the sludge was expected to increase crop yields by 30 percent.

Since 1980, not a single major new hazardous waste disposal facility has been sited anywhere in the United States. As Peter Sandman of Rutgers University has pointed out, the public perceives environmental matters not only emotionally, but also morally. "Our society," he has written, "has reached near consensus that pollution is morally wrong—not just harmful or dangerous . . . but wrong." Yet, the individuals that make up that same public are reluctant personally to assume the burdens associated with that strongly held view.

This ambivalent attitude toward the environment is not new. In 1969, the National Wildlife Federation commissioned a national survey to ascertain how much people were willing to pay for a cleaner environment. At a time of peak enthusiasm for environmental regulation, the public was asked, "To stop the pollution destroying our plant life and wildlife, would you be willing to pay an increase in your monthly electric bill of $1?" The "no" vote won hands down, 62 percent to 28 percent (with 10 percent "not sure"). That study, we should recall, was taken before the big run-up in utility bills. Perhaps not too surprisingly, the survey showed strong support for taxing business to finance environmental cleanup.

In other words, most Americans want a cleaner environment, but we are neither willing to pay for it nor seriously to inconvenience ourselves. We try to take the easy way out—by imposing the burden on "someone else," preferably a large, impersonal institution. A brief historical review of how environmental protection has evolved in the United States might be helpful before turning attention to some suggestions for improving current environmental policy.

The Growth of Environmental Protection

Environmental regulation covers a variety of concerns—air pollution, water pollution, pesticides, toxic substances, hazardous wastes, drinking water, ocean dumping, noise emissions, and asbestos in schools. The Environmental Protection Agency is the main federal organization operating in this area, and it focuses on issuing rules and approving permits. In recent years, "markets" for pollution control have been created to enable companies to seek less costly approaches to meeting environmental standards.

Early Efforts to Protect the Environment

The notion that environmental protection is a proper function of government did not originate in the twentieth century. Prior to independence, the Massachusetts Bay Colony enacted regulations to prevent pollution in Boston Harbor. Following the Revolution, most coastal states took some action to ensure that no large floating debris would obstruct navigation of the waterways within their borders.

Throughout the eighteenth and nineteenth centuries and well into the twentieth, local governments bore primary responsibility for the regulation of water and air pollution. Unfortunately, localities found themselves quite helpless to control water pollution coming from upstream, and a shift in the prevailing winds was apt to make a sleepy hamlet the unwilling recipient of smoky particles from a more industrialized town.

By the end of the nineteenth century, the connections between dirty water and contagious diseases had stimulated most states to enact water pollution laws. These early statutes were concerned with the human-health aspects of dirty water rather than with abating pollution per se. The result was a tendency for pollution issues to be buried in public health agencies that largely ignored the problem once a disease had been eradicated.

Federal involvement with the environment during the first half of the twentieth century was piecemeal. Antipollution legislation was aimed primarily at keeping interstate and coastal waterways free from debris so as to maintain the flow of navigation. The Refuse Act of 1899 forbade dumping into navigable waters without a permit from the Corps of Engineers. The Oil Pollution Act of 1924 banned oil discharges into coastal waters. Otherwise, protecting health and safety was viewed as a function of the states under their police power.

Modern Regulations Governing Pollution

The first breakthrough in federal water pollution legislation was the Water Pollution Control Act of 1948. The law did little more than provide technical and research assistance to the states, but it demonstrated a national responsibility. The Air Pollution Control Act of 1955 very much resembled the 1948 water pollution legislation. Thus, as recently as 1955 a congressional committee stated:

. . . it is primarily the responsibility of state and local government to prevent air pollution. The bill does not propose any exercise of police power by the federal government and no provision in it invades the sovereignty of states, counties or cities. There is no attempt to impose standards of purity.

During the 1970s, legislation progressively enlarged the role of the federal government in regulating the environment and committing the nation to ambitious goals. The Environmental Protection Agency was established in 1970 to pull together a variety of scattered activities and provide a unified ecological policy at the national level. EPA now administers programs dealing with air pollution, water pollution, toxic substances, waste disposal, pesticides, and environmental radiation. It possesses an impressive arsenal of powers and duties.

Activities of the EPA center around setting and enforcing standards relating to environmental concerns. EPA has several means of enforcement. Upon finding a violation, it may seek voluntary compliance. If that fails, it can order compliance and take court action. The EPA relies on both criminal and civil penalties.

The Problem: Trying to Do So Much at Once

It is much easier for Congress to express a desire for cleaner air or purer water than for an agency like EPA to fulfill that desire. To be sure, vast sums of money have been spent for these purposes in recent years. From 1970 to 1990, Congress appropriated over $30 billion for the operation of EPA. EPA employment rose from a few hundred in 1970 to over 9,000 in 1990. These numbers are dwarfed by the costs incurred to comply with the government's rules on environmental cleanup—$100 billion a year at present.

These substantial outlays have not prevented the critics from instituting an array of lawsuits whose main purpose is to get the EPA to act faster and to do more. EPA can claim important accomplishments. Between 1970 and 1987, total emissions of sulfur dioxide in the United States fell from 28 million metric tons to 20 million. Carbon dioxide was down from 99 million to 61 million. The decline in lead emissions was more dramatic, from 204,000 metric tons to 8,000. That occurred despite the rise in population and increased economic activity. Rivers from coast to coast that were nearly devoid of aquatic life teem with fish once again. Lake Erie, so laden with pollutants in 1969 that a river feeding into it caught fire, has been revived.

Despite these successes, the EPA frequently falls short in meeting congressionally mandated goals for pollution cleanup. Congress continues to pass high-sounding legislation with unrealistic timetables and inflexible deadlines, while EPA gets greater responsibility and private industry spends billions more on environmental compliance. In the words of EPA's former administrator William Ruckelshaus, "EPA's statutory framework is less a coherent attack on a complex and integrated societal problem than it is a series of petrified postures."

Economic Solutions to Environmental Problems

Dealing with Hazardous Wastes

Turning to specific environmental problems, we can start with the controversy over the disposal of hazardous wastes. Instances of toxic waste contamination at Love Canal in New York State and at Times Beach, Missouri, have brought a sense of urgency to the problem.

Emotionally charged responses are encouraged by the fact that levels of some substances can now be measured by the EPA in terms of parts per billion and occasionally per quadrillion, but the experts still debate the significance of exposure at those dosages. The headlines about chemical health hazards deal with exposures that are akin to the proverbial needle in the haystack. Actually, the needle-haystack comparison is too modest. One part per billion is the equivalent of one inch in 16,000 miles, a penny in $10 million, four drops of water in an Olympic-size pool, or a second in thirty-two years.

Eventually, society will have to face the main reason for the scarcity of hazardous waste sites—the "Not In My Backyard" (NIMBY) syndrome. Sites for the disposal of toxic substances have joined prisons and mental hospitals as things the public wants, but not too close by.

The hazardous waste disposal problem is not going to disappear unless Americans change to less-polluting methods of production and consumption. Until then, greater understanding is needed on the part of the public and a willingness to come to grips with the difficult problems arising from the production and use of hazardous substances. Of course, it will cost large amounts of money to meet society's environmental expectations. But spending money may be the easiest part of the problem. Getting people to accept disposal sites in their neighborhoods is much more difficult.

The answer surely is an appeal not merely to good citizenship but also to common sense and self-interest. In a totalitarian society, people who do not want to do something the government desires are simply forced to do so, with the threat of physical violence ever present. In a free society with a market economy, we offer to pay people to do something they otherwise would not do. The clearest example in modern times is the successful elimination of the military draft coupled with very substantial increases in pay and fringe benefits for voluntarily serving in the armed forces.

Individual citizens have much to gain by opposing hazardous waste facilities to be located near them—and there is a basic logic to their position. It is not fair for society as a whole to benefit from a new disposal site, while arbitrarily imposing most of the costs (ranging from potential health threats to depressed property values) on the people in the locality. But local resistance to dealing with hazardous wastes also imposes large costs on society as a whole. Those costs are in the form both of inhibiting economic progress and having to ship waste from one temporary site to another.

There is a way of reconciling individual interests and community concerns: providing economic incentives. The idea is to look upon environmental pollution not as a sinful act but as an activity costly to society and amenable to reduction by means of proper incentives. After all, the prospect of jobs and income encourages many communities to offer tax holidays and other enticements to companies considering the location of a new factory—even though it may not exactly enhance the physical environment of the region.

Under present arrangements, however, there is little incentive for the citizens of an area to accept a site for hazardous wastes in their vicinity, no matter how safe it is. Unlike an industrial factory, a hazardous-waste facility provides few offsetting benefits to the local residents in the form of jobs or tax revenues. But perhaps some areas would accept such a facility if the state government (financed by all the citizens benefiting from the disposal facility) would pay for something the people in that locality want but cannot afford—such as a new school building, firehouse, or library or simply lower property taxes.

Government can do much to improve environmental policy in other ways. The EPA could reduce the entire hazardous waste problem by distinguishing between truly lethal wastes—which clearly should be disposed of with great care—and wastes that contain only minute amounts of undesirable materials. To the extent that changes in legislation would be required, the agency should urge Congress to make them.

The experience of a company in Oregon provides insights into why Congress needs to legislate common sense into the antipollution laws. The firm has been dumping heavy-metal sludges on its property for over twenty years. Company officials automatically classify the material as hazardous. Why? Because it would be too costly and time-consuming to try to prove that it was not. Other companies, similarly uncertain and wanting to avoid expensive testing costs, simply declare all of their wastes to be hazardous, whether they really are dangerous or not.

A Birth Control Approach to Pollution

Over 99 percent of environmental spending by government is devoted to controlling pollution after it is generated. Less than 1 percent is spent to reduce the generation of pollutants. For fiscal 1988, the EPA budgeted only $398,000—or 0.03 percent of its funds—for "waste minimization." That is an umbrella term that includes recycling and waste reduction.

The most desirable approach is to reduce the generation of pollutants in the first place. Economists have an approach that is useful—providing incentives to manufacturers, to change their production processes to reduce the amount of wastes created or to recycle them in a safe and productive manner.

The government often taxes producers rather than polluters. By doing that, the country misses an opportunity to curb actual dumping of dangerous wastes. Switching to a waste-end fee levied on the amount of hazardous wastes that a company actually disposes of would be far more economically sound than current practices. This more enlightened approach would require a basic correction in the Comprehensive Environmental Response, Compensation, and Liability Act (or "Superfund"), but it would be a very beneficial form of hazardous waste "birth control."

More generally, a government fee on the amount of pollutants discharged would provide an incentive to reduce the actual generation of wastes. Some companies would find it cheaper to change their production processes than to pay the tax. Recycling and reuse systems would be encouraged. Moreover, such a tax or fee would cover imports that are now disposed of in our country tax-free. In short, rewriting statutes so that they are more fair would also help protect the environment—and would probably save money at the same time.

Already, some companies are recycling as they become aware of the economic benefits. For example, one chemical firm burns 165,000 tons of coal a year at one of its textile fibers factories, generating 35,000 tons of waste in the form of fly ash. The firm recently found a local cement block company that was testing fly ash as a replacement for limestone in making lightweight cement blocks. The chemical company now sells the fly ash to the cement block manufacturer. What used to be an undesirable waste by-product has been turned into a commercially useful material. Simultaneously, the companies are conserving the supply of limestone.

Creative solutions can at times convert a cost into a benefit. For example, an Allied-Signal Corporation plant in Metropolis, Illinois, created a veritable sea of calcium fluoride sludge as a by-product of its manufacture of fluorine-based chemicals. It was generating the sludge at the rate of 1,000 cubic yards a month. Analysis showed that the sludge could be mixed with another waste stream to produce a reaction. The result: neutralization of the waste and production of synthetic fluorspar that Allied uses as a raw material at another location. The $4.3 million facility to accomplish these results saves the company about $1 million a year, an attractive return on an investment that also eliminates the problem of disposal of a growing stream of sludge.

A relatively simple equipment change in any stage of a manufacturing process may promote waste reduction. When an employee discovered some gas escaping from a pressure control vent, a USX Chemicals plant in Ironton, Ohio, was able to reduce the amount emitted into the air by adding a condenser to existing equipment. The condensed gas was then returned directly to the phenol process unit. The company was able to recover 400,000 pounds of cumene, one of the plant's major raw materials. This procedure is saving the plant $200,000 in operating expenses annually. The installation cost of the condenser was only $5,000.

Incentives to do more along these lines could be provided: tax the disposal of wastes. The object would not be to punish the polluters but to get them to change their ways. Every sensible firm would try to reduce the amount of pollution tax it pays by curbing its wastes. Adjusting to new taxes on pollution would be a matter not of altruism but of minimizing cost and maximizing profit. The pollution tax approach appeals to self-interest in order to achieve the public interest.

These fees would raise costs and hence prices for products whose production generate pollution. Consumer demand would shift to products that pollute less, because they would cost less. To stay competitive, high-polluting producers would have to economize on pollution, just as they do in the case of other costs of production. Since pollution imposes burdens on the environment, it is only fair that the costs of cleanup be reflected in the price of a product whose production generates this pollution.

Nine countries in Western Europe have adopted the "polluter pays" principle. In these nations, pollution control is paid for directly by the polluting firm or from the money collected from effluent taxes. The West German effluent-fee system, the oldest in operation, began before World War I. It has succeeded in halting the decline in water quality throughout the Ruhr Valley, the center of West Germany's iron and steel production. It is also serving as a model for a more recent French effort.

Indeed, many foreign countries have shown a greater willingness than the United States to experiment with waste minimization approaches other than "command and control" measures. These approaches include: tax incentives, economic subsidies, technical assistance, demonstration projects, waste reduction and waste exchange programs.

Practical problems make changes in pollution policy difficult in the United States. Both the regulators and the regulated have an interest in maintaining the current approach. Pollution taxes have little appeal in the political system, particularly in the Congress. Many reject a pollution tax on philosophical grounds, considering pollution charges to be a "license to pollute." They believe that putting a price on the act of polluting amounts to an attitude of moral indifference towards polluters. That gets us back to the point made earlier, that many people look at ecological matters as moral issues, making it especially difficult to adopt a more rational and workable system.

Suggestions have been made for a more fundamental approach to cleaning up environmental wastes. Princeton University economists William Baumol and Edwin Mills conclude that the existing system focusing on "inspection and coercion" is useless, because there is no way of knowing who produces the wastes or who is currently storing wastes.

The Superfund experience, they contend, confirms that it is best to adopt measures that provide reasonable assurance that toxic wastes will be disposed of properly. In their view, only a financial incentive that succeeds in getting people to comply voluntarily has any chance of working. It also may prove less expensive than cleaning up the damage caused by indiscriminate dumping. Baumol and Mills would have the government identify a set of acceptable disposal facilities and pay for delivery of toxic wastes to the sites. The subsidy should not be set so high as to encourage deliberate production of hazardous waste—nor so low as to be ignored.

Yet more technically efficient solutions will not stand a chance of enactment or even serious consideration in the legislative process until the "emotional thermostat" in public discussions on the environment is lowered substantially.

Conclusion

In practice environmental economics makes for strange alliances. So far, business interests have opposed the suggestions of economists for such sweeping changes in the basic structure of government regulation as using taxes or emissions fees to reduce pollution. Despite the shortcomings of the present system of government regulation, many firms have paid the price of complying with existing rules. They have learned to adjust to regulatory requirements and to integrate existing regulatory procedures into their long-term planning.

As any serious student of business-government relations will quickly report, the debate over regulation is miscast when it is described as black-hatted business versus white-hatted public interest groups. Almost every regulatory action creates winners and losers in the business system and often among other interest groups. Clean air legislation, focusing on ensuring that new facilities fully meet standards, is invariably supported by existing firms that are "grandfathered" approval without having to conform to the same high standards as new firms. Regulation thus protects the "ins" from the "outs."

There are many other examples of regulatory bias against change and especially against new products, new processes, and new facilities. Tough emissions standards are set for new automobiles, but not for older ones. Testing and licensing procedures for new chemicals are more rigorous and thoroughly enforced than for existing substances. This ability to profit from the differential impacts of regulation helps to explain why business shows little enthusiasm for the use of economic incentives and prefers current regulatory techniques.

But the reform of regulation is truly a consumer issue. The consumer receives the benefits from regulation and bears the burden of the costs of compliance in the form of higher prices and less product variety. Thus, the consumer has the key stake in developing more cost-effective solutions to environmental problems.

Part 6
Dealing with the International Economy

32

Business and the Global Marketplace

The vague notion of globalization is focused by using facts and figures that relate to specific countries and companies and their products.

The global marketplace surely arrived when villagers in the Middle East followed the Gulf War on CNN via Russian government satellite and through a private subsidiary of a local government enterprise. Both public and private businesses were involved, and they were located on three different continents.

Other, more quantitative indicators give a sense of the global marketplace. A rising share of the products manufactured in the United States (perhaps one-half or more) has one or more foreign components. Ford's Crown Victoria has a foreign content of 27 percent, while 25 percent of Honda's U.S.-manufactured Accord is made overseas. This development was nicely summed up in a recent conversation. The customer asks the auto dealer, "Is this car made in the United States?" The salesman responds with another question, "Which part?"

A second way of looking at the global marketplace is to consider that about one-half of all imports and exports—what governments label foreign trade—is transacted between domestic companies and their foreign affiliates or foreign parents. That is roughly true in the United States, the European Union (EU), and Japan. From the viewpoint of political geography, the activity is classified as foreign commerce. But from an economic viewpoint, these international flows of goods and services are internal transfers within the same company. That is the global enterprise in full operation.

One final indicator: Despite the massive trade deficit, U.S. companies sell to and in other nations as much as, if not more than, "foreign" companies sell in and to the United States. This leads to a set of questions on which experts answer differently: Is Honda USA part of the U.S. economy? What about IBM in Tokyo? What is clear is that the consequences of the internationalization of business are profound for many firms. Half of Xerox's employees work on foreign soil. Less than one-half of Sony's employees are Japanese. More than half of Digital Equipment's revenues come from overseas operations. One-third of the profits of General Electric arise from its international activities.

Source: Murray Weidenbaum, "The Business Response to the Global Marketplace," *The Washington Quarterly*, Winter 1992.

Technology and economics are outpacing traditional ways of thinking about international politics. The standard geopolitical map is out of synchronization with the emerging business and economic map. Economic and technological forces are powerful agents for change.

A dramatic example is the Kuwaiti bank that was moved by facsimile machine. The day of the Iraqi invasion, the manager set up three open telephone lines with his office in Bahrain so that he could transmit all of the bank's key documents via fax. From time to time, the shooting around him slowed the process. But, before the end of the day, the necessary transmissions were complete. The next morning the bank opened up as a Bahraini institution neither subject to the U.S. freeze on Kuwaiti assets nor to Iraqi control.

On a more aggregate level, business planning is geared to the fundamental shifts occurring in national positions in the international economy. There are likely to be three regions of dominant economic power far into the twenty-first century. One is North America, led by the United States. Another is Japan and the other vibrant Asian rim economies. The third is the reinvigorated European Union, where change is taking place on an unprecedented scale. Business support for a North American free trade area arises in good measure in response to the competitive developments in Europe and Asia.

From all indications, the countries along the Asian rim will continue to grow rapidly during the 1990s. Japan and the four "little dragons" (Hong Kong, Singapore, Taiwan, and South Korea) are being joined by Thailand, Malaysia, and Indonesia as the newest members of the club of industrialized nations.

The European Union

The key structural shift in Western Europe is the economic integration of the members of the European Union. These governmental developments will have profound long-term effects on business productivity and international competitiveness. The big positive about this development is that the EU countries are reducing restrictions on business, trade, and labor. People as well as goods and investments will be able to move readily from one of the Common Market nations to any other. That will tend to make industries more efficient as they achieve greater economies of scale and as standardization replaces national varieties of many products and services.

Not all of the changes will be beneficial to companies located outside of the European community, however. A large negative, from the viewpoint of other nations, is that the trade wall around the EU is not coming down. Actually, the EU is toughening its external barriers to commerce. Enlightened economists are not supposed to use pejorative terms such as Fortress Europa, so let us cite some numbers instead. In 1960, before the Common Market gained momentum, more than 60 percent of the foreign trade of the members was outside of the EU. Now over 60 percent of their trade stays in the EU—a complete reversal. That ratio is bound to rise further.

This development toward a larger but more inward-looking community serves as a powerful reminder to companies headquartered elsewhere of the benefits of having strong European-based operations in order to take advantage of what is known as "national treatment." In effect, the EU is adopting the economic version of the U.S. driver's license rule, under which each state honors the licenses issued by the other states no matter how great the variation in the rules of qualification. The results will be similar.

The biggest negative is that a more inward-looking Europe is toughening its barriers to external commerce. The French government, for example, has announced new regulations on TV programming (an important service export for the United States and one of the relatively few favorable items in our balance of trade). In the guise of promoting EU-wide TV programming, the French are limiting non-EU programming to 40 percent of total air time.

In private conversations, the Europeans tell U.S. companies not to worry, that most of their trade restrictions, such as reciprocity and domestic content rules, are aimed at Japan. It is, however, far more than a mere riposte for the United States to say that it does not know how good their aim is. The same restrictions that adversely affect Japan can keep out U.S. goods. This may especially be the case for the automobile "transplants," which are built in the United States by Japanese-owned companies. Moreover, if the products of the Asian rim countries are kept out of Europe, the Western Hemisphere is their major alternate market.

The development of a European common market will produce winners and losers, on both sides of the Atlantic. Likely winners will include strong U.S. firms with an established presence in Western Europe. High-tech, well-capitalized U.S. companies are accustomed to competing on a continent-wide basis. They can use one EU country as a base to sell to the others. General Motors and Ford have more Europe-wide strength than such European automakers as Volkswagen, Fiat, Peugeot, and Renault. The same holds true for computer manufacturers such as IBM, Digital Equipment, Unisys, and Hewlett Packard compared to their European counterparts.

The winners will also include the stronger, high-skilled European companies that will be enjoying the economies of scale and growing domestic markets. They should emerge larger than ever. One category of losers will be the high-cost European firms that have been sheltered within their national markets. These tradition-bound companies will be hurt by continent-wide competition. Cheap labor and tax incentives will no longer be key competitive factors. The backward areas, such as Italy's Mezzogiorno, will fall further behind. Realistically, not all barriers to business will be down. The French are not going to make a stampede for German wine, no matter how great the reduction of formal obstacles to intra-European trade.

Finally, many U.S. businesses are likely to be losers from European economic unification. They will find it more difficult to export to Europe. They will also face tougher competition in their domestic markets from stronger European enterprises. The losers will include many companies that have not yet awakened to developments across the Atlantic.

Although the member nations are expected to be working in harmony much of the time, they will continue to have individual values, cultures, and needs. Despite the substantial amount of progress being made toward full integration, each of the EU countries will still retain its own currency (at least for the next few years), its own tax system, and, of course, its ultimate sovereignty. Perhaps even more fundamental are the differing national traditions, especially the nine languages that are spoken in the Union.

The EU is not a static concept. It started with six countries—Germany, France, Italy, Belgium, the Netherlands, and Luxembourg. Gradually, it has expanded to twelve—adding the United Kingdom, Ireland, Denmark, Greece, Spain, and Portugal. That is not the end of the line. Many other European nations are seeking admission.

Austria is a logical candidate for early entry. Although its economy is modest in size, its admission could be a strategic move, especially since Vienna often views itself as a gateway to Eastern Europe. Most likely, Hungary would then be close behind in the waiting line in Brussels. Czechoslovakia and Poland might be next or, at the least, they could apply to become "associate members."

With Denmark already a member, the other Scandinavian countries are prime candidates for EU membership—Iceland, Sweden, Finland, and Norway. With the end of the Cold War, the traditional neutrality of some of these nations should no longer be a barrier to entering into a formal relationship with the EU.

Looking beyond the initial adjustment period, an economically united Europe will become a political and economic superpower early in the twenty-first century. As Stanley Hoffmann, chairman of the Center for European Studies at Harvard, notes in his comment on the European Union:

> Clearly, the purpose of the whole effort is not merely to increase wealth by removing obstacles to production and technological progress, but also to increase Europe's power in a world in which economic and financial clout is as important as military might.

Consider the implications if and when the EU expands from twelve members to sixteen or twenty. Adding all those gross domestic products (GDPs) together shows that, in the 1990s, Western (and Central) Europe will become the world's largest market area, with concomitant economic and political power. Despite all the protestations of openness and friendship, the nations in Asia, Africa, and the Americas—and many of their business firms—will be on the outside looking in.

Business Potentials in Eastern Europe

Four decades of Communist rule have left the economies of Eastern Europe in extremely poor shape. They are experiencing difficulty converting their inefficient nationalized industries into competitive private enterprises. Because of the Marxist cliché that unemployment does not exist under communism, East European enterprises are notoriously overstaffed.

To make matters worse, Eastern Europe lacks a business infrastructure, which is so basic to the efficient functioning of a modern economy that Western nations take it for granted. These basic requisites for a private enterprise system include:

- a body of commercial law that is enforced;
- a credible accumulation of cost accounting data that can be used both for setting prices and making valuations of assets;
- personnel who can perform financial analyses;
- banks to provide credit on the basis of financial valuations rather than political determinations; and
- organizations to provide insurance for normal business risks.

In light of the criticism often hurled at these professions in the United States, it is fascinating to consider that Eastern Europe is a world with a shortage of lawyers, accountants, and insurance agents. From a positive viewpoint, that large area may provide a major new client base for many service enterprises headquartered in the more advanced economies.

Eastern Europe also needs generous supplies of capital from the United States and other capitalist nations. Attracting foreign capital in substantial amounts will not be easy. The East Europeans were brought up to hate greedy capitalists and their profiteering. But the move to capitalism (which seems to be an almost universal desire in those nations) will be difficult without capital and capitalists.

It also will be necessary for the rank-and-file employees of the East European nations to do a 180-degree turn in their attitude toward work. They must abandon their universal slogan, "They pretend to pay us and we pretend to work." Consider the thousands of East Germans who have been fired by their new West German employers because they were not in the habit of returning to work after lunch.

Not all East European nations are likely to make the transition to democratic capitalism; the most promising cases are Hungary, Czechoslovakia, and Poland. Those countries that succeed would be tough competitors for the low-tech, high-labor-cost industries in the more advanced economies. They could, however, also become subcontractors and suppliers to established Western firms hard pressed by low-cost competitors. The education of East European workers is quite good as measured by standardized math and science tests.

Russia is conspicuously absent from this discussion of ascending economic powers. It is still very much a military superpower, but its economy—aside from the military sector—remains primitive, even if the current political and social instability can be overcome. According to the Soviet Academy of Sciences, its computer capacity is less than one one-thousandth of that of the United States.

Threats and Opportunities

For the individual business firm, the rapid changes in the international economy offer both threat and opportunity. The opportunity arises as more of the developing countries enter the status of industrialized nations. Advanced economies are the best customers of other advanced economies. For example, Bangladesh is not an important customer of U.S. jet airplanes and grain, but Japan is. Yet at the same time home markets will become increasingly vulnerable to foreign competition.

There is great similarity between the domestic threat of hostile takeovers and the loss of market position due to new foreign competition. In both cases, the firm is forced to review its strengths and weaknesses and to rethink its long-term strategy. Streamlining, downsizing, accelerating product development, and organizational restructuring are often responses to both internal takeover threats and foreign competition.

Stepping back and taking a longer-term perspective makes it clear that fundamental changes are occurring in the very nature of the private business enterprise. The most domestic-oriented firm is increasing its geographic reach as its suppliers and customers are, with increasing frequency, located on a variety of continents. Joint ventures are no longer an obscure legal form. To cite one example among many, over one-half of Corning Glass's profits come from joint ventures. Two-thirds of these cooperative endeavors are with a wide range of foreign companies, including Siemens and Ciba Geigy in Europe and Samsung and Asahi Glass in Asia.

Strategic alliances are not just a theoretical possibility; they, too, increasingly involve companies located on different continents. Philips, the Dutch producer of consumer electronics, has cooperated extensively with Matsushita of Japan in developing new products such as compact discs and VCRs.

Sweden's Volvo and France's Renault also have established a strategic alliance, with an explicit division of labor. Renault is doing diesel-engine development, while Volvo is handling advanced emissions controls. The two enterprises are also moving to coordinate parts purchasing, transportation and communication, and new-product strategy. Mergers and acquisitions increasingly involve crossing national boundaries and dealing with two or more national governments, as well as a variety of state, provincial, and local authorities. In 1985, business mergers within the United States accounted for 85 percent of global merger activity. By 1990, U.S. domestic mergers accounted for less than half of the worldwide volume. Most of the U.S. companies operating in Europe do so through subsidiaries resulting from acquisitions.

Partially owned subsidiaries, associated firms, licensing, and correspondent relationships are also on the rise. Often the same companies engage in joint ventures to develop new products, coproduce existing products, serve as sources of supply for each other, share output, and compete. There is no set pattern. Various companies—in the same nation and often in the same industry—are responding to the global marketplace differently.

United Technologies exemplifies the use of geographic diversification on a global scale in developing new products. For its new elevator, its French division worked on the door systems; the Spanish division handled the small-geared components; the German subsidiary was responsible for the electronics; the Japanese unit designed the special motor drives; and the Connecticut group handled the systems integration. International teamwork cut the development cycle in half.

IBM is often cited as the role model for foreign firms focusing on high-technology markets. Potential imitators note that the corporation's basic research laboratories are in Switzerland and Japan, as well as the United States. Its thirty-odd research divisions are located around the world. Thus, the process of international technology transfer at IBM is often internal to the firm. Xerox Corporation is another interesting example of global production. Xerox has introduced some eighty different office copying machines in the United States that were engineered and built by its Japanese joint venture, Fuji Xerox Company.

The automobile industry provides a fascinating array of examples of inter-firm and intercontinental endeavors. General Motors has joint ventures with Japan's Toyota and Suzuki and partial ownership of Sweden's Saab, Korea's Daewoo, and Japan's Isuzu and Suzuki. Volkswagen reports joint ventures with America's Ford and Japan's Nissan and Toyota, and has a stake in the Czech Republic's Skoda. Virtually all of these companies compete with their partners and investors, at least to some degree.

The computer industry is not to be outdone in this regard. For example, Unisys is a customer of, a supplier to, and a competitor of IBM and Honeywell in North America, Fujitsu and Hitachi in Asia, and Phillips, Siemens, and BASF in Europe. Some lessons can be learned from the experience of companies that do well in international markets.

First, they change their basic corporate goals to conform to a global marketplace. Second, they translate a domestic advantage to create overseas opportunities by adapting their established home products to the local markets in other nations. Pall Filters, the major U.S. producers of wine filters, penetrated the sophisticated French market by designing a new French version of its filters. The company then went on to enter the Italian wine market with a second variation of its product.

In the service area, U.S. financial institutions compete internationally primarily by building on strengths developed in their domestic markets. Financial institutions in the United States and the United Kingdom have developed a high degree of technical expertise in constructing, managing, and marketing complex financial products and services. This expertise involves both the development of physical capital—primarily computer systems and software—and trained professionals and support staff with both technical and market knowledge. Japanese banks, in contrast, initially penetrate an overseas market by serving the Japanese firms doing business there.

The third lesson is that the successful global firms do not set up large international bureaucracies. One recent survey reported that the cost of the international staff rarely exceeds 1 percent of sales. Moreover, most overseas operations are run by foreign nationals who understand the local markets. Further, they start their foreign operations when the company is still of moderate size, contradicting the widespread notion that only giant companies can succeed overseas.

But it takes massive resources to provide a universal presence. Toyota, IBM, Phillips, DuPont, Bayer, Sony, and Unilever have expanded into almost all of the world's major markets. A global economy, however, does not mean that every company should try to cater to every global market. Many medium-sized firms are learning the hard way to focus on specialty products and market niches where they have special advantages. Local offices provide a company with a built-in laboratory for developing new programs and servicing techniques that can be adapted throughout the global network. The power of modern communications means that Manchester, England, and Louisville, Kentucky, are as much a part of the international marketplace as London and New York. A mix of smaller and medium-sized locations is part of a pattern that gives the modern corporation diversification and stability during periods of rapid growth and recession alike.

Public Policy Implications

The current legislative battles over trade protectionism and foreign investment restrictions are only the most obvious manifestations of the rising tension between domestic political forces and transnational economic influences. Although private enterprise is increasingly global (in purchasing, financing, research, and production as well as marketing), government policy remains parochial. Understandably, voters still care about jobs in their country, province, state, and locality, and politicians react to those sentiments.

The tension between business and government is nothing new. It has traditionally existed between large private enterprises and the rulers of developing countries. In fact, most countries restrict foreign investments in defense, public utilities, and the media. Quite a few governments require that a majority of the capital of local firms be owned by their own nationals. The tension between government and business is being exacerbated by the rapid rate of economic, social, and technological change.

There is another force involved that is ultimately likely to carry the day—the citizen as consumer. Consumers vote every day of the week—in dollars, yen, deutsche marks, pounds, francs, and lira. The protectionist-oriented voters, as consumers, purchase products made anywhere in the world. They give far greater weight in spending their own money to price and quality than country of origin. And they increasingly travel to, and communicate with, people in virtually every land. Without thinking about it, consumers are adapting to the global economy. If consumers were not so globally oriented, the pressures for restricting international trade would not arise in the first place.

Meanwhile, some of the former multinational companies with large headquarters operations and a number of overseas subsidiaries are becoming transnational enterprises with activities and responsibilities spread around the world. For an increasing number of transnational companies, profits and revenues from abroad surpass those of the country of origin. Because the interests and stakeholders of these transnational businesses are located all over the globe, some of their leaders contend that they are losing their national identities and becoming "global citizens."

The transnational business firms also develop relationships with the international economic organizations established by governments. They participate actively in the business advisory committees of the Organization for Economic Cooperation and Development (OECD), the European Union, and the specialized agencies of the United Nations (UN). The rise of international regulatory agencies, in many ways, is an expected response of political forces to the global economy.

Some types of supranational regulation are traditional, going back to the nineteenth century. For example, the forerunner of the International Telecommunications Union was established in 1865 as the International Telegraph Union.

Some of the specialized agencies of the UN have moved ahead with the formulation of codes and guidelines. Examples range from the World Health Organization's Infant Formula Code, to the Food and Agricultural Organization's International Code of Conduct in the Distribution and Use of Pesticides, to the over 300 labor standards promulgated by the International Labor Organization. The governments of the developing nations, in many cases, see a more activist role for the UN agencies than do the representatives of the more advanced economies, who are oriented to private-sector decision-making in less regulated marketplaces.

In a more basic sense, the mobility of enterprises—of their people, capital, and information—is reducing the power of government. Public-sector decision-makers around the world are being forced to understand that in a new way they have to become competitive in the economic policies they devise. Domestic policies that impose costs without compensating benefits or that reduce wealth substantially in the process of redistributing income undermine the competitive positions of domestic enterprises. The result is either the loss of business to firms located in other nations or the movement of the domestic company's resources to more hospitable locations.

Political scientists and economists have long since understood that people vote with their feet, leaving regions with limited opportunity in favor of those that offer a more attractive future. In a day of computers, telephones, and facsimile machines, enterprises are far more mobile than that. Thus, the fear of losing economic activity to other parts of the world can be expected to reshape domestic political agendas in fundamental ways.

There is a positive role for government in dealing with the global marketplace: Enhance the productivity and competitiveness of the enterprises located in the government's jurisdiction by reducing tax and regulatory burdens and lowering the real cost of capital through curbing deficit financing.

Economic education faces the challenging task of helping citizens (consumers/taxpayers) to understand the increasingly global nature of economic life. It is easier to see the impact of foreign money in the domestic economy than it is to visualize the role of one country's investment in other nations. Yet the effects flow in both directions.

A quarter of a century ago, the citizens of Western Europe were complaining that the United States was making the world one big Coca-Cola franchise. The "American challenge" was a popular topic for public debates overseas. The U.S. reply was that U.S. investment benefited foreigners by creating employment, income, and tax collections in their countries. Although the shoe is now on the other foot, the results are very similar. Foreign investment is creating jobs, income, and tax revenue in the United States. Because the financing of outsized budget deficits drains off so much of U.S. domestic saving, that foreign money is a key factor in the continued prosperity of the United States.

33

Antitrust Policy for a Global Economy

This article attempts to lay a foundation for extending the scope of antitrust policy from national to international markets. Adopting a more global focus demonstrates that seemingly concentrated national markets are often truly competitive when examined from a broader perspective.

The national and regional governments that write antitrust laws and set rules for the modern corporation are increasingly finding themselves on the defensive in the global marketplace. The individual business firm now possesses a spectrum of options to respond to government policies and enforcement practices. The reach of public sector departments and agencies is being undercut by three key factors: the internationalization of production; the increased cross-border flows of information, money, and technology; and the resultant rise of the transnational enterprise.

An extreme case of internationalization of production was cited by former U.S. Secretary of State George Shultz. He tells of a shipping label on integrated circuits made by an American firm, which reads:

> Made in one or more of the following countries: Korea, Hong Kong, Malaysia, Singapore, Taiwan, Mauritius, Thailand, Indonesia, Mexico, Philippines. The exact country of origin is unknown.

The notion that data, capital, and technological innovation cross borders quickly, at times at the speed of light, is now quite familiar. Many of the larger and more sophisticated multinational companies with strong headquarters staffs and substantial numbers of subsidiaries are moving toward a more advanced stage of organization. They are becoming transnational organizations with no single locus of decision-making. There are several "headquarters" in the enterprise. For an increasing number of transnational companies, profits and sales from abroad, and on occasion from a single foreign country, surpass those of the country of origin. In that sense, these businesses are losing their national identities.

To an outsider, the performance of the transnational enterprise is recognizable by two key characteristics. The first is the ability to attract employees, capital, and suppliers from global sources. The second is to appeal to customers all over the world.

Source: Murray Weidenbaum, "Antitrust Policy for the Global Marketplace," *Journal of World Trade*, February 1994.

Alternative Business Responses

The impacts of globalization on a government's ability to carry out its policies are profound. In the case of antitrust, tax, and regulatory issues, for example, the company can move some of its operations to a more favorable policy environment in another country. It is helpful in a world where national policies change rapidly to do business in several countries. In that event, when faced with rising government burdens in one nation, a firm can more readily shift its activities to other nations in which it operates—or more credibly threaten to do so in order to prevent government actions hostile to its interests.

When faced with onerous government obstacles, businesses draw on a variety of alternatives. For example, in 1991 Monsanto's low-calorie sweetener NutraSweet was hit with a very high duty in response to a charge of dumping in the European Union. The next year, the company entered into a joint venture with Ajinomoto, a Japanese food and pharmaceutical company, to build a plant in France to produce for the European market.

Other businesses responded by acquiring local companies. This has been a particularly important strategy for foreign firms positioning themselves in response to the integration of the European market. In 1990, Emerson Electric purchased the French firm Leroy-Somer, General Electric acquired the United Kingdom's Burton Group Financial Services, American Brands bought out Scotland's Whyte & Mackay Distillers, and Scott Paper purchased the Tungram Company of Germany. To those concerned with the antitrust consequences that may flow from the recent spate of mergers and acquisitions, it may be helpful to consider the remarks of a senior NutraSweet official:

> Although there may be evidence to the contrary, our experience only tells us that you have to be in Europe if you want to do business in Europe. . . . You can't sit offshore somewhere and ship your product in.

While joint ventures, cross-licensing, franchising and other co-operative strategies often are considered as second-best relative to exporting or to the operation of a wholly owned facility, they provide important benefits. These include, in addition to market entry, the advantage of working with a partner knowledgeable about the local situation, as well as sharing production costs and risks.

A word of warning: weak governments are not the answer to improving the flow of international commerce and investment. Inadequate patent protection laws may constitute an extremely effective trade barrier, even in advanced industrial nations.

In a real sense, the mobility of enterprises—of their people, capital and information—is reducing, but hardly eliminating, the power of government. Government continues to set and enforce the rules of the game. Besides business and government, there is another force involved in international economic matters—the citizen as a consumer. The same protectionist-oriented voters, as consumers, purchase products made anywhere in the world. Moreover, they increasingly travel to, and communicate with, people in virtually every land. In the long run, both governments and businesses will have to respond and adjust to the sovereign consumer.

Updating Antitrust to the Global Marketplace

It is necessary to update antitrust laws and enforcement to conform more closely to the new realities of the global marketplace. In recent years, antitrust authorities have been grappling with the challenge of reshaping a government policy that was developed when the largest markets were primarily national or smaller. Indeed, as the pressures of world competition grow, the increasing pressure for greater efficiency in a firm's operations takes on new weight as a reason for mergers and other actions that are likely to result in savings in cost.

The critical antitrust task of defining the relevant market includes locating the appropriate geographic boundaries in which the competitive battle occurs. Increasingly, this requires changing the traditional viewpoint as to the limit of the market. In the case of key industries such as automobiles, steel, and chemicals, the more appropriate global view means that what may seem to be a rather concentrated industry in one nation is really part of an unconcentrated and much larger group of worldwide competitors.

For example, General Motors, Ford, and Chrysler traditionally dominated the U.S. auto market. At times, the big two (GM and Ford) felt constrained in raising their market shares for fear of running afoul of the antitrust authorities—at least, that was the widespread belief in American business circles. However, the situation has changed drastically. The three U.S. firms do not dominate the list of the twenty top global automobile manufacturers. The U.S. manufacturers only accounted for 37 percent of global auto sales in 1992, and they felt the foreign competition very keenly—both at home and abroad.

Foreign competition can no longer be factored into the antitrust equation simply by counting imports as the totality of foreign firms' share of the domestic market. In many relatively concentrated industries, local firms are competing directly with foreign enterprises that may be much larger. The range of foreign government intervention in international trade must also be taken into account, including public sector subsidies to home industries and restrictions on foreign competitors. Increasingly the relevant market is virtually the entire global marketplace. It is high time that antitrust policy be updated to correspond to economic reality.

34

The Power of Enterprise:
The Case of Greater China

This article shows the progress in the economic integration of the major Chinese economies, even before the official handover of Hong Kong to mainland China. The economic (but not political) cooperation of Taiwan and the mainland is examined. The key role of the "bamboo network" of overseas Chinese entrepreneurs is developed.

In today's global marketplace, the combination of economic incentive and technological advance frequently overpowers the efforts of government to determine the course of events. The major actors in this new drama being played out on the world stage are a breed generally overlooked by students of international relations. The new major global actors are individual entrepreneurs and their private business firms. The result is decentralized economic decision-making.

This development is emphasized by the end of the Cold War. When military competition dominated international relationships, governments were the prime movers. This is not to say that the state has withered away. Rather, in important aspects, the balance of power has shifted.

Despite the many efforts of governments to restrain or even to redirect trade and investment, many businesses are succeeding in overcoming these obstacles to private decision-making. Technological advances have provided business firms with an unmatched international mobility by way of computers, telephones, and fax machines. Although the formal power of government is not to be discounted (its destructive capability has been vividly demonstrated in innumerable wars), the continuing ability of business entrepreneurs to find effective ways of responding to the combined power of economic incentives and technological advance is surely impressive.

The most compelling examples of the impact of the new competition are seen in the rise of what scholars have called natural economic territories. These are regions whose economic linkages straddle portions of two or more countries.

In many ways, this situation is similar to the numerous metropolitan economies which stretch beyond one state or province. In the United States, for example, the southern portions of Illinois are oriented to St. Louis, Missouri, rather than to the major cities of Illinois itself. Greater New York City (the

Source: Murray Weidenbaum, "The Power of Enterprise in National Economic Territories: The Case of Greater China," *Business and the Contemporary World*, Summer 1994.

metropolitan area that statisticians measure), to cite the most conspicuous example of this phenomenon, straddles three different states; but Greater New York does not contain the prime governmental functions of any of the three states.

Surely, by far the most striking case of natural economic territories crossing several major political subdivisions is provided by the recent experiences of Chinese entrepreneurs operating in proximity to their ancestral homeland.

The Rise of Greater China

Over the years, scholars have referred to the Chinas as a multiple—two Chinas, three Chinas, and more. They have in mind the fact that several of the major economies of Southeast Asia have a predominantly Chinese population. In addition to the industrialized portions of mainland China, the overall Chinese economy includes such other rapidly growing areas as Taiwan, Hong Kong, and Singapore.

This "bamboo network" transcends existing national boundaries. It is comprised of key locations where business executives, traders, and financiers of Chinese background make most of the day-to-day economic decisions. The current South China natural economic territory may be viewed as a transitional phase to a Greater China economy. This informal economy is currently the world leader in economic growth, industrial expansion, and exports. The number of its potential consumers far exceeds the markets in Europe or the Western Hemisphere.

Not all of the vast Chinese mainland can be realistically viewed as a potential for early modernization. The major economic development is occurring in the coastal provinces of Guangdong and Fujian, the special economic zones in Shenzhen and Xiamen, and the city of Shanghai. These areas are a modest fraction of the 1.2 billion population of China. Yet, in aggregate, they constitute an economy the size of France.

The Chinese-based economy of Southeast Asia is rapidly emerging as a new epicenter for industry, commerce, and finance. Economic complementarities abound and growth has been mainly market-driven. This strategic area contains substantial amounts of technology and manufacturing capability (Taiwan), outstanding entrepreneurial, marketing, and services acumen (Hong Kong), a fine communications network (Singapore), a tremendous pool of financial capital (all three), and very large endowments of land, resources, and labor (mainland China). To take a modest example, a talking doll designed in Hong Kong (and assembled in China) contains a computer chip made in Taiwan.

The informal Chinese economy differs from the more official economies dominated by large multinational firms. Of the world's 500 leading industrial companies in 1991, only one, Chinese Petroleum, is part of the greater China economy (it is Taiwanese, in 166th place). In comparison, thirteen Korean companies make the list. The largest, Samsung, is the world's eighteenth largest industrial firm.

The Chinese-based economy consists in large measure of midsize family-run firms, rather than the huge corporations characteristic of Japan, Western Europe, and the United States. Transnational networks seem to be the natural accompaniment of the Chinese trading tradition. These channels for the movement of information, finance, goods, and capital help to explain the relative flexibility and efficiency of the numerous ongoing informal agreements and transactions that bind together the various parts of the Chinese-based trading area. These arrangements generate relatively low transaction costs.

This influential network—often based on extensions of the traditional clans—is the backbone of the Southeast Asian economy. A substantial amount of cross-investment and trade takes place, often on a family basis. This is especially important in a region where capital markets are relatively underdeveloped, financial disclosure is modest, and the rule of law limited. Interpersonal networks can be critical for moving information and capital quickly. Personal trust takes precedence over formal—and more expensive and time consuming—due diligence procedures.

The earlier European experience of the House of Rothschild comes to mind—with sons and other close family members dispatched to major financial centers. The current development multiplies the Rothschild phenomenon many thousands of times.

Frequently, these cross-border business ties involve "overseas" Chinese who are dealing with people in the province of China from which they or their ancestors migrated. Thus, Hong Kong has provided about 90 percent of the investment in adjacent Guangdong, the most rapidly growing economic area of mainland China. Similarly, Taiwanese investors have been largely responsible for the expansion of the nearby Xiamen Special Economic Zone.

Government is often heavily involved in the ownership, if not the operation, of many specific enterprises. Moreover, especially in mainland China, government initiative in establishing relatively open special economic zones was a necessary although far from sufficient condition for cross-border business cooperation. Some positive inducements, such as tax concessions, have also aided in attracting foreign investment. Throughout Southeast Asia, sympathetic governmental attitudes toward foreign trade and foreign investment have been helpful.

In Taiwan, the Nationalist Party is the largest property owner, with widespread business interests. In mainland China, government owns a great variety of enterprises (often in collaboration with foreign investors). Over 75 percent of the companies listed on the Shanghai stock exchange are controlled by the government. For example, China Northern Industries Corporation (NORINCO), the largest motorcycle manufacturer in the country, is an instrument of the Army.

Enterprises owned by the Chinese government often engage in overseas business ventures. Citic (the China International Trust and Investment Corporation) has subsidiaries in Mexico, Australia, Canada, the United States, and Europe. Citic's Hong Kong subsidiary owns 12 percent of Hong Kong Telecommunications, 12 percent of Cathay Pacific, 46 percent of Dragonair, and 20 percent of a Hong Kong chemical waste plant.

The close connection between government and business in the several parts of the greater China economy is illustrated by the operations of the Shanghai Far East Container Company. This joint venture between Shanghai, Hong Kong, and Taiwan involves enterprises in all three areas to produce steel containers.

An even greater extension of capitalism occurred in 1992, when the city of Wuhan allowed Hongtex Development Company of Hong Kong to buy a 51 percent share of Wuhan No. 2 Printing and Dyeing Company. This transaction marked the first time a "foreign" company was allowed to acquire a majority stake in a state-owned enterprise, albeit an ailing one, in China. This development also illustrates the movement of industrialization from the coastal zone to the interior provinces.

Also, in 1992, China Strategic Investment, Ltd., a conglomerate run by Indonesian Chinese in Hong Kong, was allowed to buy a 60 percent stake in forty-one of the forty-two state enterprises in the city of Guangzhou. In contrast, the city of Qiaotori, in Zujiang province, has no state-owned enterprises. This metropolitan area has recently become the PRCs button-making capital. Seven Hong Kong and Taiwan companies have set up joint ventures there to produce buttons for China's growing textile industry.

Interrelationships in the Chinese Economic Territory

Numerous economic indicators illustrate the close connections being developed in the Chinese Economic Territory despite the serious political differences that exist between the governments involved. Eight years ago, the special economic zone of Xiamen on mainland China booked ten telephone calls a month to Taiwan. Currently, such calls are averaging 60,000 a month and the number continues to rise. In 1987, fewer than 7,000 Taiwanese visited the mainland. In 1992, 1.3 million made the trip. Bilateral trade, which can legally be conducted only through third countries such as Hong Kong, was $1.5 billion in 1987. The figure was $7.4 billion in 1992, a fivefold increase.

Over 5,000 Taiwan enterprises have set up production in China or otherwise invested an aggregate of $5 billion in the China mainland. Some business firms in Taiwan have relocated entire factories in remote areas of China in order to take advantage of cheaper labor and more readily available natural resources.

The state of interdependence between mainland China and Hong Kong is even more striking. Each is the other's largest trading partner and largest source of external investment. Three-fifths of all foreign investment in China has been made by Hong Kong's Chinese entrepreneurs, spread over 17,000 enterprises. A network of highways, ferries, hydrofoils, and air routes link Hong Kong and the coastal region of Guangdong.

A recent example of the joint development efforts is the teaming up of Hong Kong's Kwah International Holdings with a variety of partners in China to develop a commercial office tower in Shanghai. The array of partners is interesting—the Hwang Pu District Resettlement unit, the People's Bank of China, the Shanghai Land Development Company, and the Hwang Pu district government. This may be a novel way of financing government. Why bother to tax corporate profits? Via partial ownership, a share of the profits comes to government directly.

The People's Republic of China has invested over $11 billion in Hong Kong trade, real estate, transport, and financial enterprises. Measured by deposits, the Bank of China is now the second biggest bank in the colony. In the other direction, Hong Kong interests, including joint ventures, are responsible for 70 percent of foreign investment in China and 80 percent in the southern province of Guangdong. Approximately 80 percent of Hong Kong's manufacturing companies have branches in China and employ more than 3 million workers in an estimated 25,000 factories. There are far more people working in China for businesses owned by Hong Kong or on orders received from them than the entire manufacturing work force of Hong Kong itself (in a ratio of 4 to 1).

Investment and expertise channeled from Hong Kong have turned southern China into one of the industrial powerhouses of Asia. Approximately 50,000 managers and professionals commute daily from Hong Kong to nearby Guangdong province.

Many investments in the PRC, albeit ostensibly from a Hong Kong-based enterprise, are traceable ultimately to conglomerates owned by overseas Chinese. Perhaps the most important example is C.P. Pokphand of Hong Kong. CP owns 70 percent of Ek Chor, the mainland-based motorcycle producer. In turn, CP is owned in large part by the Charoen Pokphand group of Thailand, a Bangkok-based conglomerate founded by Chinese immigrants in the 1920s.

If current growth trends continue, Greater China could be the world's largest economy by 2010 or thereabouts. Of course, diminishing returns—or even a direct setback—could set in before that. Severe strains in mainland China arise as an economically backward, communist-led nation moves toward a capitalist regime. Most Chinese remain in poverty. Adoption of a private enterprise system, however halting and incomplete, means broadening the society's power base and considerably decentralizing decision-making. Much of the shift of economic control away from Beijing has been toward government officials at the provincial and local levels.

What Future Pattern of Organization?

The Greater China now emerging is neither a political entity nor an organized trading bloc. It is an economically interdependent area born of market and cultural forces—sharing language, customs, and history. No one can forecast with any degree of assurance the future nature of economic relationships in the Chinese economic territory. Will a counterpart to the European Union arise? Will political unification occur? Will the more modest arrangements being developed in North America be the precedent that will be followed, or will the present informal relationships be relied on in view of their substantial success?

Whatever the answer, powerful trends rarely move in a straight line for an extended period of time. Over the centuries, setbacks have occurred in the economic and political development of China. Future detours are possible. Some experts offer a rather pessimistic assessment. In that view, China can never truly prosper while the Communist Party retains its monopoly of power.

Other obstacles to continued rapid economic expansion may be economic and environmental. China seems to be running out of easily exploitable oil. Additional supplies are likely to be increasingly expensive and China's coal supply is mainly the high-sulfur, high-polluting type. As a result, China is the fastest growing emitter of greenhouse gases. In absolute terms, it is already the third largest, behind the United States and Russia. On the positive side, rapid economic development provides China with the resources to pay for pollution abatement—if it chooses to do so.

Some visitors to China report predominantly negative impressions of the new economic zones, such as Guangdong. They see primarily official favoritism, inside deals, and outright bribery. The absence of a commercial code is cited as an example of how far the Chinese have to go to modernize. In a way, the China authorities are responding to that shortcoming in a conventional Western manner. In July, they launched a crash program to train 100,000 more lawyers by the end of the decade.

Great uncertainty surely attaches to the future of the Greater Chinese economy. Nevertheless, forces of economic and business development seem likely to dominate, especially in the long run. In Eastern Europe, communism did not fall primarily because the people rejected the ideology of Marx—if they ever understood it. Rather, they saw the vastly greater benefits of democracy and private enterprise. In that vein, Guangdong—the former country bumpkin—has become the wealthiest province of China.

The Outlook

The Chinese natural economic territory furnishes a striking example of private enterprise taking the lead and government becoming the lagging influence. As we have seen, even in the face of official hostility, many Taiwanese firms and a great number of Taiwanese individuals are succeeding in establishing their business presence on the mainland. Business corporations have paced the economic development of the Greater China trading area. In contrast, government policy often generates the obstacles to cross-border undertakings. To be sure, great risks are involved in doing business in an area undergoing fundamental economic, political, and social change. But private enterprise is especially suited to taking such risks.

35

Poland's Return to Capitalism

This article was written soon after I returned from a presidentially appointed mission to Poland shortly after Solidarity took over in late 1989. I tried to show the potential of Poland's entrepreneurial private sector.

The first Eastern bloc nation to break away from the Soviet monolithic approach, Poland is now embarked on an ambitious move to a market-oriented economy. The Poles envision a movement toward a private enterprise economy, such as the one that characterizes the United States. In the short run, the required changes are extremely wrenching, especially for the entrenched officials of the state-run firms as well as their excessive labor force. Whatever economic version emerges, it will be especially tuned to the needs and desires of the fiercely independent Polish people.

We cannot overestimate either the awesome nature of the task that faces the Polish government or the resolve of the Polish people. Already, they have adopted a macroeconomic policy of austerity that has conquered a rate of inflation of 55 percent or more a month. In large measure, the inflation had been fueled by a monetary policy that was so loose that it resulted in negative interest rates being paid by the state-run enterprises. That is, interest rates were lower than the inflation rate and, thus, loans from the Treasury were being repaid with money that was worth less than the original loan.

Under the circumstances, the state-run enterprises had little reason to take the tough actions that minimize cost and enhance productivity and international competitiveness. The easy monetary policy also accommodated a budget deficit of about 10 percent of the nation's gross domestic product and resulted in a rapidly depreciating currency. "Biting the bullet," painful as it was, provided the only feasible economic response. After a final burst of price increases when price controls and subsidies were ended at the start of 1990, hyperinflation was terminated and the inflation rate fell from 78 percent in January 1990 to 7 percent in February 1990.

While trying to end runaway inflation, Poland has begun the process of dismantling four decades of communist bureaucratic restrictions on its economy. The challenge is to privatize an array of inefficient nationalized enterprises, introduce a modicum of competition, and close down or restruc-

Source: Murray Weidenbaum, "Poland: Another Middle Way?" *Society*, November/December 1990.271

ture much of an archaic industrial base. One steel complex employs 30,000 workers to make the same amount of steel for which an American company hires 7,000 people.

Examples of initial changes include eight large multi-plant meat processing firms which are slated for split-up in coming months. Another ten are scheduled for similar action next year. Current plans also include breaking up seven huge coalmining enterprises. The Polish government has to do all this while taking care to maintain the support of its people, who are starting out with one of the lowest living standards in Europe.

Prospects for Success

Let us start with the positives. The ability and dedication of the senior officials that I encountered have been in the main of a very high order. At the top level a large proportion are Solidarity union stalwarts from academia, although a liberal sprinkling of the former nomenklatura (communist bureaucracy) remains. The head of Poland's central bank is a holdover appointee from the previous administration, although he seems to be much more a banker than a politician. Among the senior officials in key ministries, prior experience is mainly in academia or in Marxist-oriented bureaus.

The nature of the task facing the Polish leadership is well understood, especially in its essential elements. More important, the basic priorities that have been set and the plans to carry them out seem to be sound. Bringing down hyperinflation is the sensible top priority. Monetary and fiscal policies are the appropriate tools for that difficult task. Perhaps even more important, the Solidarity-dominated government starts off with a broad base of popular support. The widespread expectation is that much pain will accompany the movement to a greater degree of economic efficiency and a competitive marketplace.

Longer-run positive elements in the Polish economy include a young and relatively well educated work force, and one with one of the lowest wage levels of any industrialized nation. Wages average about $70 a month. The high school education of the Polish workers is quite good. On average, their students out-perform ours in math and science (we tend to forge ahead at the university level).

Another positive aspect, or absence of an expected problem, is the availability of food in Poland. Spot shortages do occur, due in large part to poor transportation systems, but long lines have disappeared in Polish shops. The average diet in Poland reportedly now provides at least as many calories as in the United States. Poland should be self-sufficient in food during this difficult transition period. Without reference to quality, the per capita consumption of meat in the country is above the average for Western Europe. Since the partial decontrol of retail prices in August 1989, meat is visible in Warsaw's open-air markets and food is more generally available. By early 1990, prices of approximately 90 percent of all items had been decontrolled. Eventually a more productive agricultural sector will be needed to attain higher living standards and to free up resources for other sectors. At present, approximately one-half of a typical Pole's income goes for food.

The negative factors facing the country and its policymakers are numerous: ancient capital equipment, overstaffed factories, and workers used to an environment with little incentive to produce. A popular saying among Polish workers is, "They pretend to pay us, and we pretend to work." Even more damning is the frequent reference to the worker leaning on a broom. The point is that the shirker gets paid just as much as the hard-working employee.

There are a number of painful downsides that must be anticipated from the tough measures against inflation like quick balancing of the budget, shifting monetary policy from negative to positive interest rates on enterprise borrowing, and privatization that requires downsizing or closing of many outmoded and high-cost enterprises. Unemployment is already rising rapidly, interfirm disruptions are rampant, and uncertainty (that barrier to investment) is inevitable.

Many of the state-run industries are off-budget. But, nevertheless, by operating in the red, they are large contributors to the pressure for more rapid (and inflationary) monetary growth. The new focus is on reducing the numerous subsidies that account for more than one-third of the national budget. Another large part of the budget is devoted to military spending and substantial reductions seem unlikely in the immediate future. Poland's large army provides a way of disguising unemployment. With one-sixth of the population of the United States, Poland fields an army over half the size of ours. With rising joblessness resulting from closing or curtailing numerous state-owned companies, there is special pressure to keep men and women in uniform beyond any compelling military need.

A necessary complication to the effort of reducing the deficit (which has run as much as 30 percent of the entire budget) is the need for what the Poles call a "social shield" or what we term a "social safety net." In most communist states, it is virtually sacrilegious to admit the existence of any unemployment.

The lack of reported unemployment has been achieved in large part by requiring government enterprises and offices to take on far more people than needed for efficient functioning. To retain the support of the management and the workers' councils for the massive downsizing necessary to make Polish industry competitive, compassion and political reality require that serious and widespread hardship be avoided. Poland's new "social shield" is financed by a 2 percent tax on all payrolls. Initial planning calls for rather liberal benefits, such as 75 percent of the prior wage for six months to workers made unemployed by group dismissals or bankruptcies. After the first six months, the benefit is scheduled to decline to one-half of the average wage.

Similarly, any estimates of the effects of restructuring are more in the nature of forecasts rather than firm schedules. The present planning calls for a handful of pilot privatizations in 1990, with the major wave occurring in 1991 and later years. Restructuring prior to privatization would make the firms more attractive to private investors. The entire effort is substantially behind schedule. In July 1990, the Polish Parliament passed a privatization bill under which more than 7,600 state enterprises are to be transformed into limited liability corporations with shares to be sold to the public within two years. Workers will be given preferential prices for up to 20 percent of their company's shares.

The initial experiences will have to be monitored carefully. Most members of the working generation have no personal experience under capitalism. To some extent, the nomenklatura may be trying to shield the enterprises they created from the new reforms. Career bureaucrats in every country are known to drag their feet in carrying out new policies with which they disagree, especially if they believe that a policy reversal might be in the offing. An interesting twist to this point are the reports of the old-timers taking advantage of the drive to privatization by buying out the enterprises they have been running at bargain basement prices. Irwin Stelzer calls this "privatization by theft."

From a broader perspective, Poland has been the pacesetter among Eastern European nations. The courageous actions of the Solidarity union leaders have encouraged the freedom movements in East Germany, Hungary, Czechoslovakia, Bulgaria, and Rumania. Clearly, under these circumstances, it is difficult for Americans to sit on the sidelines while Poland's fate hangs in the balance.

The financial aid package passed in Congress and signed by President George H.W. Bush does not exhaust the possibilities for U.S. involvement. On a multilateral basis, the International Monetary Fund (IMF) has developed an ambitious long-term program of financial aid. As is the IMF's procedure, the recipient nation pledges to undertake a program of fiscal austerity and reform. In the case of Poland, the first step toward fiscal reform included a substantial devaluation of its currency, the zloty, which was essential to make it convertible in world currency markets.

To help in this effort, the United States and other Western nations also put together an exchange stabilization fund for Poland totaling $1 billion. The United States has pledged $200 million in crucial help that will be needed while Poland takes the difficult but painful action of permitting the zloty once again to be readily convertible into hard currencies, such as the dollar. Without such convertibility, the future flow of foreign goods and investment funds into Poland would remain at depressed levels.

The fate of the current Polish experiment will be determined by the Poles themselves. The ultimate success of privatization can only occur in the private sector. On that score, the entrepreneurial spirit among the Polish people is often underrated; 70 percent of agriculture is privately owned. Also, an array of private entrepreneurs is evident in trade, services, and a variety of small crafts. This is tribute to the ability of the people to succeed in spite of barriers imposed by a hostile economic system.

A 1989 example of Polish initiative is revealing. For some commodities, the controlled (and subsidized) price in East Germany was substantially lower than the competitive price in West Germany. The difference in some cases was so great that it paid for enterprising people to buy those items in East Germany and sell them across the border. It turns out that many of those entrepreneurs were Poles, whose business opportunities were limited in their own homeland. Subsequent events in both countries have eliminated this informal market.

Where does a people of a poor and hitherto communized society generate the capital to finance a rebirth of its private sector? The sensible answer is not from the public sectors of other nations, but from their private sectors. This is much easier said than done in the case of Poland, whose large foreign debt exceeds the combined indebtedness of all the other Eastern European nations. The likely answer consists of several parts. Some accommodation of the existing private debt will have to occur before any significant new debt is likely. In the manner of some Latin American nations, debt-equity swaps could be made. The bidders of Poland's foreign debt could be offered shares in the newly privatized enterprises. The creation of an attractive business environment is essential to attract large amounts of new private investment. An improved business climate would be a by-product of Poland's basic economic policies, notably low inflation, privatization, and elimination of regulatory obstacles to business.

The Poles have a quaint way of telling Americans that they prefer foreign investment to foreign aid. In response to frequent (and perhaps patronizing) statements by American visitors that it seems only proper that we should reciprocate for the contributions to our revolution by Generals Pulaski, Kosciuszko, etc., the Poles reply, "So now send us General Electric, General Motors, and General Mills."

Something we take for granted, the private sector "infrastructure" necessary for modern business to operate is now not adequately present in Poland. This includes so much that is almost automatically available here: a commercial banking system willing and capable of making business loans; people who can run those financial institutions and the ability of evaluating applicants; cost accounting systems and people with the knowledge to operate them; an effective telecommunications system; organizations able to train workers in advanced technological practices and executives in modern management techniques. The answers follow a common theme: The need is to invest in "human capital," in the skills and knowledge of people.

There is a bright side to the waste and featherbedding in Polish (and other state-run) enterprises. Those organizations are veritable gold mines of potential cost reduction, productivity improvement, and profit enhancement. This should attract American as well as European and Asian investors who are willing to put funds in Polish enterprises that present intriguing combinations of high risk and high profits. The Polish authorities already have approved over 400 joint ventures with companies in Europe and North America.

The recent comment by Michael Petrilli, the director of international development for the chemical company Monsanto, comes to mind: "Sure, you are likely to see increased investments over the next five years, but they'll be prudent and selective. You're not going to see any company bet the ranch on investment in Eastern Europe."

The most logical foreign markets for Polish products are the nations of Western Europe. The European Union has agreed to lift quotas and tariffs on some of Poland's industrial and farm goods. Much more could be done along those lines. Indeed, such action would properly reflect the interest of market-oriented, politically free nations to encourage Poland's march away from a centrally controlled economy. It would also reduce the possibility that the European Union would become an inward-looking market, maintaining or even expanding its trade barriers with the rest of the world.

But the interests of Europe and the United States extend far beyond the business opportunities presented by Poland and the other former Soviet "satellites." Modern history provides so many examples of nations moving from capitalism to communism. However, there is no precedent for reversing that movement. That is what makes the travails of the Polish nation so riveting to people in free nations. Poland will be taking a special type of litmus test. If the current liberalization effort works, it will have demonstrated that the effects of Marxism are reversible and communism will be seen, not as the wave of the future, but as a dismal reminder of the past.

36

The U.S. Trade Deficit:
A Misleading Economic Indicator

The true economic impact of the trade deficit is described, with some surprises for those who do not specialize in international economics. The direct economic role of trade deficits is often overemphasized, but their financing turns out to be of greater potential significance and concern.

The trade deficit is my favorite candidate for the most misleading indicator in the statistical tool kit. More often than not, bad news for the economy is good news for the trade deficit, and vice versa. In 1992, the economy was in recession and our trade deficit came down. The next year the economy revived, and the trade deficit rose.

More recently, our trade with South Korea furnishes a similar and more dramatic example of the relationship between trade and the overall economy. In 1996, the United States enjoyed a trade surplus with Korea (approximately $330 million a month). Korea's economy was expanding more rapidly and our exports to that nation were a third larger than our imports.

In 1997, however, Korea's currency and stock market crashed, and its economy declined sharply. Korea got rid of its trade deficit with us overnight (we now have a trade deficit with them, over $600 million in March 1998). Our imports are approximately the same as before, but our exports are only about one-half of their former level. All this happened without any change in trade policy. Trying now to reduce our imports from Korea would make it more difficult for that nation to return to normal.

We also pay too much attention to the much larger trade deficit with Japan. In good measure, it is a statistical artifact resulting from the fact that we have the largest population in the industrialized world. The average Japanese spends more on U.S. products ($538 in 1996) than the average American spends on Japanese products ($432 in 1996). But because we have a much larger population, our total exports to Japan are less than our imports from that country.

The trade deficit is a misleading indicator of economic success, but we should not ignore it. Looking beyond the short-run gyrations of the trade

Source: Murray Weidenbaum, "The U.S. Deficit: A Misleading Indicator," U.S. Senate Committee on Finance, *Causes of the Trade Deficit and the Implications for the U.S.* (Washington, DC: U.S. Government Printing Office, 1998).

balance and the business cycle, a more fundamental and longer-run problem does involve the trade deficit. It is a symptom of a more basic economic imbalance.

Stripping away the economic jargon, Americans invest more than we save. How do we finance our vast array of new and expanded factories, offices, and laboratories so essential to economic growth? By importing foreign capital. What do we do with the foreign money? We buy their goods and services. The result is a substantial trade deficit.

This explanation simplifies a complex economic reality, but it is correct in its fundamentals. Moreover, this explanation points us in the right direction in terms of public policy: we can reduce the trade deficit in a constructive and sustainable manner—not by erecting barriers to imports or subsidizing exports—but by encouraging Americans to save more. That will provide at home more of the funds needed to finance economic growth.

Balancing the federal budget is an important step because it eliminates a major source of dissaving. When the Treasury is not a net borrower, more private saving is available to finance private investment. Congress has made an effort to increase saving through tax reform. The Roth IRAs are a good case in point. We should go all the way and defer all saving from taxation. This means deregulating the saving process so that Uncle Sam no longer tells Americans how much to save or the exact form in which to save.

It is also useful to see international trade in the context of the overall economy. Imports are dwarfed by the total output of goods and services. Moreover, the positive effects of imports tend to be overlooked. It is more than a matter of benefiting American consumers by providing greater product variety at lower prices—and these are important positive effects. The more basic and beneficial impact of imports occurs because foreign competition spurs American companies to enhance their competitiveness by lowering costs, improving quality and, in other ways, enhancing productivity.

Any traveler beyond the borders of the continental United States quickly finds that the American economy is the envy of the world. By any objective criteria, the United States is the pacesetter of our time. The citizens of other nations are trying to copy our economic system, business practices, culture, fashions, and freedom. They do not send their young people abroad to Tokyo University or Beijing University or Berlin University—but off to get an American MBA.

Concern for those not sharing in the general progress requires a constructive response. Pressures to "buy domestic" fly in the face of economic reality—given the fact that so many "foreign" products have U.S.-made components, and vice versa. We need to make the United States a more attractive place to hire people and to do business. Tax reform and regulatory reform surely have important roles to play. The basic answer to low-priced import competition is not to "dumb-dumb" down jobs here but to raise the skill and performance level of Americans who have difficulty in finding good jobs.

It is a silly spectacle for Americans to quiver at the sight of international competition. The U.S. economy is the strongest in the world and our long-term prospects are impressive. In a great many important industries, American firms are the global leaders. Our companies rank first in sales volume in aerospace and airlines, beverages and brokerage, chemicals, computers and cars, electronics and entertainment, paper products and pharmaceuticals, soap and scientific equipment.

There is a special reason for optimism. In the decades ahead, we will be benefiting from a huge upsurge of industrial research and development (R&D) during the 1980s and 1990s. A key but quiet crossover occurred in the early 1980s—for the first time, company-sponsored R&D was larger than government-financed R&D. Primary reliance on private R&D has continued ever since, making more likely an accelerated future flow of new and improved civilian products and production processes in the United States. To envision what this might mean, we can reflect on how the fax machine and the Internet have altered customary work practices in little more than a decade.

To sum up this statement in a nutshell: we should not be so preoccupied with the statistical excess of imports over exports that we adopt policies that weaken the basic strength of our high-performance economy.

37

Globalization:
The Bright Side and the Dark Side

The shortcomings as well as the benefits of globalization are analyzed. Then an effort is made to develop some common ground between the proponents and the critics.

When we listen to the critics of globalization, we can quickly conjure up a dark vision of T. S. Eliot's term "waste land." The arguments in favor of globalization, in contrast, seem to describe a very different and upbeat world, a bright wonderland. Let us try to navigate a position in between these two polar alternatives.

Let us sidestep the semantic issue of defining precisely the very word "globalization." As one wit describes it, globalization is one of the great vacuum words of our time. It sucks up any meaning anyone wishes to ascribe to it. Let us focus on the array of impacts that arise from the increasing tendency for national borders to be crossed by people, goods, services, information, and ideas.

There is truth, exaggeration, and error on all sides of the debate on globalization. Very few look at both the bright side and the dark side. Most economists and business leaders focus on the benefits of globalization. The litany is familiar. A greater flow of international trade and investment stimulates economic growth. That rising output requires more employment and income payments and thus generates a higher living standard for consumers. Rising living standards in turn increase the willingness of the society to devote resources to the environment and other important social goals.

Global competition also keeps domestic businesses on their toes, it forces them to innovate and improve product quality and industrial productivity. After all, if competition is good, spreading it out internationally must be even better. More fundamentally, rapidly developing economies tend to generate a new middle class, the bulwark of support for personal liberty as well as economic freedom.

Finally, we are told that economic isolationism does not work. The most striking case was sixteenth-century China, where one misguided emperor abruptly cut off commerce with other nations. China had been the wealthiest, most technologically advanced, and arguably, the most powerful nation on

Source: Murray Weidenbaum, "Globalization: Wonderland or Wasteland," *Society*, July/August 2002.

the face of the globe. Yet it promptly went into a decline from which it has yet fully to emerge. My real disagreement with this line of thinking is not that the facts or analysis are wrong—but that the entire approach is sadly inadequate in terms of responding to the concerns of the critics.

The other voices in the globalization debate emphasize the dark side. Workers feel threatened by unfair competition from low-cost sweatshops overseas. Citizens generally worry about the conditions in those foreign sweatshops, especially the presence of children in the workplace. People who care about the environment see the pollution caused by the long distance movement of goods as well as the shift of production to overseas locations with low or no environmental standards. All of us witness global financial crises and widespread recession and, far worse, mass starvation amidst the collapse of whole societies in Africa.

Meanwhile, we read about the growing inequality of income around the world. Apparently, the poor are getting poorer while the rich are getting richer. Globalization may be good for the compilers of economic statistics. But, according to this viewpoint, it is the antithesis of justice and fairness. At the same time, government officials fear the loss of sovereignty, while we all face the rising power of international crime syndicates, spreading epidemics, and most dramatically the audacious attacks by global terrorist groups.

Which is it? Is globalization the bright sun or the dark side of the moon? Historians say that, measured by trade and investment flows, the world economy may have been more integrated in the nineteenth century than it is today. For example, before passports were so generally required for crossing borders, people were far freer to travel and to migrate than now.

The extent of economic interdependence across national boundaries—globalization—did not decline in the early twentieth century because of mass protests or a bad press. The causes were far more fundamental—World War I, the worldwide depression of the 1930s, and the subsequent separation of the major nations into democratic and totalitarian camps that culminated in World War II. That long period was a time of rising isolationism, both political and economic.

It is possible that the world is approaching a somewhat similar turning point. The increasingly negative public reaction to the rapid and pervasive changes generated by globalization is beginning to overtake the positive aspects—at least in terms of perception. The instinctive response by economists is to correct the substantial amount of misinformation that has fueled the backlash to opening markets and to expanding the reach of competition. However, no amount of technical brilliance is going to convince the people who are genuinely concerned over the dark side of globalization.

And surely, the education and information approach does not help with the newest negative force; the international terrorist networks. The sad fact is that the combination of terrorism and our strong response to it is making international trade more difficult and costly and international investment more hazardous and financially more risky.

It is the two more conventional sides of the globalization debate—those who favor freer markets and those who have other peaceful priorities—to which I turn. However, even here there is not the degree of trust and open-mindedness necessary for the educational approach to succeed. It is tempting to respond derisively to some of the more naive protesters. One sign in Seattle blithely proclaimed, "Food is for people, not for export." I shudder to think of the malnutrition and worse that would follow from a ban on the export of food.

Nevertheless, let us try to identify some common ground on which people of good will on both sides of the heated controversies on globalization might possibly agree. The focus is on useful but less dramatic policy changes, what we can call the "nuts and bolts" of problem solving.

Reform the World Trade Organization

A favorite target of the protestors is the World Trade Organization (WTO). Many of the criticisms are on target and deserve a positive response. The agency has become too closed and too bureaucratic. But there is no value in trying to shut it down. Its fundamental notion of advancing the rule of law on an international front is an appealing idea.

It does not diminish our adherence to free and open trade to state that the WTO has become too inbred and too rigid in its operations. For starters, the general sessions of trade negotiations should be open to the public. So should the hearings at which the various interest groups present their views. Yet, the members should be expected to go into closed executive sessions when they begin to do the actual negotiations and drafting of trade agreements. That is a common sense distinction which experience teaches us is practical and workable.

Similarly, the WTO's critical process for settling trade disputes should be opened up so that the critics can see for themselves the nitty-gritty of the workings of the WTO rules. Specifically, the dispute settlement process should be expanded to include the submission of statements by interested public and private groups. Also the hearings of the dispute panels should be open to government and private observers as courtroom proceedings typically are. This does not require that the deliberations of the panels be public events.

Help People Hurt by Globalization

Every significant economic change generates winners and losers. It does not satisfy the people hurt by globalization to tell them that far more people benefit from international trade and investment. That response is so cava-lier that it is bound to infuriate those concerned with the dark side of globalization.

A two-prong approach is needed. In the advanced industrialized nations, we must do a better job of helping the people who lose their jobs due to imports or the movement of factories to overseas locations. Simultaneously, we must grapple with the issue of the labor and environmental standards that are followed in poor (and thus usually low cost) countries by the companies that provide products for export to developed nations. Many of these overseas factories are either owned by companies in the developed world or they sell the bulk of their output to Western companies.

In the developed nations, such as our own, the most effective adjustment policy to help those who lose their jobs due to globalization—or for other reasons, notably technological advance—is to achieve a growing economy that generates a goodly supply of new jobs. In the absence of a successful macroeconomic policy, no adjustment programs will work well. Nevertheless, some more specific actions can be taken to improve the adjustment process.

Often laid-off workers need just a modest bit of help, but they need it quickly. For people who went straight from school to work and never had to conduct a serious job hunt, the most effective assistance is modest but essential: help them locate a new job, show them how to prepare for a job interview, and how to fill out a job application.

Many other unemployed people find that their job skills are obsolete or that much of their knowledge is only useful to their previous employer. They may be long on what we can call institutional information, but extremely short on the math and the language capabilities required for many new and well paying jobs. These people could benefit from some pertinent education and training. Such "trade adjustment" programs have existed in the United States for four decades, but their track record is not very inspiring.

Those public sector adjustment assistance programs need to be adjusted. They should be made more user-friendly. "One stop" registration should replace the current uncoordinated array of assistance. It is disheartening for a newly unemployed worker to feel like a ping-pong ball being tossed from bureau to bureau. There is a type of educational and training institution that can be geared to serving unemployed blue-collar and white-collar workers. It is the network of community and junior colleges that serves a very different group of people than do the more prestigious senior colleges and universities.

Older workers present an especially difficult challenge. They have limited motivation to undertake training programs that, at best, will prepare them for positions that pay much less than their customary wages—and in a labor market where they will compete against youngsters half their age. Some innovations are needed. One example of fresh thinking is the idea of providing "wage insurance" to pay a major portion of the difference in earnings between the new job and the previous position. The idea is to give the older workers the incentive to get back to work quickly before their skills become rusty. To the extent that such older workers demonstrate to their new employers their greater worth in terms of seasoned judgment and good work habits, they may find the wage gap between the old and new jobs narrowing—and thus minimizing the need to draw on the wage insurance plan.

An even more contentious area is the issue of establishing labor and environmental standards for overseas locations that make products for export to the developed nations. There are several contending groups involved, each with its own goals and objectives. The labor unions in the industrialized countries resent the competition from workers in countries with lower costs of production and hence lower working standards. Certainly compared with pay and factory conditions in the United States, it is easy and sometimes accurate to label these places as "sweatshops."

As would be expected, employers have a different attitude toward the matter. They view low cost production sites overseas as necessary to meet competition. Many Western firms report that the factories they own or buy from in developing countries pay their workers substantially above locally prevailing wages. They also claim to maintain above average working conditions.

There is a third force in this debate, which really complicates the issue. It consists of the governments of the developing countries, such as India and Brazil. They openly resent what they describe as the newly formed concern on the part of Westerners with the working conditions in their countries. They see that interest as a poorly disguised form of protectionism designed to keep their products out of the markets of the advanced economies.

In terms of action on globalization matters, unions insist on making labor standards a part of any new international trade agreement. Products produced in violation of the standards would be barred from entering other nations. The opposition to that approach is hardly limited to teachers of international trade theory. The most vehement opponents are business interests in the developed nations and governments in developing countries. The result is a standoff almost ensuring the failure of any new round of trade liberalization.

Strengthen the International Labor Organization

One global organization that warrants more attention is the International Labor Organization (ILO). It is the only international agency in which labor is fully represented. Yet unions are reluctant to use it to enforce international labor standards—and for good reason. When it comes to ensuring compliance with the enlightened standards it adopts, the ILO has been a paper tiger.

Worse yet, Congress has not gotten around to approve all of the four "core" labor standards the ILO has promulgated—the right to form unions, ridding the workplace of discrimination in employment, and eliminating child and forced labor. Ironically, compared to our own detailed and pervasive labor laws and regulations, the core ILO standards are basic but far more limited. Congress should quickly endorse all four of the ILO core labor standards. It should take the lead in urging other industrialized nations to join us in providing adequate resources and support to the ILO.

Give People a Voice via the Internet

There is a way of promoting adherence to the ILO labor standards without resorting to trade sanctions or other forms of compulsion. The ILO should post on the Internet the names of the countries that are not complying with the core labor standards. Such a "seal of disapproval" should be widely publicized and made available to the media worldwide. Consumers would then be encouraged not to buy goods made in those nations. Governments should not use force to keep out the products from the offending countries. But each consumer should get the ability to back up concerns with personal action—with that action being based on knowledge.

This approach does not provide the entertainment of puppet parading protestors. However, it may be more effective in the long run. It requires a citizenry that takes the pains to inform itself and then acts voluntarily on an individual basis. Given the widespread access to the Internet, such a consumer effort could be powerfully effective.

If I show some enthusiasm for voluntary compliance with labor standards it is because I am a member of a team of independent outsiders who check the compliance of an American toy company (Mattel) with the high standards it has voluntarily set for domestic and overseas production. While governments and nongovernmental organizations continue to debate and disagree, Mattel and other U.S. private enterprises are succeeding in improving the work environment in their factories in developing countries. Based on my own on-the-ground inspections, it is clear that Western-owned or managed factories are at the top of the scale, often setting the pace for local firms.

Why are these Western-based companies so altruistic? Certainly, a good portion of their motivation is to avoid adverse publicity as well as pressure from customers and shareholders. But you can successfully appeal to a profit-maximizing business executive who gets special pleasure from selling toys to children.

Reduce the Frequency of Global Encounters

Virtually every meeting of global leaders generates a predictable response: protesters mass in an effort to close it down. This arouses my sense of irony. The protesters are right, but for the wrong reason. The annual economic summit meeting of the heads of the major governments is not the occasion for the exercise of too much power, but too little. The phenomenon of highly orchestrated annual meetings of world leaders has degenerated into costly global photo opportunities at which presidents and prime ministers strut on the world stage—and accomplish little of substance.

One of the easiest forecasts to make in advance of any annual summit is that once again the joint communique will be disappointingly bland. Thus, the protesters are fundamentally misguided in massing at summit cities in an effort to influence a supposedly powerful decision-making operation. Few decisions of importance are made there. Today's summit meeting at its best is merely a colorful social occasion. The leaders of the major nations get to meet each other.

Each government represented feels obliged to send a huge delegation to back up its national leader. After all, who knows what technical questions will be raised? In any event, that justifies the presence of a vast array of supporting officials and staff members. Given the millions of dollars spent on these taxpayer-financed junkets, it is easy to conclude that the summit meetings flunk the simplest cost/benefit test. Under the circumstances, I offer a modest proposal: declare a moratorium on global summits. Let the leaders use modern telecommunications to communicate. In plain language, if one prime minister wants to speak to another, he or she should pick up the phone to call. Use the money saved for some worthy endeavor such as providing emergency treatment for the sick.

I predict that, aside from folks who enjoy taking expensive international trips paid for by someone else, there will be little clamor to revive the expensive custom of holding frequent meetings of world leaders. Surely no serious government function will be adversely affected by not holding a global summit meeting.

*   *   *

As the various sides in the debate on globalization continue to harden their positions, any movement to the high middle ground will become increasingly difficult. The development of a feeling of trust, or at least common understanding, is a badly needed precondition.

Meanwhile, one modest change would help. The various participants in the often-heated discussions on globalization should consider moderating their vocabularies. So often the argument seems to be carried on between "greedy profiteering monopolists" and "impractical free trade theorists," on one side, and "environmental whackos" and "corrupt union bosses" on the other. The introduction of a bit of mutual good will would surely help.

The serious concerns generated by a more closely linked global marketplace must be faced. More of us need to understand and deal with both the dark side and the bright side of globalization. Some of us may believe that international commerce (i.e., globalization) is more of a wonderland than a wasteland. But real improvement in public attitudes will not take place until we respond constructively to the genuine concerns of the other voices in the globalization debate.

Name Index

Subject Index